Henry Fonda : A Biography

HENRY FONDA
A Biography

by
Allen Roberts
and
Max Goldstein

McFarland & Company, Inc., Publishers
Jefferson, N.C., and London

Library of Congress Cataloging in Publication Data

Roberts, Allen.
  Henry Fonda.

  Includes index.
  1. Fonda, Henry, 1905–1982. 2. Moving-picture actors
and actresses — United States — Biography. I. Goldstein,
Max. II. Title.
PN2287.F558R63 1984   791.43'028'0924 [B]   84-42599

ISBN 0-89950-114-1

Printed in the United States of America

McFarland   Box 611   Jefferson NC 28640

Preface

What impelled us to write a biography of the late Henry Fonda?

Our interest in this famous American actor was really stimulated years ago when we first saw him act in John Steinbeck's **The Grapes of Wrath,** the saga describing the move of the Okies from their barren land in the South to California.

The role he enacted—that of a young man, an idealist, who concerned himself passionately with the plight of the underprivileged during the Great Depression—was a tour-de-force. His acting was so realistic that he actually was able to become the living personification of that young man on the silver screen. Our opinions about his great ability as an actor were more than corroborated by the critics.

Years later, after seeing him on stage in **Mister Roberts,** we were convinced that in Fonda our country had produced one of the best actors of our time. Joshua Logan, whom we interviewed many times, declared to us that he was the "greatest of living actors."

He was a special kind of American. Many of his colleagues and movie devotees considered him to be an All-American type who had been endowed with many virtues and few vices.

But as we interviewed many close friends and colleagues our opinion of the man was to undergo a change of opinion to some extent. Joshua Logan, a very close friend—and coauthor of the Broadway play **Mister Roberts**—praised his friend but admitted that he had a difficult time with the women he had married. One of his mothers-in-law, Mrs. Oscar Hammerstein, accused him of being remote. And in her gentle way told us that it was that trait that made it difficult for his wives to tolerate him.

On the other hand, Paul Newman, who directed him in a picture, said he was a very friendly man, not too difficult to work with and a man who relished his bourbon.

Otto Preminger admired Fonda as an artist and said that he was a perfectionist, which was hard for his fellow actors to tolerate.

Norris Houghton, who first met Fonda when they worked in a New England stock company during the summer months, said he was eager to learn his craft when they first started their careers in the theatre.

Fonda's second wife, the mother of Jane and Peter, was a very intelligent woman—and beautiful and wealthy to boot. After a few years of marriage she realized that her husband's remoteness had practically locked her out of his life. She had a nervous breakdown and committed suicide.

   Even his daughter Jane found it impossible to maintain a normal
child and father relationship with him. It was only after he married
Shirlee, his last wife, that he became the all-giving husband. By that
time he was old and not in the best of health. He now eagerly sought
a more meaningful relationship with his children, including his adopted
daughter Amy. And Jane, Peter and Amy responded to his overtures
and gave him their devotion. Jane now was a very successful and
wealthy actress. She wanted to show her father that she loved him.
Her way was to purchase the script and produce the picture **On Golden
Pond.** Henry Fonda and Katharine Hepburn were the costars.

   Fonda to all intents and purposes played himself in the picture.
The role called for an elderly man who found it difficult to communicate with his wife and daughter. Jane enacted the daughter and gave
voice to her lifelong frustrations caused by the father's remoteness.
Ironically enough Fonda was awarded the coveted Oscar for his enact-
ment of the role in that picture.

   Jane had given her father a present he had craved for years.

   During his final years he had ceased being remote and was fortunate enough to have his affections reciprocated by his wife and children—a man who loved his art but displayed little affection for those
who were related to him during his prime years found himself blessed
by fate.

                                        Allen Roberts
                                        Max Goldstein
                                        Spring 1984

Table of Contents

Prologue
The Award Dinner

The American Film Institute's Achievement Award was about to be presented to Henry Fonda on the night of March 15th, 1978, at a dinner in one of Los Angeles' most luxurious banquet rooms. It had come after a lifetime of acting in many movies. And it was the very first recognition he had received from his peers for his work— an award that had long been denied him from the Oscar Committee.

The banquet room was crowded with 1,180 illustrious guests. Among those present were prominent movie producers, stage and screen stars and other luminaries. They had all come to honor a man who, according to Jack Lemmon, "symbolized America's definitive film actor."

It was the sixth time the Institute had granted an award. The previous recipients of that signal honor were director John Ford in 1973, actor James Cagney in 1974, actor-director Orson Welles in 1975, director William Wyler in 1976, actress Bette Davis in 1977—and now Henry Fonda.

The special recognition had been given to those individuals who in "a fundamental way advanced the art of film making—whose accomplishments have been acknowledged by scholars, critics and professional peers and the general public, and whose work has stood the test of time." That was by any standard quite a mouthful, especially to Fonda who was a very shy man and who did not relish all that fuss being made about his acting.

"It would embarrass hell out of me to win an Academy Award," the actor told a reporter who had interviewed him the day before the dinner. "To have to sit there and listen to people talking about me for three hours tomorrow night is going to be traumatic." But now there was no way out of the ordeal.

When Fonda walked into the banquet hall he was piped onto the stage to the strains of "The Red River Valley." He introduced his wife Shirlee, his children Jane, Peter and Amy, his son-in-law Tom Hayden and his grandchildren. Hayden had to leave the proceedings because he had to put his child to bed.

During the evening a spotlight was beamed on the many celebrities sitting at their tables. The guests, like fans at a tennis match, were turning their heads trying to see who was there. Fonda and his family were seated at the dais. The actor by this time was displaying visible signs of acute embarrassment, and those feelings of discomfort increased as the moving light pinpointed each of the people with whom he had worked in pictures. Each felt called upon to say a few

1

words about the guest of honor. They came from his current leading lady, Jane Alexander, who was appearing with him in **First Monday in October,** a play loosely based on the career of Supreme Court Justice William O. Douglas and a fictitious conservatively inclined lady judge. There were also words from Lucille Ball, Richard Burton, Bette Davis, Kirk Douglas, James Garner, Lillian Gish, Richard Widmark, Charlton Heston, Ross Howard, Jack Lemmon, Fred MacMurray, Marcia Mason, Dorothy McGuire, Gregory Peck, Barbara Stanwyck, James Stewart, Billy Lee Williams and of course the Fonda family.

His son Peter said that the evening was "a celebration." What was being celebrated was the body of work that included his early roles in **The Trail of the Lonesome Pine, Jesse James,** his role of a colonial rebel in **Drums Along the Mohawk,** his portrayal of the dispossessed Okie, Tom Joad, in **The Grapes of Wrath,** and **The Ox-Bow Incident, Twelve Angry Men,** and the unforgetable **Mister Roberts.**

The banquet audience saw film clips of the 81 movies in which he had starred. And they heard Widmark say that he was "the frontier American, part history, part folk lore, and part pathology."

The spotlight was now trained on Kirk Douglas who rose to say that Fonda's "courtesy was one of his most endearing traits." Richard Burton, who never found himself at a loss for words, hailed the actor for his "blazing honesty." He added that it was a pity Fonda had never played Shakespeare. "What an Iago he would have made. The audience would have believed anything he said."

James Garner, who like Fonda is a very unpretentious man, said that "during 200 Broadway performances of the **Caine Mutiny Court Martial** in which I appeared as a nonspeaking actor, I sat looking at the back of Henry Fonda's neck. I learned more about acting from watching the back of Henry Fonda's neck than I ever did from anyone, anywhere."

Dorothy McGuire who knew Fonda when he was a young man in Omaha, and who had acted with him in a local playhouse production, said that his career was "the longest of any working actor," and "after 41 years it is still work in progress."

The day before the testimonial event, Fonda was sitting before a fire in his white brick house in exclusive Bel-Air, California, being interviewed. He wore a hearing aid in his right ear. There was a silver dollar bald spot in the back of his thin, straight, graying hair. Wearing corduroys and a plaid shirt he appeared more like an aging frontiersman than an actor. His weatherbeaten face reinforced his china-blue eyes. He seemed to be the very image of rectitude and probity, and then the reporter asked him about those qualities. After a few moments of silence he replied, "Those traits are based on the parts I have played because of my skinny frame I inherited from my ancestors—because of an honest face I was born with—because of a Midwestern voice I've never tried to lose, I have been cast as the honest man with integrity."

He expressed his concern about the upcoming award dinner. The people there, he said, would not be too aware of the fact that he had always been completely committed to the stage rather than films. It was a commitment that had first begun when he left Omaha for New York back in 1928 and continued through the years. He made a special point of the fact that he always returned to the stage and performed in such plays as **Mister Roberts, Two for the Seesaw, The Male Animal, Point of No Return** and **Our Town,** after consenting with a great deal of urging on the part of his agent, Leland Hayward, to act in the movies in 1934.

"To me," he said, "it's indulging myself to go back to the theater. The rewards of acting are there. The first time you do a run-through of a play is unforgettable. With the movies you start tomorrow on Stage 1, Scene 88-89. You do the scenes before lunch and that's your performance. You never get a chance to do it again. You've never played the role from beginning to end. You never feel you've created it."

Here was an actor who was about to be honored for his screen acting, and all he could talk about was his career on the stage. Indeed, he had just returned from a twelve-week run of a new play at the John Kennedy Center of the Arts in Washington, D.C.

"It is thrilling to work in the theater now," he said. "At my age, you say, I've had it. You retire like Cary Grant and James Cagney, and paint or slow down. Take small parts."

"**Clarence Darrow** [the play] happened to me when I was 70 years old. Then to have **First Monday** happen to me! The audience stands up and cheers like it's a football game and nothing can match the way I feel walking back to my dressing room."

When he was at long last called upon to deliver a speech at the Award Dinner he admitted that he had become "committed to acting as therapy for a very self-conscious young man." He recalled some old tales about several of his friends who were present that night. Among them was the "very lovely Bette Davis who once, 51 years ago, I kissed in the back seat of a car."

The spotlight now zoomed in on each of the stars as Fonda talked. Finally it moved back to the stage, revealing John Wayne who introduced a film clip in which the crew of **Mister Roberts** bade goodbye to Fonda. As they completed their farewells Wayne himself said, "Good-night Mr. Fonda." The other stars in the room joined in to say the same.

The evening was now at a close and Fonda walked from the dais leaving the award plaque behind him on the table. Perhaps it was a lapse of memory--a kind of symbolic accident for an actor who was completely lacking in pyrotechnics and flamboyant flourishes-- who despite his many outstanding movies during four decades had never been given an Academy Award. Once back in 1940 he had been nominated for an Oscar for his portrayal of Tom Joad in **The Grapes of Wrath,** but he lost out in that one to his close friend James Stewart, who had played the part of a reporter in **The Philadelphia Story.**

Chapter I
The Beginning

Noel Coward once said that "no one has a more American voice, no one has a more American face, and no one has a more Midwestern look and character, straightforward, open and unpretentious" than Henry Fonda. And yet this "typical American" stems from a family of Italian origin.

The Marchese de Fonda was a member of a highly regarded noble family who lived in the Apennine Valley near Genoa. And like Henry, Jane and Peter Fonda, he was a political maverick. He defied the Papacy and sought to establish a republic in the north of Italy. Because he supported the losing side he had to flee the country. He found refuge in Holland during the latter part of the 14th century, and for 300 years the Fondas lived in that country.

In 1642 Jellis Douw Fonda, a direct descendant of the Marchese left the Low Countries and sailed for the New World. The Fondas were among the first white people to settle in Upper New York State.

Jellis Douw Fonda first established his home in Fort Orange (now Albany, N.Y.). As the Fondas became more numerous they moved to Schenectady.

The year 1700 was the turning point for the clan. Douw Fonda was born and he in time was to make the family even more prosperous and influential. When he was 35 years old this intrepid man explored the land near the Indian settlement of Caughnawaga in the area of the Mohawk River and shortly after established a settlement there. The resident Indians naturally resented the newcomers and created some problems for them. But that was resolved in the "customary" way. The next 15 years saw a new community in the process of becoming a town. Douw Fonda was now the patriarch of the Fonda family. He was able to induce more members of the family to leave Albany and settle in his town. In time it was named Fonda. It carries that name to this day.

When the youthful patriarch was 36 years old, his wife gave birth to a man child. He was baptised Henry Fonda. Douw, as a true descendant of his ancestor the Marchese, acted in accordance with the rebellious spirit of the Fondas. Later, when the colonies rebelled against the mother country, he joined the dissidents. Two of his older sons also joined the rebellion. Their father was to pay with his life for his political beliefs. Towards the end of the conflict in 1780 a band of Indians, allies of the British, attacked the settlement. Most of the houses were set ablaze and Douw was scalped. He died of his wounds.

4

All the remaining settlers including the Fondas fled to Albany for safety. But after the war they returned to the town and took possession of the land.

The Fondas weren't quite finished fighting wars. Douw's youngest son enlisted in the army during the second conflict with England and was, in time, promoted to the rank of brigadier-general. When he returned to civilian life he became an innkeeper.

The population explosion was an ongoing problem as far back as the mid-1800's. During that period the original Fonda clan had branched out into a dozen groups. With the compulsive urge to travel to far-off places, just as their paternal ancestor the Marchese did, the Fondas migrated West.

William Brace Fonda whose mother and father lived in Fonda, New York, moved to Nebraska. In outward appearance he showed no signs of his Italian heritage. He appeared to be a typical American native, endowed with good common sense, with no aspirations to accumulate a great deal of money. By hard work and frugal living he was able to establish a printing business for himself. Shortly after setting up the business he courted Herberta Jaynes, an attractive local girl.

The marriage proved to be a successful one. The couple had three children. The firstborn was a son who entered this world on May 16th, 1905, in Grand Island, Nebraska. He was named Henry Jaynes Fonda. A few years later he had two sisters, Harriet and Jayne.

Grand Island's chief claim to fame these days is the fact that it was the birthplace of Henry Fonda. Before he was born it was known as the place where Jack Eaton, "champion gum chewer," lived. It was said that he could chew 300 sticks at one time.

When Henry Fonda was born, there were still some old codgers around who could remember the day when the entire town's population deserted it and moved to the present site some five miles away. The old site had to be abandoned because of the economic blight that hit it when the newly-built railroad just passed it by. The railroad proved to be the new town's good fortune. The trains carried the products of the state to the East and to Europe and brought back hard coin of the realm to enrich its inhabitants.

The oldsters could still remember when the Pawnee Indians waged war against the settlers. The wars were still in progress as late as 1890. The Indian power was finally broken when the men, women and children living in the reservations were wiped out by the white man's diseases—cholera, tuberculosis and smallpox—all brought in by the Caucasian usurpers.

Nebraska was to be the home of the future actor for many years, and even after years of fame as an actor he still considered it to be his real home. In fact on many of his coast-to-coast flights he made it a point to stop off there for a visit and talk over old times with his friends and relatives.

His attitudes and beliefs (his mother, by the way, was a practicing Christian Scientist) were those of a man brought up in a Western town shortly after the turn of the century. The stories told to him by his parents and relatives were almost literally imbedded in his bones.

Those tales have been told time and again by old-timers. He heard about the hardships of the early settlers and how they had to contend with fierce blizzards, long periods of drought and armies of locusts. Most dangerous of all were the vicious wars between the cattlemen and the farmers. The cattlemen wanted to maintain the open range, and the homesteaders, for basic economic reasons, had to fence the land. The bloody conflicts were finally ended when the federal government decided to grant vast, unfenced areas of the West to the settlers.

Fonda was destined to play the roles of rancher, sodbuster and sheriff only a few years after those relics had vanished in the dust-bin of history.

The fledgling was raised near Omaha. The W.B. Fonda Company was doing well. And by the time the business was flourishing the family included sisters Harriet, who was considered to be the beauty of the family, and Jayne. Interestingly enough, actress Jane Fonda resembles her Aunt Harriet.

When Henry Fonda was recently asked about his early life in Dundee and Omaha he brightly replied, "I had what I regard as a normal youth."

A glance at the family album shows Henry as a well-fed baby dressed in finely laundered clothes—a clear indication of his mother's concern over the child's welfare. Henry tells us that she was "an angelic woman." She was also a very attractive one who was musical as well. Herberta Fonda liked to sing and play the piano for her children.

The older Fonda was certainly far from being a permissive father. Today's youth might consider him very old-fashioned. But Henry always took great pride in his father and believed that his rules of conduct were good for a growing boy. He was apparently cast in the same mold.

Talking about his attitude towards his own children, Fonda has said, "I was never what is called a permissive parent. I don't believe in that. I was brought up as a disciplined person, and that's the only way to be." All of that is very commendable; yet, while his parents lived a lifetime together, their son had four unsuccessful marriages.

Henry Fonda's aspirations as a young boy were not in any way unusual, He wanted to be a cowboy, a policeman, and then a car conductor. He made a habit of visiting his father at his office daily. When he arrived there he was given five cents which paid for his admission to a nearby nickelodeon. There he loved to watch action pictures featuring William S. Hart and Charles Chaplin.

His physical appearance at the time was very unusual. He was round-faced and overweight. In time he was to reach a lanky six feet one inch and become quite thin. Despite his light weight he was very agile and strong. He managed to get on his high school track team and played center in basketball. He also made many school friends— some have endured to this day. Bill Reid, who never left Omaha, is an insurance salesman; Charles Dox left for Chicago where he became a banker; and Bill Johnson, whom he saw often, now lives in California. The four boys liked to skinny-dip in the nearby sandy pond and build shanties out of lumber taken from a building site.

A number of Henry's relatives who still live in Omaha say that he recited poems and stories at the age of four. When he was five he made his stage debut in a pageant produced by the Omaha Junior League.

It was his grandfather Jaynes who encouraged him to draw. A sensitive and cultured man, he believed that there was some talent in the boy. But it was the craft of writing that really interested Henry. He hoped in time to become a journalist.

The country's participation in World War I—the war to "save democracy" brought prosperity to the state of Nebraska and other parts of the Midwest. The nations of Europe were in desperate need of corn and meat. The continent was now a vast market for those products. The country with its bumper crops was now in a position to supply those needs, and with the advent of good times the old refrain of the homesteaders was no longer valid: "Land of the bedbug, grasshopper and flea. . .I'll tell of its fame. While starving to death on my government claim."

Henry was considered an unruly boy during the time his family lived in Dundee, but when the family moved into the large clapboard house in Omaha his behavior in school took a decided turn for the better. When he was a student at Omaha Central High School he was awarded eighteen merit badges by the Boy Scouts and made excellent marks in his YMCA Bible Study examination. His grade was 90.

But all was not serene during his early boyhood in Omaha. He was to witness an incident that remained deeply etched in his mind for the rest of his life. His father, a liberal and a very compassionate man, had instilled some of his own philosophy in his son. He took the teachings of the Bible seriously and deplored man's inhumanity to man—and found racism obnoxious that was so prevalent around him.

One day he asked his son to accompany him to his office. The two men walked into the printing plant. The older Fonda did not put on the lights. What they witnessed during the next few hours was so shocking that Fonda today found it difficult even to talk about it.

"I was fourteen at the time," he said. "A black man had been jailed on a charge of rape. Charged, I say—not tried or convicted. The jail was in the courthouse that overlooked the windows of my father's office. A riot started that afternoon. We walked over to the window and looked down and I saw what it was like for a mob to get out of control. They got the young black man out of jail, strung him up to a lampost, riddled his body with bullets, tied him to the back of a car and dragged his body all around with the bullets. They almost lynched the mayor who was trying to get through the mob. The famous lawyer Clarence Darrow, Fonda revealed, also recalled that his father told him about a similar incident. "Darrow never forgot it either."

What Henry Fonda had seen as a young boy in Omaha made him conscious of the kind of persecution some of the minorities in our country were subject to.

Henry had no time to dwell too long on the lack of social justice he knew existed in the country because he had to keep his nose to the grindstone. While there was enough money coming in to keep the family in reasonable comfort, his father, like so many other middle-class parents insisted that his son should work and learn the value of the dollar.

Fonda's father later said, "When I attended high school I always worked during the school vacations. It never occurred to me to ask why I had to do it. I just knew that I must work." And work Henry Fonda did. At the tender age of twelve his father had him on the job in his print shop, for which he was paid the munificent sum of two dollars a week.

Henry Fonda graduated high school at a time when "Silent" Cal Coolidge, the man who was obviously weaned on a pickle, was the nation's President. Coolidge believed that most of the economic problems that beset the country could be resolved by simply imposing high tariffs on imports and cutting down on income taxes. He was the kind of leader who prompted Dorothy Parker, wit and writer, to remark after being told that he died, "How does anybody know?"

Fonda enrolled at the University of Minnesota, an institution that had been established only sixteen years earlier. He majored in journalism, since writing was obviously in his blood. During the next few years he wrote dozens of short stories and a number of plays, none of which saw the light of day. He was his own harshest critic. In discussing his works he said that, while his ideas were interesting enough, his command of the language was not adequate enough to express what was on his mind. He admitted that he could not "communicate."

In addition to his studies at school he also held a number of successive jobs off campus. That routine was exactly what his father had demanded. The older Fonda supplemented whatever he earned with a weekly stipend of ten dollars for which he insisted on getting a full accounting. During that period he wrote a story entitled "The Mouse" which was published in the Dundee newspaper.

Fonda found that the work and study schedule were just too much for him to take. "I had a picture in my mind what college meant," he said, "and it didn't mean attending classes from nine to two, then working as an advisor at Unity House from three in the afternoon until 10 P.M. I was finished with my daily chores by eleven and was back in my quarters, where I quickly fell asleep while trying to concentrate on my home work. It was just too much." After enduring that rigorous schedule for a year and four months he dropped out of college.

The summer of 1925, after he had gone back home, was a troublesome time for Fonda. He looked in vain for a position that would offer some possibilities for advancement. His well-meaning father lectured him about being productive but never could come up with concrete suggestions on how to find gainful employment.

At that point in his life Dorothy Brando, the mother of actor

Marlon Brando and an intimate friend of his mother, came to the rescue. Mrs. Brando was an amateur actress of considerable ability who was connected with the Omaha playhouse. After she learned about the young man's problems she suggested that he try acting. She told him to talk to the director of the playhouse. Acting was the last thing on Fonda's mind, but with nothing better to occupy his mind he decided to try and become a thespian; it would help him to fill the empty hours of the long summer days. When he was cast to play the part of Ricky, the juvenile character in Philip Barry's **You and I** he was elated for awhile. But after he studied the script he realized that he did not have the faintest comprehension of what the director called the "typographical layout of the dialogue."

When he talked about those early days as an actor to a friend he confessed that he had never even participated in high school dramatics. But as he explained, "They were hard up for somebody to play the part and they offered it to me." After a great deal of reflection and some self-doubts about his ability to handle the part he finally said to himself, "Why not! Actually I was too embarrassed about the whole thing to get out of it," he said. And from that day he was trapped for life as an actor.

The world was now destined to see him act in plays all over the country. Fonda was never under any illusion that he had found the way to riches. He knew that an actor's life is at best a very insecure one.

The neophyte thespian continued to receive the encouragement of Dorothy Brando. He was only 20 years old when he was cast in his first role, a role she said, that suited him perfectly. She had to convince his mother that it would be good therapy for her son to act. It was she who persuaded Gregory Foley, the red-haired director who had some doubts about taking him on, to cast him in a play.

After hearing him read the part, Foley was now confident that his new recruit could interpret the character. But it was quite different with the would-be actor. Fonda was panic-stricken when he realized he was really going to appear before a live audience! He later confessed that his first impulse was to run out of the theater.

"At rehearsals I found myself in another world," he said. "It was a nightmare. I didn't dare look up. I was the kind of guy who thought everybody was looking at me. I was very reluctant. I still had no ambition to be an actor, but it was summer and I had nothing else to do, so I joined the company."

Despite his own doubts, most of the audience enjoyed what they saw. But the more knowledgeable theater buffs said that he delivered his lines like the amateur he really was. There were many people in the theater that night who conceded that there was something about his stage personality that held their attention.

Fonda agreed to work at the playhouse for two nine-month seasons. Foley, who was now certain that Fonda had some talent cast him in four different plays. In addition to acting he was told to help paint scenery and build sets. He proved to be most proficient in both of those endeavors.

While he was glowing with the praise he was receiving from Mrs. Brando and his fellow actors, his father continued to insist that he was wasting his time in a futile pursuit. The arguments between father and son were so acrimonious that Henry seriously thought of leaving home. But after thinking that out for a time he decided to take a job with the Retail Credit Company. He continued to act in his spare time. He was cast in George S. Kaufman and Marc Connelly's play, **Merton of the Movies,** a play that had been a smash hit on Broadway.

When William Brace Fonda finally realized that his son was thinking of leaving his job with the credit company to devote all his time to acting he told him that he would under no circumstances countenance his taking that road. They were at loggerheads again and there were sharp words between the two. They did not speak to each other for weeks at a time. Henry's mother decided to intervene. It was finally agreed that Henry would continue to work at the credit company and spend some time acting at the playhouse.

During the next two years Fonda played many roles. In 1927, he became the stage director of the group and received an annual salary of $500 and shortly after that he was cast as the male lead in Eugene O'Neill's **Beyond the Horizon** playing opposite his sponsor, Dorothy Brando. It was then that he decided to devote his life to acting, although he was still working as a file clerk with the credit company.

An opportunity to visit New York City now presented itself. A close friend of the Fonda family had a son who was a student at Princeton. The young man had suddenly concluded that he had had more than enough of college life. He was a rather spoiled young man-- the result of being over-indulged by a doting mother. He had no problem convincing his mother to relieve him of his arduous routine at the university. She sent him a car and suggested that he should be accompanied by Henry on his way back to Omaha. She asked Henry to do that favor for her. As an inducement she offered to pay his expenses for a week's stay in New York. Fonda, who was more than willing to get out of his job at the Retail Credit Company, readily agreed and accepted her proposal.

"There was no objection from my father," he said. "I went down to the office where I was working one afternoon and told the manager who was my boss that I was resigning. His name, if I remember correctly, was Brewer. He was petrified with shock for a moment or two." He said, "Fonda, Jesus, Fonda! Do you realize that I was planning to send you to Atlanta, to the home office!" He indicated that Fonda was being groomed for a better position and that there was every likelihood that he would become a branch manager in the near future. Despite Brewer's entreaties to reconsider, the actor's mind was now made up. Fonda left for the metropolis a few days later. During the week he was in New York he saw nine plays in six days, including three matinee performances. After a week of living it up in New York, he left for Princeton and drove his charge back to Omaha.

About a week after his return to Nebraska a friend who was

a local reporter informed him that one George Billings, who had made quite a name for himself as a Lincoln impersonator, was looking for someone to write a sketch based on the many anecdotes about the martyred President. Up to that time Billings had confined himself to dramatic recitations of the Gettysburg Address to rural audiences.

Billings had been receiving hundreds of letters from Lincoln buffs who recounted interesting episodes in Lincoln's life. He felt that the material in those letters could be used in a sketch and was looking for someone to put it together.

Before he had turned actor, Billings had been a studio carpenter and part-time actor in Hollywood. He had appeared as a double for Lincoln in a number of pictures and had become so entranced with the part that he actually managed to convince himself that he was a reincarnation of the Great Emancipator. He wore a top hat, frock coat and shawl—garb always associated with the Lincoln image.

Fonda recalled that brief conversation with his friend, the newspaperman.

Fonda saw Billings who encouraged him to write the sketch and also saw to it that there was a part for himself in the script:

"It was just putting the letters together," he explained.

One scene in the sketch has Lincoln near the battle lines during the Civil War. Fonda played the part of the President's private secretary, wearing an army uniform. The scene shows the two men reading the day's mail. One letter recalls a familiar Lincoln anecdote.

It was the oft-told one about an officer ordering the execution of a very young soldier because he had fallen asleep while on sentry duty. Lincoln was about to sign the order when his aide, Fonda, read a letter from the soldier's mother imploring him to save her son. The letter was read to the accompaniment of a pit orchestra playing the soul-wrenching "Hearts and Flowers." As he heard the words being read Billings wept bitterly. His tears rolled down drip by drip into his beard, as Fonda gazed in astonishment. Years later he told a friend he could not understand how Billings managed to do it.

The two toured all over Iowa and Lincoln's home state of Illinois for three months. Fonda received $100 every week for his efforts. "Wow!" he thought, later reporting. "That's when I saw acting as a profession for me. I was actually being paid for my work!"

It was after his third season with the local Omaha Playhouse Company that Fonda determined that once and for all he'd go to New York and make a career for himself in the theater.

He later said, "I really had no idea what I was getting into. I was unaware that it was going to be a rat race—that one could literally starve. Well, we all did starve for a while but we did survive that period."

Fonda managed to get a free ride East from some friends who were driving to Cape Cod. A few days after he arrived at the Cape he learned that there was a summer theater in Provincetown and another in Dennis. With typical provincial brashness he walked up to the box office of the Provincetown Playhouse and asked for a job. He was told to his chagrin that all casting was conducted in New York and that all the actors had already been hired. Years later he

told his friends that it was a shocking bit of news to hear. There was
nothing left but to go to New York where he was later to find out
there were no plays being cast during the summer season. But there
was still Dennis.

He trudged slowly along the beach passing the house of Eugene
O'Neill. Then he boarded the train for Dennis—a town halfway down
the Cape. When he arrived he paced back and forth at the station—asking for directions to the Cape Playhouse. On reaching there he noticed
that no one was at the box office. He walked into the theater and
saw the actors on stage rehearsing a new production. Several of the
crew noticed the tall, gangling youth staring intently at the actors.
One of the assistants walked towards him and asked why he was there.
He said simply that he was looking for a job. Once again he heard
the same refrain, "We are all cast. We cast in New York."

That response seemed to be definite enough. Fonda now decided
that he had no choice but to go to New York. He strolled around Dennis
and passed a "Rooms and Board" sign. He had planned to take the
train to New York that day and learned that none was due to leave
Dennis until noon the following day. There was nothing left to do
but to register at the boarding house. When he went down to breakfast
the next morning he found to his surprise that the entire cast of the
Playhouse, plus the director, were also guests at the same boarding
house.

"It was a community breakfast," he recalled years later. "Everybody was seated around a large oval table." He recognized many of
them, having seen their photographs in the Samuel French publications
of various plays. The cast included Laura Hope Crews, Romney Brent,
Minor Watson, Peggy Wood and many others who had previously appeared on Broadway. He found all of them quite modest. They introduced themselves to him and when he told them why he was in Dennis
they were, he recalled, very solicitous and wanted to help him. But
there was nothing they could do since—yes, he heard the same thing
again—the cast had been hired in New York. After breakfast they
relaxed on the lawn enjoying a cigarette or two. Then they suggested
that he come along with them and watch their rehearsal at the theater.
Since Fonda's train was not due to leave for New York for several
hours, he decided that it was as good a way as any to spend the morning
before departing.

He sat in the back row of the theater and watched. Then something interesting occurred; Fonda's attention was fixed on the assistant
and the stage manager who were whispering to each other. To his
surprise, the assistant walked over to him and said, "We can't give
you a job but we can keep you busy as a second or third assistant
stage manager—that is, if you can work without a salary."

Fonda, whose entire assets consisted of 100 dollars quickly
assented. He returned to the boarding house and rented a room. The
next day he was at work putting up props and carrying out other essential chores.

During the third week with the company he was told that **The
Barker,** a Broadway hit play, was to be produced. Fonda had never
read nor seen the play. The director, for reasons which were a complete

mystery to the aspiring actor, gazed at Fonda and said, "Do you believe you can handle the part?" And without any hesitation Fonda responded with a very firm "yes."

He had a change of mind however after reading the script. He sought out the director and expressed his doubts about being the right man for the part. He wondered whether the director wasn't taking too much of a chance casting him in the role. Fonda recalled that there were two other juveniles in the company who were probably far more experienced than he who had previously expressed a desire to play the role. But the director's mind had been made up; he told Fonda that he had no intentions of choosing any other actor for the part.

Later, Fonda described his experience as an actor who was working with top professionals for the first time: "In stock you open on a Monday night. You begin rehearsals on the next play to be produced the following morning, Tuesday." And so the company opened in the scheduled play on Monday night. And on Tuesday the company started working in **The Barker**. At this point the director gave Fonda the "sides" and told him, "I want you to read it this morning." He also warned him that it didn't mean that he was really getting the part. "I want you to read it during the first rehearsal," he instructed him.

The play wouldn't stand up today, but it was a smash hit back in the early 1920's. Minor Watson, a well-known star in the legitimate theater, played the role of the barker in a carnival show. He had left a son behind at the family farm before taking off on his career. He dreaded having him associated with a carnaval show. The son, however, had a mind of his own. He left the farm and appeared at the carnival—to his father's surprise.

As the company went through its paces during the first rehearsal of the play, the director suddenly turned to Fonda and said, "Why don't you go over there and sit on a barrel."

Fonda, who was very much the amateur, made a special note in his script which read—"Cross to barrel." Then he walked over to the barrel and sat down. Time appeared to be dragging for him. A typical first run-through entails deciding where each actor will stand or sit or walk on stage. Every member of the cast is intent on familiarizing himself with the routine he will have to follow on stage.

While all that was going on Fonda stood in a corner "learning his lines." He admitted years later that "It was as unprofessional as possible. I did not realize at the time but what I was doing clearly indicated that I was behaving like the rankest kind of amateur."

He was, as he put it, acting like "the guy right off the farm." His first line was "Hello Dad." The script called for the father to respond with, "What the hell are you doing here!" The angry father thereupon struck his son a sharp blow on the face. Minor Watson who was an actor of vast experience indicated by a gesture that the blow had been struck. But Fonda, on the other hand, new to the art of acting played the part to the hilt and fell on the floor. The fall had not been called for. Everyone on stage began laughing and made appropriate comments on the new addition to the company. Nevertheless, the director gave him the part.

In reminiscing about his first experiences as an actor at the Cape, Fonda recalled that "a lot of people were excited and came around saying nice things." He was now committed to an acting career and felt that he was well on his way to become a professional.

The actor who played juvenile leads left for better opportunities elsewhere and Fonda was assigned to take over his roles. There were no other actors with the company who could compete with him. The director was now convinced that he would prove to be more than adequate.

Bernie Hanighen, a boyhood friend and now a student at Harvard, was in the theater when Fonda made his debut and was impressed with what he saw. He spoke to Fonda after the curtain went down and told him that there was another stock company in Falmouth, Massachusetts, that might offer him some interesting work. Fonda decided to follow his advice and see what happened when he applied for a berth with the company.

Hanighen was a consultant to the new stock company and he had many friends among the cast. The two men arrived too late for the first act and could not sit together. Fonda was now surrounded by many of the local dowagers. The play being performed was **The Torchbearers**, Henry Fonda found it so amusing that he burst out in very loud shrieks of laughter from time to time. As Norris Houghton, one of the actors who was associated with the University Players described what happened that night: "The theater was in an uproar; Fonda laughed, but it was not just a laugh, it was a high choking sob that exploded and overflowed, shaking the old ladies for rows around." The moment Josh Logan and Johnny Swope appeared on stage as Professor Hossefrosse and Mr. Twiller, Fonda burst out with his ear-piercing laughter. And when Swope's mustache accidentally fell off and he could not retrieve it Fonda fell into the aisle. Fonda was entranced with the acting and the members of the University Players were appreciative of anyone who found them to be so amusing. Hanighen escorted Fonda backstage and the two were invited to come along with the cast for another evening's entertainment.

That evening was an eye-opener for the young man from Omaha. The real performance of the night was about to begin. Like many great musicians who like to get together to show off their act, the actors were now in their stride and displaying how good they were.

Kingsley Perry took out his dummy and did his ventriloquizing. And Logan, who was good at adlibbing went through a monologue—a monologue ostensibly being rendered by Professor Hossefrosse, the quasi-scientific lecture he had created. And Bartley Quigley, an old friend of Fonda's in Omaha, was aware that he had been in the process of creating a character whose name was "Elmer." He asked his friend to "do Elmer," an undersized but an intelligent ten-year-old who could do animal imitations in pantomime.

Fonda later said that his laughter and his Elmer act had "turned them on" so much that they invited him to join the company. He promptly accepted the offer. One member of the cast drove him back to Dennis where he gathered up his belongings and returned to Falmouth to take up his work with the University Players.

The Players were destined to work together for the next three years. Later, Josh Logan told about his first meeting with Fonda at Falmouth:

"I had no idea who this strange boy, this shy, lanky youth could be. He stood there in his white linen knickebockers. It was in the late 1920's when plus-fours were in fashion, and this Fonda chap was wearing minus-twos. His golf socks and sweater were deep black. One could either surmise that it indicated extreme good taste or Mid-western provincialism. His chest was sunken and his head and pelvis were thrust forward. I wasn't certain whether he was short or tall. But all that bad posture was forgotten when I looked at that arresting male countenance."

The majority of the actors with the University Players were from very affluent families; they were very definitely Ivy League types. Fonda felt lost among all those sophisiticated Easterners. He was, after all, a loner from the Midwest with a twang that sometimes grated on the ears of his newfound friends.

The chief catalyst in the enterprise was Charles Leatherbee. He was a world traveler, a Harvard junior and the president of his college's dramatic club. His stepfather was the Czech statesman, Jan Masaryk, whose father Thomas was the first president of the new nation.

Robert Leatherbee, Charles' father, was the proud owner of a 110-foot yacht which had been docked in Falmouth harbor. His mother, Mrs. Masaryk, had an imposing-looking mansion, "Whitecrest" at Falmouth. It included an awe-inspring view of Buzzard's Bay.

The senior Leatherbee was an indulgent parent and permitted his son to use his boat as quarters for the actors. Charlie's grandfather, Charles B. Crane, was a former United States Minister to China, a post that had been awarded him after he had accumulated a large fortune in the plumbing business.

Another member of the University Players was Brentaigne Windust, who was called "Windy" by his friends. He was to become an important Broadway director. Windy had been raised in Paris. Logan, the youngest man in the company, was still a college freshman. The other players included Alfred Dalrymple, Kent Smith, Myron McCormick, Charles Arny and the alluring Margaret Sullavan who was to be hailed later as one of the most talented stage and screen actresses. Fonda was the only college dropout, but he was accepted as a fullfledged member for the strangest of reasons.

When Fonda first walked into the theater at Falmouth he witnessed a rehearsal of **The Jest,** a drama about Florentine intrigue. The Barrymore brothers had appeared in it on Broadway. Because of the dearth of male actors it was often necessary for them to play two and sometimes three parts. Fonda was thus a welcome addition to the Players. He was told to study the role of Tornaquinci, an elderly Italian who affected a long white beard and a heavy wig. Those who saw Fonda play the part were totally unimpressed by his performance. He appeared to be a rank amateur who was fumbling at being a Renaissance Italian. In a word his debut with the company was a disaster.

Logan tried to explain what had caused the fiasco. He said that

Fonda's Nebraska drawl, odd indeed in a play based on life in Florence, Italy, and his awkward delivery of the poetic Italianate speeches "sounded like a conversation of a rural philosopher who was sitting around a cracker barrel."

After seeing Fonda's inept acting Windust wanted to fire him.

"Perhaps," he said, "we made an error in judgment in asking Hank to join the company. We should tell him he ought to go back to Dennis." But Leatherbee reminded Windust that Fonda was highly regarded in Omaha and that it was really his fault for miscasting him. "That," he said, "shouldn't be held against him. Besides, the company needs a good scenery painter." And no one could deny that he was very good at it.

The other members of the company also thought that he should be given another chance. In later years Fonda told one of his colleagues that "It (had) never occurred to me to be discouraged. I wasn't terribly clever. If I'd been smart, I would have given up and gone home."

Fonda had to wait through most of the season for his next chance to act, but it finally came. He was given the role of Chick, a punch-drunk prizefighter in Is Zat So. There was a standing rule in the company. Anyone could try out for a role that interested him. Fonda did not ask to play Chick. It was the director who thought that it was right for him.

Chick, whose visage was supposed to be battered, presented some problems for the sensitive-looking Fonda. His own features were in perfect proportion. Yet he was supposed to project the image of a prizefighter who was at the end of his career. It was a challenge and Fonda was able to face up to it with aplomb.

Fonda got a stranglehold on the role and took to it with the fanaticism of a man determined to make it work. He knew very little about boxing and was concerned about his ability to give a convincing performance in the fight scenes. His friend, Johnny Swope, had been cast in the role of a minor pugilist. The two were supposed to stage a battle that would appear to be the real thing. During the few moments they had to spare they rehearsed the battle. The fight rehearsals increased in violence as the actors staged their act in the back alley of the theater.

It was Sunday afternoon when the two actor-fighters were acting out their final set-to. The fight almost proved to be their undoing. The exchange had become so violent that it attracted the attention of local citizens who were horror-struck by the sight. Some of them rushed to inform the police. When the officers arrived, ready to take the two into custody they were surprised to learn that the two friends had only been rehearsing the bout.

As Houghton later said, it was lucky for the two that the play only ran for two performances. The two men did not know how to pretend that the fight was not for real and by the time the evening's performance was over, both Fonda and Swope were nursing bloody noses and black eyes. The local lady critic who always had waxed enthusiastic about the performances of the University Players wrote that "the fight was thrilling."

After that play Fonda's fortunes dropped again, and for the

rest of the season he was told to paint scenery.

When the summer theater season closed the actors returned to college. Fonda, the only one who was a school dropout, had only one place to go: New York.

That winter in New York was one that tried Fonda's soul. It was disheartening to discover that producers didn't have time to audition him. Fortunately for his morale he had no way of predicting that this sort of thing would go on for four winters. At first he managed to get some bit parts in a number of Broadway shows, but they closed after a few nights. The desperate economic situation of the 1930's led him to apply for a job in a neighborhood flower shop. There were over 100 applicants for that opening, but Fonda was able to impress the florist with his need for money and was hired on the spot. His duties included the task of carrying very heavy flower pots from the basement up to the store level. After a few days his knees gave way. He got up enough courage to admit to the florist that the work was too taxing. The kindhearted boss told him that he would only be required to carry the flower pots out of the store to the customers in their limousines. He found that chore somewhat easier, and he worked at the florist's shop for several weeks.

Fonda was living in a ten-dollar-a-week room in the East 60's. There were many weeks when he did not have sufficient funds to buy nourishing food, and had to live on a few pennies a day. He discovered that eating boiled rice helped ease the pangs of hunger.

Perhaps that hard life had something to do with his growing sympathy for the underpriviledged and his developing liberal political convictions. Fonda was a great admirer of the Socialist leader Norman Thomas who in 1932 managed to garner 1,000,000 votes in the presidential race between Herbert Hoover and Franklin Delano Roosevelt. Fonda carried his liberal views all his life, and shared those beliefs with his daughter Jane, although he did not approve of the way she brought them to the public's attention.

During his first winter in New York he met Kent Smith again. Fonda, who was always willing to help a fellow actor in distress, suggested that Kent accompany him on his rounds to the producers' offices. He also took him to Actor's Equity, where a bulletin board announced actor openings. One day they spotted a notice saying that two actors were wanted by the National Junior Theater of Washington D.C. The company was about to produce Shakespeare's **Twelfth Night**—a production especially designed for a children's audience. Neither of the two men was familiar with the Bard's plays, but they applied for the jobs and were accepted.

The first role Fonda was called upon to play was that of Sir Andrew Aguecheek, the apparently senile but very astute buffoon in Shakespeare's **Twelfth Night.** Fonda was later to admit that the part was not right for him and that his interpretation of the role left much to be desired, but the audience seemed to like what they saw and the directors of the company were satisfied. They asked both Smith and Fonda to stay on for the remainder of the season.

Fonda lived a somewhat monastic life in Washington D.C. and did very little socializing. While he was physically attractive and had a flair for telling amusing stories, his funds were always too low for the normal boy-girl dating of a young man in his early twenties. Besides, Fonda's mind was on acting.

His friend, Bernie Hanighen sent him a wire toward the end of his first year in Washington and suggested that he come to Cambridge and try out for a role in a musical then being planned by Harvard's Dramatic Club for its summer program. Hanighen felt that the group could overlook the fact that he was not a Harvard undergraduate. Fonda did not need any strong urging. He made the trip to Cambridge, auditioned for the part and was accepted.

A number of Radcliffe College girls were engaged to sing in the chorus, an essential part of the production. Margaret Sullavan, who was only 18-years-old at the time, was a member of the chorus. She was also studying dramatics at the Copley Theater and taking dancing lessons from Ruth St. Denis and Ted Shawn. A piece of stage business in the play called for the ladies of the chorus to slap their male counterparts in their respective faces. The boy Margaret slapped was Henry Fonda. That was the beginning of a lasting relationship. Fonda later told an interviewer how he got the part in the first place.

"I was working in a repertory company in Washington D.C. when I received a wire from a friend of mine, Bernie Hanighen who was president of the Harvard Dramatic Club. I used to do a character at parties called Little Elmer. Bernie had written Little Elmer into

Kent Smith, Mrs. Smith and Henry Fonda at the Stork Club, 1948.

his musical, but he couldn't find an undergraduate at Harvard to play the part. This show was supposed to be strictly undergraduate—so he wired me and cast among the other girls—this girl. She was a character even the first time I met her. This was a typical burlesque type of comedy and one of the pieces of business was for her to cross the stage while I go in the other direction. I do a big take, make some gestures or comment. She turns around and slaps me and just keeps walking. But when this girl slapped me every time at rehearsal and every performance it was a solid rock slap. You would have thought I could only say, 'Who is this bitch? Get her out of my sight.' But it didn't work that way, see; she intrigued me."

Margaret Sullavan was indeed a very attractive young woman as well as a provocative one. She was about five feet two inches in height. Her eyes were her most striking feature—a sparkling grey. Her hair was golden brown and her skin was flawless white. She was born in Norfolk, Virginia to a family of comfortable means. Her father was a stock-broker. Despite any plans her parents may have had for her she had definite ideas of her own. Even at the tender age of six she let everyone know that she intended to be an actress. She began her career in the theater with the University Players.

The Players were now faced with a very perplexing situation. It was a problem that could have seriously affected the group's season in Falmouth. Mr. Robbins, the owner of the Elizabeth Theater, suddenly decided that he could reap bigger profits by showing his movies every day of the week. He informed the University Players that it would have to vacate the place. He was, he told Leatherbee, no longer interested in signing a new contract with the company. Thus, the summer of 1929 found the Players without a theater to work in. Mr. Crane offered to help the stranded actors and give them some land which he owned in Quisset to build their own showplace. But the wealthy neighbors in the area strongly protested having itinerant thespians in the area. A new place had to be found in a hurry. The profits from the previous season amounted to $1,200—hardly enough to fund building or buying a new theater. Mr. Crane, Leatherbee's grandfather, came to the rescue. He loaned the company $20,000, more than enough money to buy the land and build a theater.

Leatherbee found an old and abandoned plant that had been previously used by the local power and light company. It was located near Falmouth's Inner Harbor and was quite spacious. In fact, there was enough space for an auditorium, stage and lobby facilities and a cage and dance floor. Leatherbee had checked on it during the Christmas holidays and decided that it would do. His father promised to talk to the townsmen and try to convince them that a theater would prove an asset to the neighborhood. Once again there were the rich summer people who did not want any gypsy troopers galivanting around in the exclusive residential area.

Their reasons for not wanting the actors around were hardly convincing. The patrons, they said, would be imbibing too much hard liquor and would be speeding around in their cars killing many of the children on the streets. They never tried to explain why children would be on the streets at one-o'clock in the morning. The University

Players could not make any headway with the townspeople. A vote was taken and the proposal to build a theater was turned down by two-thirds of the voters. It appeared that the last chance had gone down the drain and the company would have to disband.

But all was not lost. The directors of the company finally managed to find a suitable site for their theater in Old Silver Beach just across the railroad tracks from Falmouth. Mr. Crowell, the owner of the place, said that the company would be allowed to build the theater there. He told them that he would not sell them the land and that the building would be turned over to him five years hence. At that time, he said, he would consent to discuss a future arrangement.

The place had an old clapboard dance hall somewhat the worse for wear and tear. But Leatherbee was not discouraged by its appearance. He hastily took possession of the land and the building and started construction of a theater. The dance hall was converted into a combination bar and restaurant. The profits that were expected to accrue from that venture would help, defray some of the expenses that would be incurred by the company's theatrical productions.

Another problem presented itself. Who was to be the ingenue in the first play? Once again Leatherbee came up with a suggestion. He proposed that Margaret Sullavan should play the part. True, she had practically no experience for such an important role, nor did she satisfy the company requirement that every member attend college. Sullavan appeared to be out of business before she had even begun her career, but during the interview someone recalled that she had attended a small college in Bristol, Virginia, for a year. When some of the actors expressed some doubts about her experience, Windust, the director, said—"Well, one has to start someplace and it might just as well be the University Players."

Margaret Sullavan was a very ambitious girl; she could hardly contain her enthusiasm when she was told that she had been chosen for the role. She confided that she planned to make "a million dollars, have five children and be a star on Broadway by the time (she) reached 35."

The summer season was now about to begin, but the building that was to house the actors and their plays was not much more than a few stakes in the sand. Fonda arrived from Dennis there about that time and started painting murals in the adjoining dance hall and restaurant bar. His friend Kent Smith helped him.

The workers were doing their best to have at least a temporary theater ready for the opening night. They had only three days to go. Fonda slaved away, installing a large grid which was to be used to suspend the scenery and the counterweights.

Margaret Sullavan's appearance at rehearsal just before the first production led to some angry words. She had been told that bobbing her hair was not consistent with her stage role, but that was exactly what she did. Leatherbee berated her before the entire company; she in turn retorted with some very earthy language.

Fonda was still busy with his scene painting on the day of the opening. After completing that job, he cleaned himself up and got ready for his own role in the play entitled **The Devil in the Cheese.**

It was the first time Fonda and Sullavan played together. The plot called for the two to be married and for the hero eventually to become President of the United States. Quite a tall order for any hero! Fonda played the juvenile lead Jimmy Chard, while Sullavan did the ingenue Goldina Quigley. The plot was really an involved one that made little sense. Chard, a ship's steward, is ordered to eat a piece of cheese so that he can set off a mysterious bio-chemical process and conjure up an ancient Egyptian God who will reveal the secret of eternal youth. Goldina, the daughter of a very wealthy father, is touring Europe when the two meet.

The play, if it could be called one, was a goulash of impossible and unpredictable situations. Besides trying to cope with unbelievable dialogue the actors—to their astonishment—were faced with a series of disasters.

In act one the Quigleys are shipwrecked and transported to a Greek island in a basket. The family is tossed onto the island from a trap in the basement—literally dumped onto the stage. Some crumpled and printed old newspapers are supposed to simulate rocks on the island.

Miss Sullavan's opening line, hardly an immortal one, was, "Mother, everything will be all right." She just managed to say the words breathlessly as she landed on the stage and delivered her words with such assurance that director Logan who was standing in the wings, exclaimed while shaking Leatherbee's hand, "What a wonderful actress we have!"

"I have to sit down," says Mrs. Quigley. She is supposed to sit on a stool, but there is no such prop in sight onstage. Joshua Logan, always at the alert (he was playing the role of the head monk in the play) quickly produces a grocery carton and tosses it from the wings. The overweight Mrs. Quigley sits down. The carton naturally collapses.

Chard nee Fonda has now turned airplane pilot. He is supposed to walk on the stage to the sound of the airplane motor in the background. To produce the required aircraft noise, director Windust had a prop man back a truck near the stage door and start its motor roaring. With that sound bursting the ears of the audience, Fonda strolled on stage. He scrambled up a ladder while the audience gazed in awe at his great daring. He then flung himself down and said, "Here I am, Goldina."

Act two also brought on a series of near-disasters. The first scene called for the approach of the yacht or something that looks like one. Goldina in a dream sequence saw a boat. She also visualized herself as the future Mrs. Chard enjoying a honeymoon with her new husband. She even sees a baby in the sequence—actually fondling an object that resembled one. It was really a chiffon handkerchief knotted in one corner.

As the curtain rose the audience saw her cooking dinner in the wilderness. The prop man had neglected to provide an object that looked like a make-shift stove. And so, a real stove was shoved in from a nearby restaurant.

The performance progressed from bad to very bad. In this act Fonda's appearance was preceded by the sound of running water—not what the script called for and the audience heard shrieking from the women's dressing room in the basement below the stage. At that moment the prop man conjured up a live sea robin, the spiny-finned fish, as a part of the play's realism. It was splashing around in a twenty-gallon milk churn that had been filled to the brim with sea water. In addition, more water was now pouring onto the stage with the force of a tidal wave. It was coming from the Marine Biological Laboratory at Woods Hole about twenty miles from the theater and was surging up through the stage planks, soaking the women.

Fonda was supposed to carry the fish on stage in his net. However, when he tried to lay his hands on the sea robin he discovered that its protective spine prevented him from doing it. Hurriedly, he asked the stage hands to hold the net while he upended the churn. As he did, about half of the water in the churn splashed into the planks of the makeshift stage floor and almost drowned the young women in the dressing room below. The rest of the water gushed out onto the stage and frightened the audience out of its wits.

But Fonda didn't lose his "cool." He managed to get hold of the net which was supposed to contain the elusive fish and as he did, he shouted, "Just caught him up the mast."

"Good," his light of love exclaims, "put him in the kettle and we'll have him for dinner."

The fish, unfortunately, was not cooperating and refused to leave the net. Fonda, not a bit put out by the annoying behavior of the fish, shoved the net into the cooking pot. The audience saw the protruding handle of the net and laughed. The young couple then triumphantly toasted each other—or tried to. Fonda and Sullavan raised their glasses, nearly shattering them in the process and Fonda gulped the water and promptly turning a ghostly pale. The prop man had absent-mindedly filled both glasses with salt water.

The next scene brought forth even more complications. The couple was now on a desert island. In came Fonda in grass pants, carrying a live turtle.

"Speared him in the bushes," he said.

"Good," responded the well-poised Goldina. "Pop him in the kettle and we'll have him for dinner."

The turtle, however, had other ideas. While the two performers spoke their lines, it managed to crawl out of the pot and fall to the stage floor. He waddled across the sea water puddle that had formed in the footlight trough and landed in the center aisle. The turtle continued its course straight towards Leatherbee's grandmother, Mrs. Charles B. Crane, and started to crawl up her leg. Her shriek startled the audience.

While the traveling turtle received the attention of the audience, the actors continued playing their parts unaware of what was happening. There were just too many things going on on-stage to occupy their attention. Miss Sullavan was preparing to enter wearing a grass skirt and a brassiere made of artificial flowers. The hero, Jimmy Chard, who was supposed to be studying the local flora, suddenly came across a most unusual specimen. In the play he is expected to exclaim—"Aha, some flowers for my wife," and plucks them. But the prop man had neglected to provide the necessary flowers. Standing in the wings waiting for his cue to go on was Joshua Logan. Observing Fonda's predicament, he quickly turned to Miss Sullavan who was standing nearby and tried to tear some of the artificial flowers from her brassiere, not realizing that his effort would cause the entire bra-combination to come apart. The actress wasn't having any of this; she tried to fight him off. After a futile attempt to get at her brassiere, Logan managed to tear the straw bracelet off her wrist and throw it on stage as Miss Sullavan nee Goldina walked on. While her outward demeanor was calm, inwardly she was churning. Goldina, a trained botanist was now supposed to cry out, "Drop that! It's the deadly camellia flower that brings on sleeping sickness." Instead she shouted: "It's the deadly camellia straw!"

Undaunted, Fonda pretends to be affected by the flower's poison and goes on with the act:

"I'm feeling sleepy," he murmured.

"Lie down," Goldina whispered, "and I'll just cover you with this grass mat." But that was easier said than done; there was no grass. Wracking her brain for the right words, she came up with—"No, I don't guess I will."

Fonda and Sullavan also appeared in **Merton of the Movies** that season but their performance did not raise any enthusiasm from the critics. For the first time in their brief stage career they started to entertain some doubts about their acting abilities, but that state of mind was soon dissipated as their skills improved.

The second week of that second season was quite peaceful—a sharp contrast to the near catastrophe of the previous week. The day after the curtain rung down on **The Devil in the Cheese** Fonda was at work again, this time directing an Owen Davis' mystery play, **The Donovan Affair.** It was a typical who-done-it that had been staged many times on Broadway. The play, while it did not evoke the admiration of the University Players, was chosen because it was a hot box office item, and it did bring the customers to the theater as expected. A production of a good mystery play was always a sure fire way of bringing the exchequer of the company into the black. During the time the University Players produced their plays in Falmouth at least fourteen of the productions were mysteries which paid off handsomely. The cast said that their repertoire was "Two for the Sailors and One for Us."

The next play in which Fonda acted was Sutton Vane's melancholy but moving work about our **Progress Into the Next World,** with Josh Logan as the director. Alfred Lunt had played the major lead in the Broadway production and the reviewers recalled how perfect he had been in the part. As Norris Houghton said, "Many of us there remembered the hoarse agony of Lunt's voice and the biting sarcasm of his desperation, yet even with this criticism already set up we found nothing lacking in Mr. Fonda's acting of the part of Tom Prior."

During the run of the play a car with a Louisiana license plate with two women arrived at the theater. A very young and very pretty girl stepped out and walked into the lobby. She glanced furtively around her, seemingly confused. At that moment Fonda appeared. He asked the girl if he could do anything for her.

"Can you tell me where I can find Josh Logan?" she asked. Fonda stared at her, looked at the car in the street and ran away shouting, "Josh, Josh, you've won, you've won!"

The girl was astonished by the seeming irrational actions of the man. She waited in the lobby for the next fifteen minutes. At last Logan appeared. The girl was his teen-aged sister, Mary Lee Logan.

Explanations were now in order. It appeared that the Logans and the Fondas had left Omaha and Shreveport at the same time and were traveling to Silver Beach to visit with Josh and Hank. The actors and actresses of the University Players decided to place bets on which of the two would arrive first. The winners of the bets arranged for a party to celebrate.

Fonda was now at a point when he began to believe that his skills as an actor were now on a professional level. His acting in **Merton of the Movies** had, of course, not been an unqualified success. He was later to admit that he had not been able to lose himself in the character of Merton. He stood, he said, "outside the character."

Houghton, who was a junior member of the company at the time, stated that Fonda was actually becoming technically more professional without realizing it. He was unconsciously following the Stanislavsky system (Lee Strasberg pointed that out years later), a System based on "emotional memory." Shakespeare's **Hamlet** doesn't expire every evening. The simulation of pain or pleasure and the ability to recreate it time and again are basic to an actor's art.

"That is the mystery of acting. The actor, if he is a Fonda or anyone else, has to be able to be both at the same time in the same way."

Fonda, of course, was dead wrong in his appraisal of his performances with the University Players. He was, according to Josh Logan, just right for the part of Merton and in all probabilities better than he had been when he acted the role in Omaha.

After Merton there was an appearance with Margaret Sullavan, Leatherbee and other members of the company in **Crime,** another mystery thriller. The play had the usual ingredients including a polite thug and his band of thieves, second-story burglars, forgers and so on. The two pure-minded characters who were caught up in the assorted mayhem being perpetrated by the gang were played by Fonda and Sullavan. That drama of high crime had the distinction of being the first time the two had had a love scene. It took place on a moonlit summer's night in Central Park and called for a good deal of ardent embracing. The actors standing in the wings were aware that Fonda and Sullavan were becoming increasingly enthusiastic in their embraces at successive performances. It was obvious that a romance between the two was in the works.

The final production of the season was **The Constant Nymph,** a dramatization of Margaret Kennedy's novel. Fonda played the male lead in that play with Sullavan as his paramour. In the meantime their offstage courtship that had begun when both appeared in **Crime** continued apace. If one is to believe what their fellow actors said about their liaison, it seemed to be more a conflict than a courtship.

They fought and made up again and again. There were days when they did not speak to each other. But onstage, both played their love scenes with relish and realism. Off stage Sullavan did not confine herself to hurling verbal missiles at her lover. She once threw a pudding in his face in a seaside restaurant, then ran out, skipping over the Cape Cod sands with Fonda in hot pursuit. She ran into the ocean with her clothes on, he following her. He was frightened, thinking she was about to commit suicide.

And so it continued for weeks. By this time the entire company was cognizant of the fact that Fonda was passionately in love with the five-foot-two bundle of femininity. At the same time it was apparant that both were unpredictable and that anything could happen when they were together.

One of the members of the company described their emotional outbursts as something which had to be seen to be believed. After their daily arguments at the theater the two usually went to the restaurant next door. All their differences were quickly forgotten when they sat down to order their food.

During the 1930 season at the Cape, Fonda rebelled against the Establishment which was, according to him, directing the company in a most undemocratic manner. Logan was his more than willing ally in the assaults against the entrenched power. The two could always be counted on to vote against Windust or Leatherbee. Their revolt was basically motivated by a difference between two factions. One group believed that it was necessary to abide by the basic rule that had been set by the Players, namely not to accept any new member if he or she had not attended college. The problem was brought to the fore by Ross Alexander, a talented young actor who had appeared in a number of Broadway plays. He had gone to West Falmouth to be near his inamorata, a young woman who was working with the University Players. A few of the actors said that he should be invited to become a member of the company. But there were others who raised objections because he had not gone to college. Leatherbee did not share their opinions. He wanted to have Alexander in the company simply because he was talented. He thought that was more than enough to justify his position in the matter.

Alexander had made himself at home in the men's quarters and was also entertaining customers in the nightclub. His sense of humor appealed to Leatherbee, but Windust was being very stubborn and he continued adamant in his determination to keep Alexander from joining the company. One exception to that iron rule had been made when Fonda was allowed to become a member. He had been a college dropout. But in Windust's mind it did not create a precedent. The fight between the two factions almost wrecked the company. Windust it must be said, had logic on his side. The reason the company had been organized in the first place was to provide theatrical experience for men and women who were going to college and hoped to make a career for themselves in the theater. If they had not gained the experience, it would have been impossible for them to face up to the fierce competition they would encounter from the actors who were already working.

Windust continued to insist that the basic rule must be adhered to without exception. Strangely enough, Fonda, the college dropout, went along with Windust. He should have been the last man to blackball anyone who wanted to join the company. He may have had his reasons for taking that position, but he never bothered to explain what they were. In fact, he said that if Leatherbee kept on insisting that Alexander be accepted as a member of the Players he would ally himself with Windust and do his best to set up a competing company.

The University Players was now split down the middle; half of the members stood with Leatherbee and the rest with Windust. It was another civil war. Disaster appeared to be in the making. Former friends were no longer on speaking terms with each other. The battle of West Falmouth was becoming more intense with each passing day.

Just when the situation seemed to be insoluble, Logan returned to West Falmouth. He had been delayed in coming because he had had to prepare some term papers for a summer course he had been taking at Princeton. He was astonished to learn what was happening. Both sides tried to enlist him as an ally. Logan, however, saw himself as a peacemaker.

He said: "It would be ridiculous to break up. You wouldn't have as good a company. You'd have to go through all the pain of finding another theater. This season is lost. Why not come up with another rule. Take as many college people as possible but if there's some outstanding noncollege man, hire him."

Although Ross Alexander soon had a change of mind and left the Cape for New York, both Windust and Leatherbee were very grateful to Logan for providing what amounted to be a graceful face-saving formula. So good a deed could not go unrewarded. The two leaders decided to make Logan director of the company. It was a great step forward for a man who had only been an occasional actor and a standup comedian.

Yet to Logan's surprise and chagrin, Fonda suddenly developed a distinct distaste for him. Now that Logan was a director he had become part of the Establishment, and that did not sit well with the young rebel. Utilizing his talents as a pantomimist and script writer of sorts, he needled the new director, performing satirical imitations of him to the delight of the other members of the company.

As if that wasn't enough, he accused his friend of giving answers without actually believing what he was saying. He had never taken Logan seriously—Logan was only twenty-one years old at the time. Fonda had a tendency to harbor resentments for real or fancied slights. The strained feelings between the two continued for more than a year.

In the meantime the love affair with Sullavan was moving along a very rutted road. Sullavan who could always be counted upon to do the unpredictable, was making life very difficult for Fonda. He knew that she liked Leatherbee and that he, in turn, loved her. It was assumed by those who knew the three very well that Fonda's professional criticism of Leatherbee was somehow related to their competition for Sullavan's affections. But she did prefer Fonda because, as she put it, he was the more amusing of the two.

"As I looked at them," one of Fonda's colleagues said, "they seemed to prove the adage: she couldn't stand to be with him, she couldn't stand to be without him."

As far as appearances were concerned Fonda was the more handsome of the two. In time the directors of the company became aware that he had certain qualities that made him a charismatic leading man. He did very well with romantic roles and at the same time had an aura of male sexiness and a kind of unpretentious demeanor that seemed to tell his audience that he was completely unaware of his attractiveness. It was sometimes difficult to hear him enunciate his lines on stage because he had a dislike for "stagey" talk. And after a particularly good performance which aroused an enthusiasm and admiration on the part of the audience, he often failed to acknowledge its applause.

Leatherbee meanwhile had finally realized that he was at a distinct disadvantage in his striving for Sullavan's love. He now fixed his attention on Logan's sister, Mary Lee, who had by this time become a member of the company. He eventually married her.

Sullavan and Fonda discussed the possibility of getting married many times during those early days in West Falmouth. Later, in New York, they actually went down to City Hall and got a marriage license. After some reflection they decided to wait for a while. Their combined income was to say the least negligible and for that practical reason they decided to wait for a more propitious time to tie the knot.

Some time after they had arrived at that decision Sullavan started to earn more money. But Fonda, an old-fashioned male chauvanist who was raised in a state where the male of the family was expected to be the main breadwinner couldn't see himself being supported by a wife. As if life hadn't created enough problems for him, Sullavan's career suddenly took a new turn for the better. She managed to get a job as an understudy in the touring company of Preston Sturgis' smash hit, **Strictly Dishonorable.** The production was directed by the fabulous Antoinette Perry, the same Antoinette whose name is now immortalized in the "Tony Award." Ms. Perry was impressed with the young girl's abilities as an actress and when Sullavan was later invited to appear with the Princeton Theater Company she released her from her contract. It was there that Lee and J.J. Schubert's talent scout saw her and persuaded the two brothers to sign her to a contract. Soon afterward the Broadway audiences saw her in a play entitled **The Modern Virgin.** The staging play occurred May 1931. The critics did not like it and made no bones about it. But Sullavan had a personal triumph. One critic wrote that she would "cut a figure in the theater both in Hollywood and on Broadway." And all that happened when she was only twenty-one years old.

Fonda, on the other hand, was still plodding along trying to gain some kind of foothold in the theater. After what seemed to be an endless time of trudging the city streets contacting one producer after another he finally gave up the ghost for the time being and went back to act in the National Junior Theater in Washington D.C.

While working there he adapted **The Wizard of Oz** as a musical—actually composing the music, designing the sets and even helping direct the show. Shortly after that he decided to return to New York to try his luck again.

Fortunately his colleague Leatherbee's apartment in Tudor City was not being used. Leatherbee, the moving force behind the University Players, had gone to Moscow at Grandfather Crane's expense to study with the famous Stanislavsky. The apartment was furnished with expensive Chinese prints and green velvet curtains. Fonda enjoyed the luxurious atmosphere of his temporary home. The cruel world outside and its hard-boiled theatrical agents and cynical producers were erased from his mind when he walked into the place. He thought it was his own Shangri-La.

Fonda was now back to his austere and heart-breaking way of living, existing on rice and water. That way he eked out an existence in the city that winter and looked forward to the comparative serenity he always found at the Cape in the summertime.

When Fonda returned to West Falmouth later that year, Logan wanted to discuss his plans for the company with him and Leatherbee. The latter, in turn, was anxious to impart all that he had seen and learned at the Moscow Art Theater. They were now grandiosely planning for a summer theater that would become a regular stock company.

Fonda, who had left his bride-to-be in New York where she was appearing in **The Modern Virgin** was not in a happy frame of mind when he arrived in West Falmouth for the summer season. He was aware that he was not getting anywhere as an actor, while Sullavan was well on her way to success.

When the New York play closed, Sullavan left for West Falmouth, not completely empty-handed but with a run-of-the-play contract that called for her return to Broadway when the production reopened in August.

Fonda was standing behind the "flies" when she walked into the theater. She was kissing and being kissed by everyone there that day, and also receiving congratulations for her professional good fortune. Fonda looked on with intense mixed feelings. As she walked directly underneath the "flies" he shouted, "Hello there!" She looked up and said, "Fonda, shave off that silly moustache." She always called him Fonda even during their most endearing moments.

The two were cast in a southern romantic play called **Coquette**. Their stirring performance moved the audience and the other actors to tears. Josh Logan's little sister, Mary Lee, who was standing just off stage waiting for her cue to walk on for her brief moment, was so taken with the two that she forgot what she was supposed to do. She was nudged by a stagehand and with tears still streaming down her face she said her lines.

The season was about to end, and the last play was about to be staged. It was Sir James Barrie's **A Kiss for Cinderella**. Fonda was to direct it and design the scenery. He was also to play the role of a soft-hearted policeman.

Susan Gill, a Radcliffe girl, was to play opposite him. She was vacationing in Europe and had been told that the role would be hers when she returned to Falmouth. But her very busy social life abroad was so consuming that she had no time to learn her lines. During a rehearsal it became clear that she would have to be replaced. That role was given to Sullavan.

As usual between rehearsals Sullavan and Fonda waged their regular donneybrooks. And in between the battles they conceived all kinds of silly gags. For example:

They sat on the steps near the box office several minutes before the theatergoers arrived. Fonda sat cross-legged while Sullavan squatted on his shoulders, her bare feet entwined under his chin. She also wore three hats one atop the other. And she pretended to have a sore toe, which she had tied up with a tattered rag and a fancy bow tie on top. The two just sat there not moving a muscle. The astonished patrons stared at them, not quite certain what to make of it. When the bell rang signaling that the curtain was about to be raised in "fifteen minutes" she leaped off his shoulders, and the two pranksters rushed into the theater.

As Houghton said, "In watching the two at play and in an argument one could only conclude that Sullavan could not abide being with Fonda and, on the other hand, would like to be with him forever."

The last play had now been produced. It was now time to leave West Falmouth. The company organized a special celebration. A treasure hunt was proposed. Quigley and Perry, two members of the company, were told to conceive the clues and decide where the treasure would be hidden. The hunt was to be confined in the area of Buzzards Bay and Hyannis.

When the final curtain was rung down the cast drove off posthaste in several cars. One automobile raced towards Woods Hole where they hoped to find a clue that would lead them to Leatherbee's camp; another car sped in a different direction towards the Pocasset railroad station. In a few minutes all the cars were off and running.

The last clue for each car led them to the Cape Codder Hotel which had been empty for a very long time. It was located on a buff over the bay, and it had the appearance of a typical haunted house.

Car No. 1 drove up to the deserted hotel. The driver and his companions rushed inside the place. There were no lights. The electricity had been cut off a long time ago. They stumbled through the dark hallways. As they turned a corner, a white figure suddenly fell in front of them. There was a long gash across its throat. Upon investigation they discovered that it was none other than Liz Johnson, a member of the company. She had dabbed her throat with ketchup. Tightly locked in her hand was another clue. It indicated that the treasure was hidden nearby.

As the other cars arrived at the hotel the horrors there were increasing in intensity. The first arrivals were now trying to frighten the newcomers. After the fun was over Fonda found out where the treasure had been hidden and won the prize. It was a bottle of Cointreau. That kind of liquor was very hard to come by during Prohibition.

The actors and actresses then drove back to the theater where tables laden with food had been prepared.

The following day as the boat was pulling away from the New Bedford slip the members of the company who were on deck saw a figure rushing up. It was Fonda. They could hardly hear what he was shouting:

"What's the combination of the safe?" he wanted to know. The bottle of liquor was locked in it.

With the summer season at an end, the directors of the University Players decided that it would be feasible to open in Baltimore. They took a lease on the Maryland Theater which was located on Franklin Street. The theater had been built during the latter part of the 19th century and was similar in appearance to the Paris opera house. The only jarring note was the brass spittoons near the staircase. The theater had a horseshoe tier of mezzanine boxes. There was a balcony above that, and a gallery—and it had 1500 seats.

The directors of the company believed that the stage presented a bit of a problem. On the side there were dressing rooms that gradually ascended to the gallery. There was a very old switchboard which was unlike the modern counterweight system at the Old Silver Beach in Massachusetts. But the bottle-green velvet and faded gold leaf decorations dominated the front of the theater.

Just next door there was the Kernan Hotel. The members of the cast had registered there because the rates were reasonable. It was also close to the theater. The company rented a seamy-looking basement nightclub that was located in the hotel. It had been vacant during the day and was used for rehearsals by the company.

The directors now felt that with their new status as professionals, a new name for the company would be appropriate. They called themselves "The University Repertory Theater."

Chapter II
Acting in Baltimore

Everyone within the vicinity of Sullavan and Fonda knew that the love affair between the two was still an ongoing phenomenon. They grew accustomed to those emotional outbursts that erupted at unexpected moments, then stopped. A great deal of fire and fury was manifest in those outbursts, but quoting the Bard, "It was all full of sound and fury signifying nothing." Their anger was quickly forgotten when they sat down in the restaurant next door to the theater.

At the nightclub where most of the cast entertained the patrons or worked as glorified domestics, one found "The Harvard Rhythm Kids" led by Fonda's good friend, Bernie Hanighen. On most nights one could sense the slightly sickening, sweet, pungent odor of marijuana permeating the club. The musicians smoked it because they thought it helped them create better music. Fonda, the staid Midwesterner, tried to smoke a "joint" but didn't like it. He enjoyed drinking beer however. The members of the company were experimenting with a brew of their own. The liquid was bottled and put away in the pit of the theater's orchestra. And that led to a startling occurrence.

The Czech playwright, Karel Capek's somber play, **The Makropoulus Secret** was being staged one night. Fonda and Peggy Wood were in the midst of an engrossing scene when a series of loud explosions rent the air inside the theater. Pieces of glass flew in all directions. The frightened men and women scrambled to the nearest exits while the actors on stage were momentarily petrified with fear. The cause of the unexpected sound effects was soon found; it was the yeast expanding in the stored bottles, causing them to explode.

The amateur brewers made the beer primarily for their own use, but there was an even more potent concoction. The ever-creative Charlie Leatherbee made a special kind of cocktail that he called "Orgeat." It was a mixture of barley water derivative plus almonds, egg whites and lemon juice. The mixture was to be shaken at least eighty times before serving. According to those who tasted it, it had more kick than 100-proof vodka.

"Orgeat" was selling quite well at the nightclub. There were many calls for the concoction. As a result it had to be put into five-gallon milk churns to meet the demand—the very same containers that had been used to keep the sea robin confined in **The Devil in the Cheese.**

Fonda was now performing his well-known Elmer act at the nightclub. He had no need to imbibe "Orgeat" to feel high. His success in the playlet had been more than enough to make him feel that way.

Elmer, the bright ten-year-old character he had assumed, was certain to provoke loud guffaws from the audience and his fellow actors. He enjoyed doing his Elmer act.

Logan always worked with him during those early days; he played the part of a barefoot Professor Huxley Hossefrosse who gave pseudo-scientific lectures in his own special style. He also played the same character with Fonda in a skit at the supper club. The act called for Fonda, a slow-witted stooge pretending to be an innocent member of the audience. He was asked to come onstage to assist the professor in some stage business. Logan would give him a large cake of ice and then insist that he hold it tightly. While the alleged cretan shuffled around the stage gazing at the audience with an agonized expression on his face, the professor would deliver a long monologue on some incomprehensible subject in a rather incoherent manner. No one could make out what he was trying to say. The comical situation reached its peak when Fonda, still clutching the cake of ice, floundered around the stage trying to dispose of it.

Logan still says that his friend's talent as a pantomimist which he displayed to such great advantage in the Elmer-Professor routine would have matched the art of even a Marcel Marceau. He also said that it was "close to genius." Under the circumstances he could have earned a good living with Mack Sennet or as a face in a circus. I believe that it is lucky for Charlie Chaplin, Harry Langdon, Buster Keaton and Emmett Kelly that he didn't join their game.

The male members of the company were all very "macho." Those were the days before Women's Liberation had become a serious movement. They did most of the entertaining at the supper club and relegated the menial tasks of waiting on tables and sweeping the floors to the women. Margaret Sullavan wasn't being cast in many of the productions, nor was she willing to sweep floors and work at the other menial tasks. She finally waged a miniature revolt and told the director bluntly that she was "an actress not a kitchen maid."

The Baltimore season of the University Players opened on November 10, 1931. The audience, according to Logan, was a very distinguished one. But the play that was staged was a disappointment. It was the company's hardy perennial, **The Devil in the Cheese.** To the amazement of Leatherbee the audience enjoyed it. Even the reviewers found it entertaining. On the following night for a change of pace the company presented a thriller—**The Silent House.** The reviews of that production were good.

The company now considered itself a full-time repertory group. Yet despite the good reviews there was a dearth of customers at the box office because the paying customers would come to see one play and then discover another had been substituted. The plays were changed every night. European audiences are accustomed to such rearranged schedules, but since the local citizens did not know what to expect they just stayed away. Something had to be done to remedy the situation, but the stubborn directors refused to face up to the problem and did nothing at all. They were determined to educate the public and teach them to expect unannounced changes.

Meanwhile Margaret Sullavan's play closed on Broadway. A few days after that she joined the company in Baltimore. The manager of the theater, encouraged by the appearance of the Broadway actress, was able to convince the directors to make a change in their policies and stage one play a week. Thus the company once more was stock instead of repertory.

The local theater buffs started flocking to the box office again when the critics wrote rave reviews about the production of **Death Takes a Holiday**. It starred Sullavan and Kent Smith. The directors with rare astuteness reduced the price of the tickets to fifty cents for matinees and a dollar for the evening performances. That did it! Hordes of citizens rushed to the box office the next day, and for the first time since the company had opened in Baltimore the entire house was sold out. Fonda, Sullavan and Smith were now considered super-stars in Baltimore at any rate.

Shortly after that prosperous moment for the company it was learned that Sullavan and Fonda had applied for a marriage license again. Sullavan at first denied it. On Christmas day, precisely at 11:00 A.M. the members of the company crowded into the dining room and saw the two being married at long last by none other than Horace Donegan, the Episcopal rector of Christ Church. He happened to be a college classmate of Leatherbee. After the two had been legally joined together in holy matrimony, Windust sat down and played a rather lacrimose love duet from the score of **The Constant Nymph**. Sullavan and Fonda made a few trite remarks of appreciation. Everyone there was quite touched by the speeches.

On that very day a matinee of **The Ghost Train** was staged, with Fonda playing the lead role of the bridegroom. News of the marriage was leaked to the press by the lady ushers. When the bridegroom pulled a handkerchief out of his pocket—it was a part of the stage business—and some rice poured out of his pocket and on to the floor, the canny audience burst into overwhelming applause.

While everyone was happy about the marriage of the battling twosome, disaster loomed for the University Players. The Group Theater of New York had shut its doors after the failure of **The House of Connally** and was on the lookout for a more promising area to show its wares. The Group chose Baltimore because its very attractive ingenue, Margaret Barker, the daughter of a prominent local family, was bound to attract the city's theater patrons. The Baltimore press now ignored the University Players company and devoted all of its free space to the rival group. The Players felt that something of a drastic nature would have to be formulated and acted upon. As usual Leatherbee came up with a brilliant idea. Some weeks previously, a burlesque adaptation of Aristophanes' classic play, **Lysistrata**, had been closed down by the Puritan-minded police in Los Angeles. The actors and actresses were jailed for the night. Newspapers all over the country ran blazing headlines about the incident. Leatherbee pointed out to the cast that that was a way to get publicity and as a result it would effectively eliminate The Group as rivals. All instantly voiced their approval of his idea that **Lysistrata** should be the next production of the company. All, that is, with the exception of Sullavan and Fonda. That prudishly-inclined pair professed horror at the very thought of staging so bawdy a play. There were some who doubted their sincerity and said that they really wanted a vacation so that they could enjoy a honeymoon. That is exactly what happened. They drove off in a second hand car that they had recently purchased.

Meantime the company began producing the play with zest. The next four days were spent setting up scenery and rehearsing a cast of 100 actors. In that short time it was necessary to mount a tremendous production that should have taken many weeks. The directors managed to recruit would-be actors, models, society girls and sundry other stage-struck men and women to take part in the play. The costumes were dyed in caldrons, and gilded papier-mache shields and helmets were made in a hurry. Strong wooden swords were carved and painted silver. Dance teachers associated with the Dennis-Shawn Company of Washington D.C. were transported to Baltimore and they helped to choreograph the elaborate bachanal. The background music was provided by a recording of Stravinsky's Le Sacre du Printemps to accentuate the basic sexuality of the play.

Lysistrata attracted thousands of people. It was sold out on opening night and several nights after that. There were also eighty standees at every performance. The directors were more than pleased, especially when they were told that the rival Group Theater's production had only attracted a pitiful 190 people. When the entire week's productions were sold out, it was decided to extend the run of the play for another week.

Fonda and Sullavan were not aware of what was happening in Baltimore. Their honeymoon had gotten off to a bad start when their car broke down just outside Washington. There was nothing to do but return to Baltimore by train. In a way they weren't too unhappy with that turn of events because they were longing to see all their friends again at the theater. Upon their return they were put up in a room at the Kernan and were left pretty much to themselves. No one annoyed them. In fact they were left incommunicado. But every day members of the company would pick up messages they left for them—messages that berated the directors for staging a dirty play.

Despite their misgivings about the play's plot, the demand for tickets continued unabated. The company decided to extend the run for still another week. It was also decided to move the show to the Auditorium Theater because it could accomodate more people.

After that success the company staged James Barry's **Mary Rose**. The stars in that play were Sullavan and Fonda, and the director was Logan. This very charming play told a story about a young girl who was torn between the reality of life and the strange world outside it. Both Fonda and Sullavan, according to Logan, were "unsurpassable."

The next play produced by the company was S.N. Behrman's **The Second Man**. The cast included Fonda, Sullavan, Kent Smith and Elizabeth Fenner. This too was one of the company's better efforts.

Success did not create an atmosphere of peace among the Players. A problem arose that had Fonda demanding that his good friend Logan be dispensed with as a director and replaced with one from New York.

The episode started early one morning. Leatherbee telephoned Logan and implored him to rush right over to the rehearsal room. "Windy," he said had become ill with tuberculosis. "He will be in the hospital for a long time."

When Logan walked into the room Hall Bassett, the stage manager, gave him a script. Leatherbee said, "You've got to take over right away." Logan had never read the script nor had he seen a performance of the play. He told Leatherbee that he did not want to undertake the responsibility of directing a work that he was not familiar with. "The actors," he said, "will have no confidence in me."

Leatherbee told him to "do the best you can. The cast is aware that you will do the best you can. They also know that we must have it on the boards next week."

When the cast was assembled they displayed distinct signs of doubting Logan's ability to direct a play. Leatherbee, sensing their state of mind, told them to exercise some patience; all would work out. Logan read the script and then started to follow instructions—those on the printed script that had been used previously by a New York based company. For example, he would read the following: "Hank move to behind the sofa," and "Peggy, sit on chair stage left" and so on. After a few minutes had gone by Fonda raised his voice in protest. "Actors," he exclaimed, "shouldn't be told where to move when the director doesn't know why." Logan was hurt and told Fonda that he wasn't being very patient. He appealed to the cast:

"Let's just blunder through the business as indicated in the script today and after I've read the play tonight I can make some sense out of it.

Logan was about to declare that the rehearsing was to be called off for the day when Fonda said:

"Just a minute. I don't think anyone should leave until Charlie gets here. We've sent for him." Leatherbee appeared on the scene almost instantly as if he had been conjured up by a magician's trick. Fonda, acting as the self-appointed spokesman for the cast, said:

"This is a protest and I'm speaking for the entire group. If Windy is ill we've got to have someone who can direct the whole company. Josh isn't experienced enough for that. It's all right for him to direct a single play once in a while, but not our entire season. To put it bluntly, we won't work with him."

Displaying a considerable degree of insensitivity, Fonda did not look at his friend when he was delivering the ultimatum. At that moment Logan felt that with a friend like that a man indeed doesn't need any enemies.

Leatherbee displayed a loyalty that is all too rare in the world of the theater. He refused to bow to Fonda's threats and made it quite clear that he intended to stand by Logan.

He declared, "Come hell or high water, I'm not sending to New York for anyone. It would disrupt our whole company. Josh can handle this and so can you if you try. If at the end of the week it isn't working out, we'll talk about other arrangements."

During the following week Logan, somewhat intimidated by Fonda's behavior, was resisting a compulsion to get on a train for

New York. It was now important that he make every effort to regain the confidence of the cast. He suggested that they allow their imagination to run freely and that he would be more than willing to edit if necessary. They followed his suggestion and told Logan that they were enjoying the new freedom he had allowed them and that they now had full confidence in themselves. In a sense he was learning the hard way how to be a director. His method worked well. The next two plays found him in full control with no questions raised by anyone.

The Trial of Mary Dugan was the next play on the schedule. It was a melodrama written by Bayard Veiller. In addition to Fonda and Smith, a new and talented actress was engaged. Her name was Mildred Natwick. Fonda and Smith had worked with her at the Children's Theater in Washington D.C. It was Natwick's debut with the company, and Sullavan's last appearance with the Players.

The aura of success was still in the air. Since the next play would be staged during Lent, the theater manager suggested that the company produce a religious play that would depict the last days of Christ on earth. The director selected **The Dark Hours** by Don Marquis, the author of **Archie and Mehitabel.** But it was a dismal failure.

The company had been working for seven weeks in Baltimore. Despite its many successes the actors felt letdown for reasons they were unable to explain to themselves. Fonda, who according to Logan, had "never been the same after Baltimore," announced that he was finished with the University Players. He left the company rather abruptly. He was now determined to make his own way in the New York legitimate theater.

Chapter III
Struggling in New York

Fonda left in a huff after the Baltimore season of 1931 was over. He said that he was dissatisfied with the way things were going and would in the future try and find a place in the theater elsewhere.

After he left the University Players he attracted the attention of Broadway producer, Arthur J. Beckhard. The latter had recently produced and directed the New York hit play, **Another Language** authored by Rose Franken and starring Dorothy Stickney. At least ten years older than most of the Players, Beckhard managed to persuade the directors to try out some of the plays the following summer. It was considered to be quite a feather in the cap for the Players to be working with so prominent a man. In the end however, the company found itself ruthlessly exploited rather than helped by the extremely suave Beckhard. He utilized all their facilities to try out some of his plays. Logan and associates had actually believed that a time would come in the near future when the company would be working in New York and be able to establish a permanent repertory company there. But their hopes were quickly shattered. The catastrophe occurred after the company was persuaded to stage Frank McGrath's play, **Cary Nation.** "The play," Logan said recently, "was a groaning bore." It had first been tried out at Old Silver Beach. In this new production Beckhard demanded a 50-50 split of the profits and insisted that it should be staged at the Playhouse Theater in Baltimore. When the company's directors told him that they did not want to do it, Beckhard threatened to take it to New York with most of the cast. Reluctantly Logan and the other directors agreed to accede to the producer's demands. It was a very bitter pill for them to swallow especially when the large expenditures that had been defrayed for the production put the company in a financial bind.

The play opened at the Biltmore Theater in New York on October 29, 1932. Esther Dale was the star. The cast included James Stewart, Myron McCormick, Mildred Natwick, Barbara O'Neill and Josh Logan. The company's worst fears were realized. The critics did not like it. They treated the effort with well-deserved derision. That blow, plus a deserted box office, caused the play to close. And it also brought about the demise of the University Players. The vision the directors and the actors had all shared with Fonda, that a repertory company of their own which would make a definite mark on the theater in America vanished overnight. It was the end of a dream brought about by naivete, a lack of good business sense, and a producer who was so well portrayed by Zero Mostel in the picture of the same title—**The Producer.**

The cast was now at liberty. Beckhard, seeing an opportunity for himself came to the rescue. In need of cheap labor, he offered several of them jobs in his organization. Logan was hired at the munificent salary of fifteen dollars a week. But, as he later recalled, the fifteen dollars did not stay in his pocket too long. Producer Beckhard, who was always short of loose change, often asked Logan to pay for his taxi fares or lunches. Poor Logan, who knew he was being used, was afraid to object since jobs were scarce during those depression years. Beckhard, always the schemer was offered many directorial jobs and, in turn, he farmed them out to Windust, Logan and the others. On still another occasion Logan was picked to direct another of Beckhard's assignments. He made certain that he would receive all the credit for the work done. Thus Logan did the work and Beckhard benefited as usual.

Beckhard, like an old-time sweatshop boss, had a good thing going for him. Logan found himself indebted to Beckhard for two jobs—that of company manager at night and assistant at the box office during the day. For both chores he received the grand sum of $50 a week.

James Stewart managed to make $35 a week and McCormick, $30. With all that affluence the three decided to rent a modest-sized apartment on West 63rd Street, just a few steps away from Central Park West. The decrepit apartment had not received a coat of paint in years. It included a bedroom with two twin beds, a living room with two studio couches, a bathroom with a shower that had a permanent odor of decay and hordes of cockroaches. It also had an oversized kitchen stove that took up practically all the available space in the hall.

Fonda was still out of work at the time. Despite the fact that the three men could have used some additional revenue from another occupant they decided to invite the impoverished Fonda as the fourth man in their apartment. Fonda was the only one of the foursome who had been married, but that marriage was over almost before it had been consummated. Fonda called the apartment "Casa Gangrene," a well-deserved description of the rundown place.

Central Park West in New York City is an avenue of luxury apartment houses with upper middle class tenants mostly. At that time, however, houses right off that avenue were inhabited by a motley array of tenants, often the poor or gangsters. The building in which the latter day version of the Four Musketeers lived, stood right across the street from the Young Men's Christian Association. Anyone who looked out of an apartment window there, would see a special kind of business flourishing on the street. Hookers were approaching potential customers while their pimps inside the building kept a sharp eye on their "merchandise." The girl friends of the notorious local gangsters paraded in all their finery. Gun battles between rival gangs were the order of the day. The infamous Jack "Legs" Diamond, racketeer extraordinaire and well-heeled bootlegger, was gunned down on the street during the time the four actors lived there.

Shortly after moving into the apartment, Fonda left for a short stay in Omaha. The director, Gregory Foley, had asked him to star

in a play at the local theater. Fonda readily accepted because he
wanted to see his parents, his old friends, and most important, because
he was going to be paid for his work.

The director suggested that Fonda pick the play he would like
to appear in. He chose Barrie's **A Kiss for Cinderella**, a play that
had previously been produced by the University Players. He had directed, designed the scenery and played the role of the tender-hearted
policeman in the Barrie comedy. At that time his wife of two months,
Margaret Sullavan had played the female lead in the production.

In the new staging at the Omaha Playhouse the lead was played
by a teen-age girl named Dorothy McGuire who was later to become
a very successful stage and screen actress.

After a few pleasant weeks in his home town, Fonda returned
to the apartment on West 64th Street. But times were still difficult
and once again he was tramping the streets of the big and unfeeling
city looking for work along with thousands of other victims of the
Depression.

After weeks haunting the offices of the theatrical agents he
finally landed a job as leading man with a stock company. He was
now in an exuberant mood despite the fact that he would have to
take the ferry to the flatlands of Jersey City every day. He boasted
to his fellow-lodgers that the money he expected to receive for his
labors would be fantastic if not obscene. He had been promised ten
percent of the gross receipts at the box office. The three friends
were deeply impressed. Fonda was now in the same league with such
super-stars as Alfred Lunt, Lynn Fontaine, Ethel Barrymore and Katherine Cornell. Or so they thought. They were among the few thespians
who were able to get so advantageous an agreement.

"Well, I suppose we're in clover," he boasted to his friends. But
their expectations for a better life were quickly shattered. The facts
were most disappointing: The tickets had been priced ridiculously
low and there were very few customers. In all, Fonda pocketed seven
dollars a week. However, whatever the shortcomings of his rent pay-
ments he made up for in his achievements as cook and handyman.
Logan admits he was a bit jealous of his friend's talents.

"He mastered everything he tried his hand at," he said. "He
could paint and build scenery, he was a talented artist, and a master
of the culinary arts. And what's more," said Logan, "he could also
do amazing things with his supple body."

The two often frequented the "Y" across the street where Logan
watched Fonda exercise with his palms flat on the floor. He would
then flip his feet into the air and with no effort at all paddle all over
the room his legs either bent or stretched straight out. Logan was
now determined to prove to his friend that he too had some gymnastic
ability. Noticing a rope suspended from the gymnasium ceiling he
asked Fonda whether he would like to see him climb it. Fonda nodded
his assent and watched Logan make his way hand over hand to the
top. But when he reached that point he was stricken with an attack
of his chronic vertigo. He was quite frightened and a cold sweat covered
his body. He finally was able to work his way down the rope and land

safely on his feet. With this accomplishment he turned to Fonda and
said:

"Did you see me go up?" The taciturn Fonda responded with—"I
didn't think you could do it." And without another word he turned
and walked away.

Life at Casa Gangrene continued for a while without any further
incident. Fonda was still earning the munificent sum of seven dollars
a week and preparing appetizing portions of Mexican rice, beef and
Swedish meatballs. The meatballs were made of ground veal and milk-
soaked bread crumbs, a recipe he had received from his mother.

Three of the Casa's inmates had only modest appetites. The
sole exception was Jimmy Stewart, who despite his rather slim frame,
consumed vast amounts of food. At one sitting his amazed friends
watched him swallow eighteen meatballs. Stewart's appetite created
a serious budgetary problem for the others even in those pre-inflation
days.

Since money was in short supply, someone had to devise ways
to increase the exchequer. Fonda, imaginative as always, came up
with a clever suggestion which he claimed would bring more cash
into the coffers. His plan was to set up beer parties which would
be held once a week. The four pooled their meager resources and
rented a cellar in a speakeasy on West 40th Street. The decor was
very primitive. The floor was of earth. But that was a part of its
attraction. It was a correct assumption that the local young people
would be attracted to the place where the admission price and most
of the food was minimal.

Fonda kept cuts of steak on an iron grill. Ross Alexander, the
young actor who had created some problems for the University Players
when they worked on the Cape, assisted the new restauranteur in
cooking the meats for the patrons. The price of a steak and unlimited
steins of beer totalled one dollar.

Later, one of the actors recalling those days, said:

"The club was a good place to spend an evening. The food cooked
by Hank was superb."

Even after many years and many starring roles, Fonda's skill
as a cook was still enjoyed by his friends. He liked to invite close
friends to a Sunday-night meal at his California home. And they still
swear by his skill as a cook.

Fonda's talents as a scenic designer would prove to be a handicap
for a time. One summer while looking for a job he was asked to try
out for a play that was to be staged on Long Island. It was near enough
to the city to attract the critics, but it didn't happen that way. The
director had chosen Fonda to appear in the play, but the author had
other ideas; he wanted another actor to play the part. Fonda was
left, as he said, "high and dry."

The summer theaters had already engaged all the actors they
needed and Fonda was now in a desperate situation. When an agent
friend proposed that he should accept a job as a handyman with a
theatrical company in Surrey, Maine, he accepted the suggestion
with considerable reservations. His duties called for the driving of
a station wagon, taking care of the cast's trunks from the railroad

station to the theater and doing some work backstage. That meant taking care of the props and other necessary stage chores. And for all that he was paid thirty-five dollars a week, including room and board.

However, when he traveled to Maine he was told that a scenic designer and electrician had already been hired by the company. In the smaller summer theaters only two men are usually hired to do whatever has to be taken care of backstage. The two men have to design, construct, paint, set up and take care of the lights on stage. Fonda had done all that before, but now he was given one choice—to work as a third handyman. Toward the end of the season the scenic designer had a battle royal with the producer and resigned in high dudgeon. Fonda, always alert for any opportunity, contacted the producer and convinced him that he was more than capable to fill the job. Thus he became the scenic designer for the last few shows of the season.

The season ended with the Broadway hit play, **Michael and Mary.** The play of British origin starred Edith Barrett in New York. She was touring with a package deal which she now offered to stock companies. Miss Barrett was expected to arrive in Surrey momentarily to take part in the dress rehearsal. The company at the summer theaters generally rehearsed all with the local cast. Barrett would then "pick it up at the dress rehearsal."

The play had three sets. That created some complications for a small stock company that did not have a loft. Nor did it have any wings. Fonda had to find a way to cope with those problems. How was one to solve them? There were three sets to handle. He managed to resolve it by painting the flats on "both sides" so that one side would be the fireplace for another scene in the play. Turn it around and it became the fireplace in still another scene. Ingeniously, he also saw to it that a window could be turned around and become a window in a different scene. Fonda managed to work the props in such a way that the sets functioned smoothly.

The star, Edith Barrett, was greatly impressed with the skill Fonda displayed as a scenic designer and praised his work. She knew nothing about his experience as an actor, and then and there, began to broadcast far and wide what a talent she had discovered. Even his friends who should have known better, advised Fonda to stick to that craft and make it his career in the theater.

"Fonda, face it," they said. "For Christ's sake you're a scenic designer. Why don't you accept that fact. Be happy that you have been given that gift and just settle for it. You're not going to be an actor."

After listening to that well meant but uncalled for advise, Fonda said:

"I can't accept that."

But one must eat and the only work being offered him at that time was that of a scenic designer at the Westchester Playhouse in Mount Kisco. The town is only forty-five minutes away from Broadway. Fonda was aware that it was easily accesible for the New York critics. That was the major reason why he accepted the job offer.

Toward the middle of the summer the company had an open week. The two producers of the Playhouse approached Fonda and asked him to suggest a one-set comedy, preferably with five characters, which they would like to stage. They wanted a set that could be made cheaply. As Fonda explained--"The royalties aren't very large. The cast isn't big and one set keeps the cost down also."

Fonda remembered that the University Players in Baltimore had produced a one-set, five character comedy entitled **It's a Wise Child.** He also recalled that one of the characters, the iceman, appears on stage for a few minutes in the first act and briefly in the third act, and had provoked a great deal of laughter from the audience. While not the most important part the audience usually found the most amusing one on stage. "He stood out."

Fonda told the two producers that he could "save" them "a salary of an outside actor because I've played the iceman." They agreed to let him act the part. And after his first appearance he proved to be the most talked about actor during the run of the play. He was invited to come back to the Playhouse the next season because of the success he had had in playing the character.

Fonda liked waxing philosophical about the accidents in life that can determine a future career. He implies that we are all creatures with a will of our own, but that life can deal out unexpected cards. A step backward in his case, such as accepting a job as a handyman, was in a sense the way he was able to get a job as a scenic designer at Mount Kisco. And that led to his renewing his career as an actor. It was not planned that way, he says. But it did happen. Who could have foreseen such an outcome?

"Imagine," he said, "because I did accept the job to go to Surrey, Maine, to drive a station wagon, which was a real comedown for me after I had been acting for many years, I found myself playing important parts again only two years after that experience at the Westchester Playhouse and actually playing solid parts." "Is it fate," he asks, "Or do we ourselves set in motion a series of events without any knowledge of their outcome?"

But we are running ahead of our story. It was the third winter in New York--the winter after his first summer season at the Westchester Playhouse. Fonda was now sharing new quarters with Jimmy Stewart and both men were now going to producers' offices looking for work. They heard that Leonard Stillman was doing a revue called **New Faces.** It was being rehearsed at some out-of-the-way place. Stillman was then easily convinced to take on the two actors. He had nothing to lose since he was rehearsing without having to answer to Equity (union) rules and thus did not have to guarantee salaries to anyone who worked for him.

Stewart, always the more fortunate one, worked with the revue for a week. He was accepted for a role in **Yellow Jack,** a play about army doctors fighting yellow fever outbreaks in Panama where the Canal was being built. Guthrie McClintic, husband of Katherine Cornell was the director. But Fonda remained with **New Faces** and did some pantomimes with Imogene Coca and sketches with other members of the cast.

Fonda's work came to the attention of Leland Hayward, demon agent whom he had been introduced to years earlier. Leland signed him to a contract. The following summer when Fonda was acting at the Westchester Playhouse again and, for a change, playing important roles there, Hayward was on the coast on a business trip—his headquarters were still in New York—when he offered Fonda an opportunity to act in the movies. Fonda however wasn't in the least interested in motion pictures. He told Hayward that he had no intention of going to California. But Hayward the best convincer in the business, would not take that turndown seriously. He sent Fonda a lengthy telegram telling him in detail why it was imperative for him to go to the coast. He assured him that he would not have to stay there. After reading the telegram Fonda sent one in return. It contained one word, "No." It was his way of being amusing. But Hayward persisted and finally managed to persuade Fonda against his better judgment to come to Hollywood.

Fonda had a week's vacation coming to him. Since Hayward was paying for his travel and hotel expenses, he felt that he had nothing to lose by going to Tinsel Town.

Hayward was waiting for him at the Los Angeles airport with a very impressive-looking car. He drove Fonda to the very posh Beverly Wilshire Hotel where he engaged a suite for him.

It was mid-summer. The day was both hot and humid. Fonda's first step was to go into the bathroom to shower. After he had dried himself and donned a robe he walked into the living room to find Hayward talking to a stranger. It was none other than movie producer, Walter Wanger. The name Wanger meant nothing to him since he knew very little about life in movieland nor about the men who were running the studios.

The year was 1934. The country was still suffering the effects of the Depression, tens of thousands of able-bodied men and women were unemployed—some were selling apples on street corners. Others were lined up at Salvation Army soup kitchens in order to keep body and soul together. And all over the country one saw the so-called "Hoovervilles," makeshift shacks in the town dumps with once fairly prosperous Americans living there. And yet despite the economic blight that had hit the nation the giant movie studios were racking in tens of millions of dollars at the box offices every day of the week. People were looking for some escape from the miseries they saw about them and the screen factories of Hollywood were busily engaged in manufacturing the fantasies they craved.

Fonda, who had tasted the bitterness of poverty during four dreary winters in New York, was vulnerable to the siren songs being whispered in his ears by Wanger and Hayward. The two men were at their most persuasive best that afternoon in the hotel suite.

At first the actor demurred. He told them that his first and only love was the legitimate theater. But before he knew what he was doing, they had his signature on a contract. He had insisted, however, that he should be allowed to have sufficient free time between pictures to go back to New York and play on the stage. It was all like a dream. The sum of money he was to receive for his acting was unbelievable. He could not comprehend why a tough-minded Hollywood producer aware of the fact that he was unknown could offer him $1,000 a week.

In later years, when he discussed the incident with a friend, he mentioned that he walked down Wilshire Boulevard with Hayward, the super-salesman and exclaimed:

"There's something fishy about this."

It just did not seem plausible for a man in his right mind to offer him all that money.

He turned to Hayward and said:

"How do I get out of it?"

Hayward, he later said, always teased him about that remark. The contract Hayward reminded him, allowed Fonda to work in New York during the winter season. After the deal had been consummated Fonda returned to the Westchester Playhouse. He had previously committed himself to act in two more plays that summer.

He appeared in Molnar's **The Swan** in which he played the part of the tutor; Geoffrey Kerr had the role of a prince and Francesca Brunning was the princess. And therein hangs a tale—a tale of how an unforeseen happening changes a life and a career.

The Broadway star, June Walker was married to Kerr and frequently came to Mount Kisco to see her husband and watch him act. Kerr and Fonda were occupying the same dressing room when June walked in and whispered something to Kerr.

"I heard a few words she was saying to Kerr," said Fonda years later.

She said, "Wouldn't he be wonderful as the farmer?" Fonda was still unaware that he was the subject of that conversation. He erased it from his mind since it apparently did not concern him. Or so he thought at the time. But the following week he received a telephone call from playwright Marc Connelly. He had written and was about to direct a play called **The Farmer Takes a Wife.** June Walker had been signed to play the female lead in the play. Connelly asked Fonda to come down to New York to discuss some business with him. Fonda went to the playwright's hotel, and about an hour later he was reading the male lead part for him. Connelly was more than impressed with the reading.

"What's your salary?" he asked in a gentle manner. Fonda replied, "$35 a week at the Westchester Playhouse." The playwright told him to go to producer Max Gordon's office and ask for $200 a week. He also advised him that he would call Gordon and alert him that he would be at his office momentarily. Fonda did not encounter any problems with Gordon. He signed a contract to act in the upcoming production.

Perhaps an explanation is due about the various kinds of contracts an actor is offered by producers. There is a run-of-the-play contract and a two-week minimum standard one. The latter enables the producer to fire an actor with a compulsory two-weeks' notice. The actor also must give the producer two-weeks' notice before quitting. Fonda had that kind of a contract with Gordon.

The show opened in Washington D.C. and was a great success

with both the audience and the critics. The following day when Fonda arrived at the theater for a run-through of the play he was approached by Gordon's business manager. Fonda, not entirely naive, realized that the manager was about to offer him a run-of-the-play contract. That prompted him to surmise "If he wants that kind of contract I'll ask him for a bigger stipend." The manager read his mind and said:

"How much did you have in mind?"

And Fonda said: "Well, two and a quarter."

There was no haggling. The business manager readily agreed to that demand. Fonda later realized that an agent would have had Gordon pay him at least $500 a week or more likely $750.

The play opened in New York and received unanimous approval by the critics. It was a hit. Following that successful opening the William Fox Company bought it for a film. That happened before Fox was swindled out of his own company by the financiers.

The powers in charge of the company were originally considering either Joel McCrea or Gary Cooper for the farmer's part, but they finally decided to have Fonda who was an obvious choice in view of his outstanding success in the Broadway production. When the movie moguls discovered that he was under contract to Wanger they had some trouble persuading the producer to loan him out for the picture. Wanger was to receive $5,000 a week for his actor's services. He in turn gave Fonda $2,000 dollars above the 1,000 he was paying him. That left $2,000 which landed in the producer's pocket.

The play's premier on Broadway occurred in October of that year. The local critics said that Fonda portrayed the character of Dan Harrow to the life, giving him "the manly virtues of an admirable American." The use of such glowing terms as "strong," "lustrous," "an artist to his fingertips" and "typical of the country as its Uncle Sam image" were not thought to be exaggerations by the theatergoers. Thus Fonda was off to a good start in the public mind both as an actor of an unusual talent but as a fine American. After the debut in that play the image he projected and has projected ever since in the eyes of his fellow-Americans that of an idealized man, dependable, honest, with an integrity that made him unique. He became and was regarded, to quote President Carter, "national treasure."

Modest as ever, Fonda felt that this image of himself was not entirely true-to-life. At the time he was portraying the character of "Mister Roberts" on stage—another version of Dan Harrow—he said, "I'm not trying to suggest I'm a son of a bitch, but I wouldn't want the world to think I go around thinking I'm the kind of guy I portrayed in **Mister Roberts**." Nevertheless the world still regards him as that kind of person.

Max Gordon, a man sensitive to violence, tried in his own way to tone down the realism of the play in one instance. The hero, Dan Harrow, was embroiled in a fist fight with a tough hombre—the leader of the canal gang. The thugs encouraged the two antagonists to commit mayhem on each other. One of the members of the gang enthusiastically urged Dan Harrow to "kick him in the privates." The line was spoken so inaudibly that Fonda could not hear what he said. Marc Connelly also wondered why the line he had written could not be heard. In time he was told that Gordon had asked the actor to reduce his voice to a whisper. He thought that the words were too offensive for the stage.

While the critics praised the play to the skies, the theatergoers reacted negatively to it. They enjoyed seeing Fonda in the role, but found it to be somewhat old-fashioned. It closed down after 104 performances. Connelly, Gordon and Fonda had expected the play to run much longer, but its demise did not sadden the hearts of the trio altogether. It had, after all been sold to the movie company for a substantial sum of money.

Fonda knew that his career had advanced a big step. Here was an actor who had only a short time before been a scenery designer and a general handyman in the theater. Now, he was playing with another star in a Hollywood "blockbuster" along with Janet Gaynor who had won an "Oscar" for her acting in **Seventh Heaven.**

That sort of good fortune happens quite rarely to stage people, even in the best of times. Years later when **My Fair Lady,** the Broadway musical, was being cast for a film Warner Brothers overlooked Julie Andrews, the star of the original production because she wasn't famous enough. Audrey Hepburn, who couldn't sing a note to save her life, was starred in the picture. She mouthed the words while another actress sang the songs. Fonda, who was more fortunate, managed to be assigned the lead role—both on the stage and in the movie.

Fonda encountered some problems trying to adjust to the new medium. He explained years later that Connelly, a very good stage director, had guided him through his first starring role on Broadway. Actors learn to appreciate that kind of direction. Up to that time Fonda's experiences in the theater had been limited to playing in stock companies where the cast rehearses for as little as a week with very limited guidance from the director. Windust was still learning how to direct, and his advice could hardly been taken as the last word in the art when Fonda was associated with the University Players. But now, he had the advantage of four weeks' rehearsals before opening on Broadway. That also included three to four weeks of performances on tour where he could polish his lines. Fonda liked to cite an example of how he and Connelly worked together:

"Dan," he said, "had a particular reply when the heroine Molly wanted to know some facts about horses."

"Do I like horses," Harrow says, "Yes ma'am. Mostly I admire cows." Connelly knew that there was something in the lines that would provoke laughter from the audience. After rehearsing for a while, both Fonda and Connelly found that the only way laughter could be induced was to pause between the words "Yes ma'am" and... "Mostly I admire cows."

During the filming of the play, Victor Fleming the director, asked Fonda to cut out the pause after the words "Yes ma'am." "Just shorten it." Fonda raised strong objections to the change of stage business. He said, "Vic, it took eight weeks for Marc Connelly and me to discover that's the laugh line. The key to the laugh is the pause."

Fleming was a man who could change his mind when the occasion called for it. He said "okay." Fonda included the pause in the next "take." But he could have spared himself the effort; the pause was eliminated by the film editor in the cutting room.

Fonda also mentioned that he had encountered some other problems while working in the movies. The play script, he said, is always written so that in the middle of a page you will find the character's name and his dialogue just under it. The stage instructions are generally in parentheses between the name and the dialogue. But movie scripts are arranged in a different way. When he first began to act in the movies he found it rather disconcerting to see that the scripts had two columns—the left side of the page for the character's name and the dialogue, and the right side for the action and stage direction.

In one of the early scenes in the hotel lobby you see Molly waiting for Dan to walk in. The two converse with each other and go to the dining room. The script at that point reads Dolly. Since he knew that there was no character whose name was Dolly in the stage script Fonda was momentarily at a loss to know what to make of it. It occurred to him that someone had changed the original script and introduced a new character. He walked over to Fleming and asked him who Dolly was. She appears in every scene he said. Fleming exploded with laughter and explained that the word was simply applied to the camera direction.

The first day's shooting was conducted outdoors. It was a new experience for Fonda. He had played Dan Harrow over 100 times on stage. And there was, he said, no water there. There were artificial trees and something that looked like a blacksmith's forge. Now he was acting in the same scenes only there were real trees, a real boat, and live horses who were actually pulling the boats along a real canal. There was a professional blacksmith who was working at a real forge. "It was," he admitted, "an exciting experience."

At one point the cameraman was about to shoot a scene when Fleming motioned Fonda to walk over to him. He tried to explain him the differences between stage and screen acting. Tough guy Fleming was not the most sensitive man, some said. His behavior on the set was reminiscent of the conduct one would expect from a bleary-eyed dock worker who had been imbiding too much hard liquor. But he knew his craft and Fonda respected his opinions.

"You're exaggerating it," said Fleming. Fonda who was the most reserved of actors had now been told that he was overdoing it. He was disturbed, but listened attentively to the director.

A stage actor has to project his body movements as well as his voice in order to have it reach the topmost balcony. Fonda was told that while that was necessary in a theater, it must be dispensed with on a movie set. The camera does all the projecting needed. A movie actor speaks his lines like a man who is carrying on a conversation with a friend. The microphones take care of the sound.

Fonda, who was always a dedicated artist, could never be accused of being opinionated. When his intelligence told him that a director made sense he listened and followed his advice. That is what happened after Fleming had pointed out what he should avoid in the movies.

Fonda and Janet Gaynor in "The Farmer Takes a Wife," 1935.

He knew that Fleming had offered his advice and that by following it he would become a natural performer. He had tried to have his stage acting appear natural and realistic to a point. He was intent on making his audiences believe they were seeing the real thing and not just another actor who was practicing his tricks to befuddle them.

Fonda tried to bring more naturalism in his work. Frequently he whispered a silent prayer to himself in which he expressed the hope that the audience would believe that he was playing the character for real—not that he was simply using all the techniques at his command to appear authentic.

The Farmer Takes a Wife was produced by Fox in 1935. While such future stars as Jimmy Stewart, John Wayne, Gary Cooper, Clark Gable and other actors had to play comparatively minor roles in the first picture they appeared in, Fonda achieved film stardom in his very first effort. Fonda, who was always generous to a fault, attributed his film success to director Victor Fleming.

Janet Gaynor, one of the super stars of the early 1930's, was still one of the mainstays of the Fox studios, but she shared top billing with Fonda in that picture. She was well cast for the part of Mollie Larkins, a role that called for a small statured girl with teenage enthusiasms who still had to display some degree of maturity.

The cast included the red-haired Irishman Charles Bickford, the grotesquely elongated Slim Summerville, and the whiskey-voiced Andy Devine. Others in the cast included John Qualen, Margaret Hamilton, Roger Inhof and the very young Jane Withers. It was Henry Fonda however who made the greatest impression on the critics with his acting abilities.

New York Times critic, Andre Sennwald waxed positively poetic in describing the sentimental warmth and the cogent charm he found while viewing the film. He wrote that it "is a rich and leisurely comedy of American manners and its roots are deep in the native soil." However he did find that the performances of Gaynor and Summerville were not as good as those of Herb Williams and June Walker who had played the stage roles.

It was only Fonda and Bickford who managed "to approximate the superb performances of those stage players." "Mr. Fonda," he wrote, "is the bright particular star of the occasion." And looking into the future he continued—"As the virtuous farm boy, he plays with an immensely winning simplicity which will quickly make him one of our most attractive screen actors."

Richard Watts, Jr., critic of the **New York Herald Tribune,** wrote—"Mr. Fonda is that rarity of the drama, a young man who can present naive charm and ingratiating simplicity in a characterization and yet never fail to seem both manly and in possession of his full senses."

And the **New York American** (now a defunct newspaper) said, "Henry Fonda's day dawns...He dominates the scene and emerges from his film debut with a certain film success and one of the really important contributions of stage and screen within the past few seasons."

Chapter IV
Success in Tinsel Town

As one of the recognized brightest new stars in Tinsel Town on the Pacific, Fonda was now frequently asked to come to the most exclusive parties in the movie capital. One of the first functions he attended was in the home of the always scintilating Carole Lombard. His producer, Walter Wanger had managed to get the invitation for him.

An actor in Hollywood was accepted on the basis of the money he made. The more he was paid the more highly he was regarded. It was quite a triumph for Fonda to be asked to come to the Lombard abode. He had been in only one picture and his salary was still below the figure that was considered to be a proper entrance fee, at least among the elite of movieland. His natural demeanor and handsome appearance, as well as his sardonic sense of humor aided him in cementing some lasting friendships. In time he made such friends as Robert Montgomery, Tyrone Power, song writer, Hoagy Carmichael, the Gary Coopers and many others who were considered to be members of the upper strata in Dream Town.

His forthright honesty and his resistance to the demands of the studio magnates puzzled his new friends. The men in control of the studios demanded that he pose for publicity pictures, escort female actresses under contract to opening nights, grant interviews to sob sisters working on the newspapers and fan magazines and reveal every detail of his life to them. Fonda catagorically refused to play the Hollywood game. He was not the kind of man who carried his heart on his sleeve, nor did he feel any real liking for the female stars he was asked to accompany to movie premieres. He was bored with the artificial manners of some of the actors and studio moguls. Most pleasing of all to him, at least, was the money he was making. It made more tolerable the kind of life he had to lead in California.

During the next three years Fonda was assigned a variety of roles in pictures that could only have been considered potboilers. The sole exception was **The Trail of the Lonesome Pine.**

After his success in **The Farmer Takes a Wife** he was cast in a remake of a sad tale entitled **Way Down East.** The original version of the film had been produced in 1920 with David Wark Griffiths as the director and Lillian Gish and Richard Barthelmess as the lovers. It was considered a screen classic, even though dated at the original filming. The new version however lacked the sensitivity of the old film. Janet Gaynor was offered the part previously played by Miss Gish, but she had to turn it down because of illness. Rochelle Hudson, who replaced her, gave a performance that was at best mediocre—the critics were very unkind about one scene which had her hopping about on some prop ice floes. Seenwald of the **Times** wrote "...your first impulse is to applaud the production as a sly and uproarious burlesque of the celebrated tear drama. But the film possesses genuine charm in its earlier scenes on a New England farm."

Fonda fared better at the hands of the film critics. One critic said, "In large measure this is a personal triumph for Henry Fonda, whose immensely winning performance as the squire's son helps establish an engaging bucolic mood for the drama in its quieter moments."

Fonda's reputation as a fine actor was still intact despite the film's defects.

By this time Wanger knew that he had a "hot" property in the actor. Why produce pictures when one could make more money loaning the star to other companies? He loaned him to RKO which cast him opposite the petite operatic star Lily Pons in a bit of fluff that did not amount to very much. Miss Pons was treated gently by the critics, but it was Fonda who was praised. The **New York American** said, "Lily Pons has the advantage of splendid support that approaches the brilliant, especially in the part of Henry Fonda whose performance is absolutely stellar. Such simplicity, directness and ability to create living characters is a talent that cannot be analyzed and certainly cannot be dismissed as accidental."

After assignments in a number of pictures he did not like, Fonda said:

"Some of my pictures aren't that good. I could name you many pictures without drawing a breath that I'm ashamed of."

After he had completed another Grade C movie with the operatic coloratura soprano, he had a strong urge to go back to New York and act on the stage. But three more years were to go by before that became a possibility. During those early years in Hollywood he lost his father and mother. Their deaths affected him deeply because he had always felt a strong attachment toward them. They did see him perform on stage at the Omaha Playhouse and had gone East to see him work with the University Players in West Falmouth. He had hoped that some day they would see him in a Broadway play.

Fonda was now a bachelor again. His marriage of two months with the temperamental Margaret Sullavan was now almost a forgotten episode in his life. Most of his friends found it hard to remember that he had ever been married. He set up his California home in an apartment that did not satisfy him. He moved to a number of other places until he decided to share quarters with his old friends John Swope and James Stewart. The latter was now under contract with Metro-Goldwyn-Mayer after he had been screen-tested and turned down by the Fox Company.

The troika was now ensconsed in a house with a gang of demanding cats. The place was now called "The House of Cats." It appeared that a feline whose name was George had acquired a mate whose name was Cerisse. The two had kittens. In time dozens of homeless cats made themselves at home in the house. Whether the army of cats were the hosts who allowed the out-numbered homo sapiens to live there was now a moot question. Reminiscing about those bygone days, Fonda said with a smile on his face that his old friend Jimmy Stewart is given to fabricating when he weaves fanciful tales about their lives in "The House of Cats."

Stewart apparently enjoys telling tall tales. Discussing the difficult ties they encountered with the stray cats that infested the place, Stewart said that he came home one night and saw Fonda, who had been drinking trying to shoot the furry pests with a bow and arrow.

"There were 35 of them," said Fonda. "They were wild and were breeding like cockroaches and they were a menace to the people in the neighborhood. It was a very serious problem.

"We called the Society for the Prevention of Cruelty to Animals and they promised to come and pick up the cats provided we would put them in boxes. But how could we catch them—they were dangerous. But the bow and arrow part of the story is apocryphal. I think that that's the nicest word to use.

"I had a target in the front yard and I did shoot arrows. I didn't shoot cats. I couldn't have hit a cat if I'd aimed at it, but I have to admit that it made a good story."

Stewart says that Fonda and he were living in the Brentwood, California, home when Greta Garbo rented a house adjoining theirs. He said that she had a stone wall built around it in order to have more privacy.

Stewart, a minor league Baron Munchausen further claims that he and Fonda were irritated with her actions. In a spirit of revenge they dug a tunnel under it so they could spy on the actress. Fonda, who was a stickler for truth, confirmed that Garbo had indeed moved next door but that she only had had a fence built—certainly not a stone wall. "He talked about digging a tunnel, but we didn't do it. Stewart tells that we dug and dug and dug until we hit a water main and flooded the whole place. It gets to be a beautiful story but it ain't true."

During his early years in California, Logan was working on the same movie lot with his friend Fonda. When Walter Wanger was about to start shooting the film **Vogues of 1939** with eight very glamorous models, Logan says that he observed him concentrating on a slip of paper on day. Turning to Logan, Wanger gave Logan a slip of paper which had the following information: "Tomorrow morning at ten we are testing Miss Aldredge, Miss Cawley, Miss C.D. and Miss E—."

As Logan read it he said, "I sure would like to meet the girls." Wanger pondered for a few moments and then said, "I've got the set up. You'll give a party, all of you at the house. I don't want any of these Hollywood press agents to make the girls feel commercial. This affair has to have class. I'll send over the food and drink but you've got to distill the guest list. No other girls. Fuck them. At least two men to every girl and they must be 1—single, 2—tall, dark and handsome, and 3—gentlemen in evening dress and if possible famous and, above all, eligible. Now call me if Jimmy, Hank and Swope agree."

Logan followed his instructions to the letter. Fonda and his friends accepted Wanger's stipulations. In fact, they fell all over themselves trying to go along with the producer-agent's wishes. One of Logan's friends was even willing to jilt his girl friend of long standing until the party was over.

"We did not countenance that sort of behavior," Logan said.

Logan was on the telephone for hours describing the girls' beauty and their culture. He fantasized about their charms and said that they were ethereal creatures who had descended on a rosy cloud from a Wagnerian Venusberg which he said was located about halfway up a rainbow. In addition to his pals Fonda, Stewart and Swope, Logan also invited the stocky Dick Foran and convinced Bogart to come along and enjoy himself.

The great day arrived at last. The male guests had never met any of the girls. Eight of the men were asked to pick them up. Dressed in white ties and formal wear, Swope escorted Katherine Aldredge and Logan chose Olive Cawley, a perfectly proportioned brunette. Kate was taller, a blonde and quite vivacious. The six other girls were equally endowed with the necessary physical attributes.

After all the guests had arrived Logan served drinks. The girls asked for lemonade instead, and the men indulged themselves with tumblers of whiskey.

Logan now says that the girls looked "like beautiful petals that had just fallen off a perfect magnolia blossom." The men for some reason were at a loss to know how to behave. Their language, usually quite earthy, was suddenly gone with the winds. They spoke like gentlemen that had just come out of a cloister; there were no expletives uttered that night. Logan suddenly had a thought that the men, ill at ease with the girls who were behaving like typical Salvation Army lassies, would run out of the house screaming that they had been conned.

Surprisingly enough the men stopped drinking the hard liquor and began to play charades and musical chairs with the girls. Stewart did a number of card tricks. Fonda made some small comment about the weather. After the party was over the boys drove the girls home and then returned to the house. By that time the other guests had left, with the exception of Bogart who was acting as if he was about to commit a murder. Logan apprehensively surmised that Bogart had been expecting a good deal more from the ladies and was angry because what he did get was some lemonade and innocuous conversation. Stewart, Fonda and Logan tried their best to lift his spirits and offered him a drink.

"Was it all that bad?" they asked him.

Bogart looked at the trio and then quietly said:

"Anyone that would want to screw one of those girls would probably toss a rock through a Rembrandt."

Chapter V
More Happenings in Dream Town

Fonda was enjoying his bachelor existence in southern California. One of his neighbors was Jeanette MacDonald who one unkind commentator once called "The Iron Butterfly." Fonda dated her and described his experience—that is, if it could be termed one. During the early evening he behaved in a very formal manner and addressed her as Miss MacDonald. As the evening progressed he became bold enough to call her Jeanette. It was all quite innocent, but the publicity man at the movie studio and the local gossip columnists had them engaged to each other. That news was based on the one date they had. The actress-singer was only one of the many young women he dated in those days.

There were other girls of course. He squired Shirley Ross around town for a brief period of time. The girl who really made a special impression on him, however, was Virginia Bruce, a talented actress with a charm all her own. All three male friends moved in on the stunning-looking actress with the enthusiasm of football players pushing hard for a touchdown. When Fonda's fourth picture, **The Trail of the Lonesome Pine,** had its premier at a local theater in Hollywood all three men escorted the fair lady.

It can now be revealed that the late Al Capp, famous for his **Li'l Abner** cartoon, admitted that it was Fonda's portrayal of David Tolliver in the picture that inspired him to create the very popular comic-strip character.

Friend Swope, more patient than Fonda, didn't get around to marriage until a decade later when he finally led Dorothy McGuire to the altar. Stewart, even more the reluctant dragon, did not become betrothed to the magnetic Gloria Hatrich McLean until he was 43. But we are moving ahead too fast. Fonda's fourth picture, **The Trail of the Lonesome Pine** (Paramount 1936) directed by Henry Hathaway, was the first outdoor color film produced in Hollywood.

For the first time Fonda was called upon to portray a character prone to violent impulses. In his previous films he played introverted country boys, but in **The Trail of the Lonesome Pine** he was a mountain hillbilly who was basically tender-hearted, considerate of his mother and acutely sensitive to the feelings of his sister and his girl, but ready to shoot to kill his family's enemies. Life in the mountains as revealed in fiction and the movies was in another time and place. The only thing lacking in the hills of Kentucky was culture and graceful living.

Fonda not only played Dave Tolliver; he was David Tolliver. The cast included the very appealing Sylvia Sydney, ex-saxaphone player Fred MacMurray, former tap dancer Fred Stone, the very vinegary Beulah Bondie, and Nigel Bruce who apparently was taking time out from playing Dr. Watson in the Sherlock Holmes pictures.

The picture had been previously produced in 1916 and again in 1923. The book on which the movie was based, was a best seller for years and the stage version had been a bread-winner for many touring companies. However, the Fonda picture wasn't just a repeat of the previous productions. Henry Hathaway's direction was responsible for creating a film that critics seriously considered to be a minor classic.

Frank S. Nugent of the **New York Times** had the following to say about it:

"...this is no turgid drawing room drama with a superabundance of dialogue and a minimum of action. It is none too generously endowed with story values. For all its gunplay and fist-swinging its plot considered alone would be unimpressive and a little more meaningful that the elemental fodder on which most Class B melodramas feed. But when to that story is added a cast of unusual merit and a richly beautiful color production then it becomes a distinguished and worthwhile picture."

And Regina Carwe of the **New York American** wrote:

"Henry Fonda contributes another fine cinematic portrait of the galaxy he has given in the role of the somber mountaineer whose heart is filled with murderous tradition and who is sometimes warmed by sunnier emotions."

Despite his fear of being interviewed by the local sob sisters of the movie fan magazines Fonda couldn't entirely avoid them. **Photoplay** magazine was a popular publication at that time. After an interview the publication ran a story in which Fonda was described as a typical pater-familas who wanted above all else to marry and settle down with a dutiful wife in a suburb and start breeding children. In a way the writer of the articles was being prophetic.

After his experiences with the fascinating but unpredictable Margaret Sullavan, Fonda was now searching for a more dependable partner. The second Mrs. Fonda was soon to appear in his life. Her name was Frances Seymour Brokaw. The Seymour lineage was an illustrious one. Frances' mother claimed to be a direct descendant of John Adams. Her father, even more the blueblood was, he said, a direct descendant of Edward Seymour, Duke of Somerset who was one of King Henry VIII's toadies. It was Jane Seymour who married that monarch and was in time beheaded by him.

Through her paternal grandmother, Frances was related to the Stuyvesants, the Stoutenburgs, the Howards and the Biddles of Philadelphia. Despite her highborn origins money was in very short supply for Frances. But there was a cousin, Henry Roger, a Standard Oil vice-president who was eager to help his ambitious and beautiful niece. He offered to pay her way through college. But she considered a higher education a waste of time and she chose instead to go to the Katherine Gibbs School where she was taught stenography and other office routines.

As she once succinctly put it, "So I can go down to Wall Street and marry a millionaire."

Frances' first position was with a bank in Fairhaven, Massachusetts. She labored there for a brief period and then departed for New York where she found an opening with the First National Bank. It was there that she met multi-millionaire George Tuttle Brokaw who had recently divorced Clair Booth, later to snare Harry Luce for herself. Brokaw was an alcoholic; he also beat his wives.

Frances had one child with her difficult husband. Shortly after its birth Brokaw died in a Hartford, Connecticut rest home where he had been attempting to regain his mental equilibrium after a strenuous bout with alcoholism. He left an estate valued at between four and five million dollars. His widow was his sole heir. She also collected on his $750,000 insurance policy.

Frances had always aspired to marry a wealthy man and she had succeeded in getting one. Now, in addition to being an independently rich widow she was also a very attractive one with astute financial skill. After the untimely demise of Brokaw she left for a European vacation with a young woman who was engaged to Ford de Villiers Seymour, her brother.

Fonda, whom fate had selected to be her next husband, was still living in California and enjoying his newly-acquired prosperity and success as an actor. The good life agreed with him. Long gone were the days when he had had to exist on a meager diet of boiled rice and water. Having lost his beanpole appearance he was now regarded by the Hollywood glamour girls as a handsome and very desirable bachelor. At that time he was cast in a picture with his former wife, Margaret Sullavan. Entitled **The Moon's Our Home,** the flick was an off-beat comedy with Sullavan in the role of an heiress and movie star who had been spoiled rotten by her many admirers.

It was the first time in film history that a divorced couple had been cast in the roles of lovers. It was the story of a temperamental actress and an adventurer-writer, Fonda, who are in love and get married without either of the parties being aware of the other's background. Sullavan outdoes herself as a talented comedian and plays the unpredictable lady to the hilt, throwing lamps and other weapons at her hero and barely missing him.

Fonda however did not fare very well with the critics. In a sense the picture was a minor Waterloo for him. One critic found him to be "engaging, although not too persuasive." Fonda accepted the criticism gracefully and said that you can't win them all.

The two former members of the University Players also made another film together, **Hotel Imperial.** Henry Hathaway who directed the picture vividly recalled how they behaved on the set:

"They were playful. She didn't care how ugly she looked. We worked three or four days and then the fun began. She wasn't married. She and Hank and some other Hollywood actors were always out on the town. She and Hank were kids who had grown up in the theater and were, as I said, very playful. She had a water pistol and she'd squirt him in the face and he'd scream and laugh and then squirt her and they'd fall over. He'd rib her about her ugly hair and face and costume and she'd chase him and he'd chase her in and out of the scenery.

"They fell over a pile of wires. She broke her arm and the studio bosses called me and said, 'Do we have to get Dietrich back?'

"I said, 'God told me twice not to finish this picture. A heroine with an arm in a sling scrubbing a floor and going to her wedding in a sling! It's ridiculous.' " That picture incidentally was finally cancelled out. Later on, another version was directed by Billy Wilder. It was called **Five Graves to Cairo.**

After the fun was over Fonda was offered a starring role in a picture with the French sensation, Annabella. It was his decision to accept that offer that led to his going to Europe where he met his future wife, Frances Seymour Brokaw. And it was the European filming of the picture that led him into the arms of Frances.

Fonda sailed for Europe in the spring of 1936. As his friend John Springer later explained he had "a strong desire to travel abroad and see both Ireland and England." That was why he decided to play in the picture.

Fonda was fascinated with Ireland where some of the scenes of the picture were shot. He had also looked forward to working with Annabella who happened to be a very sophisticated and outgoing kind of a woman.

It was while he was playing in the picture at the Denham Studios just outside London that he first met Frances. She wanted to see how a movie was being made and asked a friend to take her to the studio.

Wings of Morning, the first color film was being produced in England. Frances was quite taken with the handsome American actor who was playing the starring role in the picture. She knew that he was just what she was looking for in a husband. As usual, Fonda was the pursued rather than the pursuer. Apparently that was to be his fate for the rest of his life. As one good friend said to him. "You have never married anybody. They all married you!" But truth to tell he was beguiled with her charm and her upper-class manners. She was gentle and shy—two characteristics which she shared with Fonda. At the time of the first meeting Frances had a five-year-old daughter from her marriage to Brokaw. She hoped to have more children.

After his work in the picture was finished, Fonda left for a grand tour of Europe with Frances. They stopped over in Paris, Munich, Berlin and Budapest and savored what each of the critics had to offer.

During their tour of the continent they discussed the subject of marriage. There she was, beautiful and intelligent—and wealthy. From an actor's viewpoint she was a good security risk. While his own financial situation was good enough he had not forgotten those lean years of struggle in New York and, like most actors, he had learned

Top: Annabella and Henry Fonda in "Wings of the Morning" (1936). Bottom: Jackie Cooper and Henry Fonda in "The Return of Frank James" (1940).

Top: Fonda's second wife—mother of Jane and Peter—Frances Seymour
Brokaw Fonda. Bottom: Henry Fonda Enlisting in the U.S. Navy.

through bitter experience that life as a professional entertainer was at best uncertain financially.

Frances' parents announced their engagement on August 24, 1936. And several days after that Frances and her friend Fay Devereaux Keith who was engaged to her brother Roger sailed from Le Havre for New York. It was now September 16. Fonda remained behind for a brief period of time and then left Europe for New York where he arrived all alone. Josh Logan, who had driven down to the pier in an old beat-up car was there to welcome him home. He asked Fonda whether he had been impressed with the girl:

"Girl?" Fonda asked somewhat puzzled by the question. And then after a pause he said, "She's wonderful. We'd go for long rides in the buses, then get off and wander into some old English inns. We went dancing and looked into shop windows like a couple of kids."

"Isn't it wonderful to find a girl like that to marry," Logan said.

"Marry!" exclaimed Fonda. It was then that Logan was told that he was talking about Annabella.

Fonda set himself up temporarily at the Gotham Hotel on upper Fifth Avenue. Three months after Frances had been introduced to him at the Denham Studios she became his wife. There were a number of snobbish members of the Seymour family who said that she was marrying a man who was socially beneath her. A Seymour, they said, should not become the wife of a mere actor. They did not know that Fonda was a descendant of an Italian nobleman.

The ceremony took place at St. Bartholomew's Church on fashionable Park Avenue, with the Reverend Ralph Stockman officiating. There had been quite a problem getting a clergyman to perform the Episcopal ceremony because the groom was a divorced man, but that was resolved in time.

A large crowd of excited teenagers and some older persons waited outside the church to catch a glimpse of the groom. They cheered him to the echo when he arrived dressed in a morning coat and top hat. His friend Josh Logan was there. Fonda was attended by his agent, Leland Hayward, while the bride had her sister Marjory Campbell Seymour as her maid of honor. Fonda's two sisters had come all the way from Nebraska to see their brother being married for a second time.

The glowing bride wore a powder-blue tulle and an off-the-face hat and held pink roses and blue delphinius. Her brother Roger and sister Mary stood close by as the Reverend Stockman intoned the traditional ritual.

A reception for 150 people was held on the roof garden of the Hotel Pierre on 61st Street and Fifth Avenue. The couple then left by plane for Omaha where the new Mrs. Fonda was to meet with other members of her husband's family. The actor's mother and father had passed away and thus never lived to enjoy their son's success.

After a brief stay in Omaha the couple flew to Los Angeles where Fonda was to work in three films. They settled down in a small house and immediately began to look around for a more permanent place. They spent days on end driving around the Los Angeles area looking for some land where they could build their house. They found what they wanted in the Brentwood section, but the owners were reluctant to sell the land. It was not until Frances had given birth to her first child that the Fondas finally were able to induce him to sell the land to them.

The couple had very definite ideas on how to utilize the land they had purchased. They planned to have a garden and a great deal of thought was given to where the house should be constructed. Fonda wanted a Pre-Revolutionary War type New England house. It would be a colonial building with all the modern conveniences.

Unlike most home owners Fonda wanted his house to harmonize with the terrain. Shortly after he had acquired the land he set about building the house located on Tigertail Road along a path that wound up through the hills past a post-and-rail fencing. Right under it was a cupolaed porte-cochere that separated it from the garage and the servants' quarters. It also had a number of wings and a wood-shingled roof at a different level. The garage entrance was in the rear and was covered by a forest of shrubbery in front. There was also a breeze-way that connected it to the house and the old barn exterior that gave the feeling of being attached.

A playhouse was constructed a short distance away from the house—a bit to the rear and right across the lawn. The playhouse was meant to serve as a cabana and a swimming pool. The building was in stone—wood stucco style similar to the house. The gardens, a smaller playground and a jungle gym for the children they hoped to have were also laid out. Frances also wanted to have two painted wooden carousel horses which she had purchased in the East placed in the playground. But let us go back to the time when the couple first settled down in their first apartment in Los Angeles. Fonda started working in a new picture—**You Only Love Once.** It was being produced by Walter Wanger and directed by Fritz Lang. The leading lady was Sylvia Sydney who had played with him in **The Trail of the Lonesome Pine.**

Fonda did not realize that he, like the biblical Daniel, was about to walk into the lion's den. The rapacious beast in this instance was director Fritz Lang who, as he once said, had the disposition of a Prussian Army sergeant.

Fonda was to portray Eddie Baker, a young escaped convict who was being relentlessly pursued by a latter-day Javert for a crime he had never committed. After escaping from prison he tried to get away across the state line with his devoted wife. The story ends tragically with Eddie and his wife shot down by the relentless police while in flight. It happened just before the couple had reached the state line and safety. It was a very grim drama. The somber mood of the picture was more than matched by the feelings of the actor who was being subjected to cruel and inhumane treatment by the tyranical director. Fonda said that Lang terrorized the entire cast and crew, but he also emphasized that he had no negative feelings about the majority of the foreign directors with whom he had worked and that he always had maintained good relations with most of them.

Fonda conceded that Lang had directed some films that were very good. In trying to explain why the director behaved the way

he did Fonda said that Lang had begun his career as a movie director
when there were no sound pictures being made. He believed that
Lang preferred to work in silent pictures because he was able to order
his cast around verbally. He saw himself as the director of a cast
of puppets. He behaved like a latter-day Svengali who mesmerized
his actors at will. In a sense this master manipulator believed that
his actors should be handled like retarded children and carefully guided
through their chores. Behaving like a frenzied Leonard Bernstein,
the orchestra conductor who is justly famous because of his violent
gyrations on the podium, Lang also had a tendency to wave his hands
frantically and prance around the set, and managing to distract the
actors. Fonda found all that very irritating.

He once told a colleague about an incident that involved Lang.
He said that Charles Boyer, the French actor, was at a party and
recounted to him what had happened when he was working in a film
that Lang had directed. It was an adaptation of Ferenc Molnar's play
Lilliom. In one scene Boyer was supposed to be expiring. He was
lying on the bed, his feet bare. The camera was moved forward for
a closeup. Lang, who was standing a few inches away from Boyer
said, "When I pinch your toe close your eyes. When I pinch your toes
again roll your eyes."

"Can you imagine that," Fonda declared. "He was actually cueing
Boyer by pinching his toes. Well, that's not the way I like to be directed.
I fought with that man all the way until my work was completed."

Despite Fonda's annoyance with Lang he admitted that the
film had turned out well. Lang had obviously brought out the best
in Fonda. Howard Barnes, the critic for the **New York Herald Tribune**
wrote: "Mr. Fonda achieves a fine balance between the romantically
engaging and desperate aspects of the role. He does a brilliant job."

And Blanche Johanson of the **New York Daily Mirror** wrote
that "Fonda is flawless. Skilled in the impressive art of representing
the befuddled and confused, he put on a show which resounds with
sincerity and integrity."

Having at last found what they wanted in a home in Brentwood,
Fonda, who should have been happy to have settled down with a wife
whom he loved found himself growing more restless. He was longing
to go back to Broadway and act in a play. Frances told him that she
was pregnant during that spring of 1937. He was more than pleased
with the news. But that did not give him a more cheerful attitude;
he was bored with his movie acting and discussed returning to New
York with his good friend, Leland Hayward who in turn saw to it that
he would be asked to play in a work entitled **Blow Ye Winds.** The
opening was scheduled for Broadway in September. Fonda was now
at loose ends. He had no more pictures to work in so he decided to
travel East and join his fellow actors at Mount Kisco and appear in
that hardy perennial **The Virginian.** The play was to open at the West-
port Playhouse and be followed with a one-night stand at Mount Kisco.

Frances and Henry flew to New York at the beginning of the
summer season. She had made arrangements to sell the antique furniture and art objects that she had bought after she had married Brokaw.

And Fonda, in turn was busy rehearsing in **The Virginian.** After he had appeared in that play he worked in **Blow Ye Winds.** All his labors in that one were in vain. The play opened to very poor notices and was closed down in record time. Despite that disappointment the activity had been a change of pace for him, which helped. He could now go back to Hollywood feeling refreshed and start playing in **Jezebel** with Bette Davis.

Fonda should have been quite content now. The family house on Tigertail Road was now fit for habitation and he knew that he would enjoy living in it.

The couple's first child, Jane, was born on December 21, 1937, and was named Lady Jane after her mother's ancestor Jane Seymour, Henry VIII's third wife. Jane was called Lady Jane for years until she made it very clear that she did not like that name. Her brother Peter was born two years later. Like his sister he had the same three godfathers—James Stewart, John Swope and Joshua Logan. Logan still recalls his first visit to the Brentwood house. Peter was a baby in swaddling clothes. Mrs. Fonda, who was about to leave the house to go shopping, told him to go upstairs and take a look at her infant. He did and was amused by what he saw.

"Peter was looking out and started laughing. It was as though Henry Fonda was inside the tiny child, looking out, and saying, 'Save me!' The baby's blue eyes were identical to those of his father."

Because the family lived so far away from an urban center and neighbors both children had to depend on each other to a large extent for companionship. They had their dogs, a cat, rabbits and some chickens. Not too far away from the house were the bobcats, coyotes and dangerous rattlesnakes. The youngsters were always dressed in Levi's. Jane cannot recall anytime during her early years when she actually wore a dress around the house, but she did have one when she was eight years old.

Fonda, a man of many interests, readily adopted the role of a part-time dirt farmer. He enjoyed plowing his fields with a recently purchased tractor, he loved the outdoor life and was an early advocate of organic farming.

Jane and Peter could always be found near the swimming pool. They also enjoyed riding two mules which had been loaned to them. Often they rode horseback in the nearby hills.

Fonda, strictly the dirt farmer at home usually left his movie-star self at the studio. The two children did not know how their father made his living for quite a number of years. Jane remembers seeing her father wearing a beard for a few weeks, then shaving it off. It happened frequently and puzzled her. When she finally asked her mother why her father did that, Frances explained that his roles as an actor called for frequent changes in appearance. As they grew a bit older, both she and Peter would fantasize about fighting Indians, roping horses and trailing villains in the primeval forests. When they were finally allowed to see some of their father's flicks, they tried to imitate his acting.

One movie that made a strong impression on them was **Drums**

Along the Mohawk. John Ford directed the film. He was a fanatic for realism. He had Fonda running into a forest pursued by savages who were bent on scalping him. At war against the invading whites the Indians had been slaughtering many of the colonists in the Mohawk Valley during the Revolutionary War. The two children were terrified as they looked at the screen and saw their father puffing and panting and running away from the pursuing Indians. Both children really believed that their father was in imminent danger of being killed.

Jane said, reminiscing, "It was the longest movie of my life!"

Jane may have had her differences with her father, but she deeply loved him and tried to emulate him in speech and manners. She actually yearned to be a boy during her young days. She said, "I didn't start wanting to be a girl until I was in my teens. I was embarrassed; I was shy with boys." She even had her hair cut in boy's style.

Jane and Peter loved to watch their father enact his various roles. In those parts he was often a true-blue American, honest and courageous. But while they lavished their affections on him he always seemed to be too preoccupied to pay them any attention. He never fully responded to them. There were moments of intimacy between father and children, but they were few and far between. Nor could the children feel a close emotional attachment to their mother whose main interest appeared to be financial security. Jane now will admit that Frances was a very generous woman and she also revealed that she bought a house for her mother who was 80 years old at the time.

Both wife and children, especially as the youngsters matured, saw a different kind of man than the one who was admired by millions of moviegoers. Brooke Hayward who, along with her brother and sister, were close friends of the Fonda children, recalls that the actor was "melancholy and saturnine, always about to explode or become angry for no apparent reason." Another observer of the family scene said she always "felt he was a time bomb ready to explode. But it was many years later when we actually saw him lose his temper over some forgotten trivia. He was booming purple-faced with veins sticking out of his temples. It was the only time I was ever privileged to see what may have been a constant for Lady Jane."

No one who saw the screen character would ever believe that. That screen image was that of a calm, taciturn but engaging man. Someone explained that it was because of his hypercritical nature that he was able to mold his own image.

In time, from a feeling of adulation for her father Jane began to fear him. Those fears were often expressed in nightmares.

"As a young girl most of my dreams evolved from the basic need of being loved and being frustrated in fulfilling that need," she confessed. She also said that she was constantly dreaming of being a guest at a banquet and not being able to reach the huge mountains of food. She saw herself chasing butterflies which she was never able to catch. In contrast to the lovely butterflies she always wore rather drab clothes. Her hands were five times' normal size. When Fonda finally left California for New York to rehearse the play **Mister Roberts,** she was happy to see him leave.

Chapter VI
More Pictures

In the years he spent in Hollywood before he accepted the offer to play in **Mister Roberts** in New York, Fonda also appeared in **Slim**. The cast included Pat O'Brien, Stuart Erwin and Jane Wyman who was later to become the first wife of Ronald Reagan. It was only a fair-to-middling film. Fonda wasn't particularly pleased with the role but the critics, notably Archer Winston of the New York **Post** said that it was "better than good."

During 1937, the year his daughter Jane was born, he played in **That Certain Woman** with Bette Davis who insisted on having him as her leading man. Because she was the leading star on the Fox lot, she got what she had asked for.

In the two pictures in which they co-starred **That Certain Woman** proved to be a total loss. But **Jezebel** was quite good. The critics were generous in their praise of the acting of the two stars. Davis won an Oscar for her work in the picture.

Fonda was not under contract to Fox when he was co-starring with Davis. He had been more than willing to appear in a picture with her after he had read that script. He felt even more secure in his judgment when he was told that Willie Wyler was going to direct the flick.

Fonda had at first been rather reluctant to act with Davis after his experience in **That Certain Woman.** There were some problems that had to be resolved before he consented to play in the film. He knew that his first child would be born on December 21. The date was certain since Frances was to have a Caesarean section at Doctor's Hospital in New York. Fonda insisted that he be with his wife when the operation was to be performed. He was aware of the fact that Wyler usually took a minimum of sixteen weeks to complete a picture. There was no way Wyler could do it in less time. Fonda knew of course that he would not be able to be in New York in time to see his child being born and still be able to continue acting in California. The offer was made. He turned it down at first. But Wyler was a persistent man; he promised that he would finish his work in the film by December 21. After being assured of that Fonda agreed to stay on in California.

Wyler attacked his job like the proverbial Trojan. He had his actors running around in circles. Fonda was able to leave for New York on time. But Wyler had only started to direct the other actors after Fonda had left. Here is how he did it: He stopped filming scenes after the star's presence in a particular segment was no longer needed.

And then he picked "something else in which he was needed." In other words he did not direct the scenes in sequence, but had Fonda play the scenes he was required to be in. After he left, Davis did whatever she was required to do as did the other members of the cast.

Despite his well-justified fame as a brilliant conversationalist and extraordinarily gifted director Wyler was disliked by most of the actors who worked in his pictures. One reason for their attitude was his insistence to shoot dozens of "takes." Fonda recalled Bogart's warning him not to play in any of Wyler's films because he had had some difficult moments with him.

Bogie said, "Jesus, don't touch it. Don't go in there." But Fonda disregarded his advice and did play in **Jezebel.** After he had finished his chore in the film he said that it had been a "rewarding experience."

Wyler and Fonda were good friends all their lives. The actor admitted that Wyler had indeed insisted on filming far too many "takes." But he also said that there was always good reason for his way of directing. On the other hand a director like John Stahl according to Fonda, shoots "takes" by the dozen and never troubles himself to tell the cast why he needs that many.

Stahl gave everyone the impression that he held most actors in contempt. He never admitted to conceal his feelings about them. As Fonda once reflected, "It seemed as if Stahl was thinking 'if they're going to hand me actors like this, what are you going to do.' "

Things were different with Wyler. He would say, "This time in the middle of a scene, react to a mosquito bite."

Ideas of that kind came easily to him. The actors responded despite their differences with him and generally they enjoyed the experience. The results were good. The Wyler association proved to be a rewarding one for both Davis and Fonda.

In **Jezebel,** Fonda played the role of Preston Dillard. Bette Davis was Julie, a Southern belle with a great deal of bitchiness in her character. Fonda was not lagging too behind in his interpretation of a patient, yet suffering swain.

Howard Barnes of the **New York Herald Tribune** said, "It was Miss Davis' show but she has valiant aid from the other performers. Henry Fonda makes an adequately disgusted hero."

At that point in his career Fonda considered that some of his work in pictures was good, although he confessed he was ashamed of some films while others were very good. But he was not a superstar yet.

The year was 1938 and it was at a time when John Ford walked into Fonda's life. During the years 1938–39 Ford was setting Hollywood on fire with such masterpieces of the cinema art as **Stagecoach, The Young Mr. Lincoln, Drums Along the Mohawk** and **The Grapes of Wrath.** It was in **The Young Mr. Lincoln** that Ford and Fonda worked together for the first time.

When the picture was first proposed to Darryl Zanuck, head of the Fox studios, he said that the subject had been done to death. Who, he wanted to know, would pay their good money to see another film about Lincoln. Broadway had had two shows on the same subject— **Prologue to Glory** and **Abe Lincoln in Illinois.** Enough was enough,

Zanuck declared. After reading the Lamar Trotti script he changed his mind. It was too good to be filed away. Fonda was asked to play the title role, but he was too much in awe of the martyred President to feel secure enough to take on the part. After being pressured continuously by Zanuck and Trotti he finally consented to submit to a test. It was shot a few days later; Fonda was dubious about his acting the part when he saw himself on the screen. There he was for all to see with an overly large proboscis, too much hair on his face and head, and warts all over his face. In a very determined manner he told the two men that he did not intend to play Lincoln and that he meant what he said.

The following day Ford summoned him to his office. The fiery-tempered Irishman sat behind a large desk chewing away at a big cigar. Fonda later said that he felt like a lowly sailor standing before an admiral of the fleet. Before he could open his mouth Ford shouted, "What's this about not playing Lincoln. Man, you're not going to act like a President with beard and all, freeing the slaves at long last. You are being asked to act like a young squirt of a lawyer who hasn't got a penny to his name and is just trying to make something of himself in the big wide world."

After he was subjected to that harrangue Fonda changed his mind and said that he would play in the picture.

But while it took some hard convincing to get him to work, he was more than anxious to act in **The Grapes of Wrath,** John Steinbeck's saga about the Okies. Fonda had long enjoyed his independence as a freelance actor. But the Fox Company that was going to produce the picture insisted that he sign a long term contract. He recoiled from that suggestion but Darryl Zanuck, High Mogul of the Studio laid down the conditions, and there was no way of beating him at his game. Zanuck, a five-foot-two dynamo and a fellow Nebraskan was born in Wahoo about thirty miles from Omaha. He more than made up in bombast and "chutzpah" what he lacked in height. And he oversaw his domain with an iron hand. His hands touched everything that was related to his picture making. He read and passed final judgment on the scripts, edited them and saw to it that the casting was conducted according to his will. He was not particularly interested in films as an art form; he was solely concerned in reaping huge profits for the studio and its stockholders.

There were many naive souls in Hollywood who believed that Zanuck had suddenly seen the light and decided to produce the Steinbeck because he had become a bleeding heart. But his concern about the plight of the Okies was minimal. He did admit that they were courageous and that their suffering would make for a good dramatic movie.

In his biography of Zanuck, Mel Gussow of the **New York Times** relates one incident that occurred during the filming of the picture.

Zanuck was in the midst of a conference with Steinbeck when one of his toadies rushed into his office and said that Shirley Temple had lost a tooth. Zanuck was panic-stricken. He felt he was being confronted with a catastrophe:

"Is it her front tooth?" he gasped.

He was informed that it was.

"Then do something," he commanded.

"But, but," the 'yes' man spluttered.

"Well out with it," Zanuck shouted.

"They want you to come over to the set and tell them what to do."

During that tense interlude Steinbeck sat there hardly believing what he was hearing. When Zanuck finally said that **The Grapes of Wrath** was of minor importance at that moment, the author chuckled to himself and later told a friend that he was now aware for the first time that everything he had heard about Hollywood, about the irrational behavior of the moguls who ran the Studio, was true.

Fonda who is a liberal Democrat by conviction and who had been instilled with a feeling of compassion towards the underprivileged in our society by his father, did not have a high opinion of Zanuck. He wanted to play the part of Tom Joad not only because of the money he would be getting but because the film, as he saw it, would be an eyeopener for those Americans who did not know what was going on in the country. He also liked to work with John Ford.

Zanuck at first proposed that Tyrone Power should play the role of Tom Joad. "He is," he said, " a big box office draw and that is important." That Power was no more a Tom Joad than Fonda was the Archbishop of Canterbury did not phase him at all. He continued to insist that Power was just right for the role. The reason he was pushing for Power was quite obvious. Power had always been his pliant tool and could be depended upon to abide by his wishes without questioning. Ford in turn was convinced that Fonda was perfect for the part. He thought Power was a pretty boy and a decent man, but he did not respect him as an actor. But Zanuck had no intentions of giving up on Power. He now proposed that Don Ameche should be hired to play the role. He still hoped to have Power but believed that suggesting another actor would confuse the issue and he would in the end have his way. This time it was Steinbeck who raised very strong objections to Zanuck's choices.

Ford, who was once called "a perverse son of a bitch genius," by Fonda, was the kind of Irishman who loved to keep everyone guessing. That was what Fonda believed. He usually had his script superviser, his assistant director and everyone else on the set in a constant state of confusion. And yet despite his insensitive treatment of them, his staff remained loyal to him.

Fonda once said that working with Alfred Hitchcock was quite a contrast to being associated with the pugnacious Ford. Hitchcock would always listen to the suggestions made to him by his staff and by the actors. When he told his cast to do a certain scene they knew what to expect from him and what he was after. Ford, on the other hand, "wouldn't talk about an actor's part." When a brave soul once ventured to ask him what it was all about he simply ignored that person for the rest of the filming.

"I saw him do it," Fonda said. But Ford was an instinctive genius. For example--In **Grapes of Wrath** when Tom Joad is bidding goodbye

Henry Fonda and Jane Darwell—"The Grapes of Wrath."

to his mother, played by Jane Darwell, it was a moment of high emotion.

"Jane Darwell and I (Fonda) recognized it for what it was without talking about it. It was a fairly difficult scene technically because the camera had to come out of the tent and then take Pa and Tom down the side of the tent until they finally sit down on a bench besides the outdoor dance floor. So just to get that movement—there was a pan and a dolly I believe—it took an hour or more for the cameraman to set it up and be sure that he knew all the motions and could anticipate them."

"The actors had rehearsed the camera movements for many hours. At one time they sat down on a bench where the scene would begin and the camera was in position and Ford would cut. The cast had never rehearsed the same dialogue or the same scene where Tom Joad says goodbye to his mother. Ford never made a point of that or would say, 'look' I don't want you to use it up. He never spoke about it. He just cut like he had something else he was going to do or for reasons he never explained to me and the other members of the cast."

"After rehearsing for a few hours up to that point Jane Darwell and I felt like two race horses ready to take off. Ford knew that we were more than ready."

"I guess Ford knew what he could expect from Jane Darwell and me. He'd worked with the two of us in other picture. When everybody was about ready Darwell and I were so uptight when we got to that point that both of us broke down with emotion so that we had to hold it back and not let go. And because of that we just shot the scene. Ford was satisfied. He just got up and walked away. He knew that there would be no more 'takes.' Imagine that! Not a single rehearsal! I think that he was the only director who worked that way."

The Grapes of Wrath is now believed to be one of the best films ever made. Nunally Johnson, a conservative Southerner, had been criticized by liberals because he stressed the personal and dramatic area of the novel rather than the political. Steinbeck, after all, had written a strong indictment of American society and had wanted to emphasize it in the film. Johnson just had the characters talking about the dawn of a New Deal for the average American citizen, and he also ended the script two-thirds of the way through the book with the scene in which Tom Joad is saying goodbye to his mother and goes off to become a labor organizer.

Zanuck said that the ending would not go down very well with the moviegoers. He insisted on adding an epilogue. Everyone who was connected with the making of the picture was now up in arms and said that they would fight him to the death if he tried to dilute the message in the novel. But there was no predicting what the Czar of the Studio would do; he surprised everyone with the dialogue he wrote that ended the picture.

Ma, Jane Darwell, castigates the parasites of society and says, "Rich fellas come up and they die, and their kids ain't no good an' they die out, but we keep a' comin'. We're the people that love. Can't nobody wipe us out. We'll go on forever 'cause we're the people."

The picture ended with that upbeat note, and Zanuck was quite correct in his judgment that an audience would react as he had predicted it would. The moviegoers were stunned by the impact of the message and by the lines he had written.

With so spectacular a characterization of Tom Joad and the rave reviews he received from the critics in newspapers all over the country, a question was asked—Why had he not been awarded the coveted Oscar? Fonda had been nominated for the Academy Award along with Charlie Chaplin for The Great Dictator, Raymond Massey for Abe Lincoln in Illinois, Laurence Olivier for Rebecca, and James Stewart for The Philadelphia Story.

Everyone who was present at the Award event was certain that Fonda would receive the Oscar. Even James Stewart voted for him. But to the surprise of many and the chagrin of some, his old friend Stewart was the recipient of the Award for his work in The Philadelphia Story, a film that had been quite correctly called Katharine Hepburn's picture.

But if Fonda was somewhat disappointed in not receiving that ultimate recognition from his peers, he could still feel some satisfaction in the praise he received from the critics.

Pare Lorenz, the McCall's magazine critic wrote:

". . . it is quite a movie. Ford did have in Fonda an actor who gave him one of the finest performances I have ever seen: in fact, you may forget Fonda is in the company—his performance is so tough, undeviating and simple you may think he is one of the extras, or one of the actual migrants..."

And Howard Barnes had the following to say: "The players from Henry Fonda as the embittered Tom Joad to Dorris Bowdoin as the bewildered Rosa Sharn act their parts like figures in the main stream of history rather than puppets in a small bit of make-believe.

"Mr. Fonda has never been better on the screen than he is as the surly but reasonable Tom. . ."

And Frank Nugent of the **New York Times** who was just as enthusiastic about Fonda and the other actors as his fellow critics said:

"Henry Fonda's Tom Joad is precisely the hot-tempered resolute saturnine chap Mr. Steinbeck had in mind.

"What we are trying to say is that **The Grapes of Wrath** is just as good as any picture has any right to be; if it were better we just couldn't believe our eyes."

Fonda was now chafing at the bit. He wanted to get out of Hollywood and go back to his real love, the legitimate stage. He really had no reason to apologize for taking the time to work in pictures. His acting in **The Grapes of Wrath** was an artistic accomplishment of the first magnitude, and because he had appeared in it there was more than a justification for his having prolonged his stay in the film capital.

The picture truly reflected the social unrest and the privations suffered by many Americans during the dark days of The Great Depression. It is still considered to be a social commentary of those bygone days and its message is still pertinent today. Fonda's portrayal of Tom Joad has since gone down in film history as a prime case of an unusually gifted actor in the right role at the right time.

Chapter VII
No More Freelancing

Fonda had to pay a high price for agreeing to play the role of Tom Joad. Zanuck demanded his pound of flesh and forced him to sign a long-term contract with his company; that was the price he demanded for giving him the part. Fonda knew that he would have to work in many pictures that would not be to his liking. Zanuck, always the entrepreneur, would be loaning him to other film studios like a chattel slave whenever he chose to do so. Fonda's resentment against Zanuck persisted until the end of his life.

Fonda admitted, however, that he made some very good pictures after he had signed the contract with Zanuck. But they were for the most part produced by other companies to which he had been loaned out. He said that **The Lady Eve** (Paramount 1940) and **The Male Animal** (Warners 1942) were "good experiences" for him. Another loan-out which he said was a good one was **The Big Street** (1942) in which he was co-starred with Lucille Ball. That film was based on a Damon Runyan story about the denizens that abounded on Broadway. Fonda remembered that the only Zanuck production he liked working in was **The Ox-Bow Incident.** It should be noted that Zanuck had no great belief in its artistic possibilities but later took all the credit for producing it when it had been acclaimed by the critics.

The star was praised for his acting in **The Return of Frank James,** although the picture was not considered outstanding by the critics. Fonda still shuddered when he remembered the difficulties he encountered with director Fritz Lang. Having had many bad moments with Lang on previous occasions, why did he consent to work with him in another film? He explained in this way: "It was because he came to me with tears in his eyes and said he had learned his lesson."

But old dogs never learn new tricks. Lang behaved like the Prussian Junker he had always been. Fonda was unable to comprehend why Zanuck had assigned the German director to work on a Western. Years later he still insisted that he did the right thing in hiring him. Often forgetful of the basic themes in the film the man always became engrossed in getting the proper camera angles; he literally "painted with his camera."

In the film **You Only Live Once** there is a scene between Sylvia Sydney and Fonda which shows the two at supper just after they had married. The camera starts with an insert of the marriage certificate that had been put against a vase. It had been moved far enough away in order to show the audience enough of the couple's plates to make the moviegoers believe that they had just finished eating their ice cream and cake. After it had been backed away far enough so that the audience could see them looking at each other, they delivered their lines. Lang had Fonda and Sydney working on that little scene for two days.

"Can you imagine that!" said Fonda. "Spending two days filming that minor episode! He could do that one time; then he would come in and take a spoon and change the way the ice cream was in the dish. Then he'd change the way the spoon had been placed. Then he'd stand and blow cigarette smoke into the shot. That went on for hours at a time."

And that was the way Lang worked again when he directed Fonda in **The Return of Frank James**. One scene called for Fonda to walk into a burning barn. John Carradine, a former Shakespearian actor, who was playing the role of the cowardly assassin had shot down Jesse James in cold blood. He was supposed to hide in the barn. Frank James (Fonda) went into the barn to find him. He looked all over the place. The scene was supposed to end with Frank James finally walking out of the barn. It was just a simple piece of film shooting. But Lang enjoyed making life a problem for everyone around him including himself. He had no intentions of completing that scene the easy way. He ordered countless "takes" for the next five hours. Why did he do it? Lang never explained. He just went on and on and there was no stopping him. He insisted on having cobwebs hanging from an overhead beam down to the post that had been put there. Fonda had to pause for a few minutes while Lang had a man from special effects blow cobwebs all over the place. The man blew dozens of holes in them. They all collapsed. And the special effects man had to repeat the process. Fonda was both irritated and amused by the antics of the director.

He said, "By that time I knew Lang so well I would make bets with the guys that we would be three hours fucking with the cobwebs in a scene where I come in and stand around for two seconds and then walk out."

During the filming of **The Return of Frank James**, Fonda and the other members of the cast were on location in Lone Pine, California. It happens to be one of nature's wonderlands. There are very high mountains and century-old trees reaching up to the skies.

One of the trees that had been struck by lightning and had collapsed years ago was now just a very long trunk with spurs sticking out of it. It was the right prop in the right place, and it would have served the right purpose if Lang had only let well enough alone.

As usual, he had to improve on nature. By the time he had his camera in position he decided to have the log moved. The entire crew labored valiantly to move the trunk—a trunk that measured at least four feet in diameter at its base and was 80 feet long—to another spot. After it had been put there Lang had the crew build a platform and then put the camera in another position. It was really quite complicated.

On the other hand, Ford, the very stubborn Irishman, knew his craft and didn't blow the minds of his actors or his crew. He would have had the tree trunk lie where nature had left it. Then he would have made a study of the area and said, "Nuts," and put a tripod down and filmed the scene. But that was not Lang's way of doing things. The man among other things was responsible for the sudden demise of four horses. They had been unable to stand the high altitude. The poor animals had been forced to run uphill at a fast gallop again and again. It was just too much for their hearts to stand. They just fell down at last and died.

Fonda summed up his experiences with Lang:

"I didn't enjoy working with Lang." But he had to admit that the picture was not bad.

Bosley Crowther of the **New York Times** said that Henry Fonda as the tobacco-chewing Frank James was "a beautiful characterization."

Chapter VIII
More Problems for Zanuck

Zanuck, the boss of the company, was not the kind of man who would be impressed with films that were made for the elite. We know that his God was money, and from that point of view he was quite correct in his judgment about the kind of pictures the average movie-goer would be attracted to. His idea of what constituted good box office features were such second or third-rate efforts like **Sweet Rosie O'Grady** with Robert Young and Betty Grable. That picture was little more than an adaptation of **Love Is News** in which Tyrone Power and Loretta Young were starred. It was a piece of cinematic tripe in its original version and in its later re-production.

Nor did it take too much mental effort on his part to produce **Coney Island.** The original film had been entitled **The Bowery.** Zanuck produced a rash of such pictures. All he did was to examine old films, have the scripts changed slightly, and make them over again.

And now we find Fonda waging a battle to force his nemesis to approve the filming of **The Ox-Bow Incident.** After many weeks of acrimonious debates between the two, Zanuck apparently gave way and agreed to produce the picture. However, there was a very big "but." Fonda had to promise that he would work in **The Magnificent Dope.**

The Ox-Bow Incident was based on a novel by Walter Van Tilburg. The incident described in the book was about a mob led by a sadistic former army colonel who was determined to lynch three innocent men who had been accused of murdering a local cattleman. The men were lynched. Proof of their innocence was later revealed after the men had been hanged.

Fonda could identify with the murdered men. We know that he had witnessed the lynching of a black man in Omaha when he was a young boy. And that it left its mark on him.

Fonda was familiar with the type of men who were being portrayed in **The Ox-Bow Incident.** As a young boy he liked to listen for hours to the old settlers telling their stories about life at that time when the state of Nebraska was still a territory. Fonda knew that his older friends were similar in character to the men who were described in the Van Tilburg novel. The actor was tremendously attracted to the type of man he was being asked to portray. The role called for a man who was cynical and yet courageous enough to stand up to the mob who was bent on enjoying a lynching holiday.

Zanuck still continued to say that the lynching scene would cause the moviegoers to stay away from the box office. He was reading the minds of the average American correctly. The country was engaged in a great war at the time, and the people were fully aware of the horrors that were being perpetrated by the Teutons. They were looking for an escape from the harsh realities of their existence. And paying their good money to witness a lynching party on the screen would hardly give them any peace of mind. The movie, as Zanuck had predicted, was a failure at the box office.

After completing his acting in **The Ox-Bow Incident,** Fonda decided to enlist in the Navy. He was about to board a bus for San Diego when he learned that Zanuck had managed to cajole a number of important men in Washington D.C. to have him deferred. Fonda, as he later said, "was never so mad in (his) life." Zanuck, always the devious one, was determined to have his star stay at home and play in his production, **The Immortal Sergeant.** The very thought of a producer going so far as to keep a man from fulfilling what he believed was his duty to his country was something that Fonda found hard to understand.

Zanuck won that time and Fonda had to act in his picture. The film was about a shy young journalist who became a leader of men during the military campaign in the western desert in Africa. Despite the trite plot, the film, as Zanuck had predicted, was a financial success. But as Fonda later confessed, "The experience was a most unpleasant one." That was largely due to the fact that John Stahl was the director. Stahl, he said, "was a real son of a bitch." He liked to shoot dozens of "takes" and when an actor asked him why it was necessary he said:

"Well, I have to do it over again because they gave me lousy actors." And in saying that he managed to insult Thomas Mitchell, Maureen O'Hara and Fonda, all who had worked in the picture.

Fonda said that "everybody hated him. I finally chewed his ass out on the set and my co-workers gave me a silver cigarette box with all their initials engraved on it. I still have it somewhere."

After he had completed his work in **The Immortal Sergeant,** Fonda was free at last. He enlisted in the Navy. His friend Jimmy Stewart had already been accepted as a recruit in the United States Air Force after being previously rejected because of his weight. Stewart stood six-foot three inches in height and weight a mere 145 pounds.

Fonda served in the Navy for three years. He held the rank of quartermaster third class for the first nine months of his enlistment. After graduating from the Navy Training School in San Diego he was assigned to a destroyer which was about to sail to the Pacific Theater of War.

After a tour of duty he was recommended for an officer's commission by his executive superior and shortly after that he was on his way to service headquarters in New York City. On his arrival there he was promoted to the rank of lieutenant, junior grade, and ordered to proceed to Washington to assist in producing training films. He let his superiors know that he had not volunteered to serve in the Navy just to find a snug harbor for himself. After giving voice to his feelings of outrage—it was loud enough to be heard in the highest

official circles in the capital. He was ordered to leave for the Marian-
as where he was to serve as an assistant operations officer oh the
staff of Admiral Koohler. In time, he was awarded the Bronze Star,
given a Presidential Citation, and promoted to senior lieutenant.

When an inquisitive individual once asked him what motivated
him to join the armed services when other so-called patriotic actors
were still working in Hollywood, he said that his reasons were "private."
He did not want to elaborate on those reasons. He did add that the
men who could continue working there without feeling any sense
of embarrassment about not serving their country in the war against
the Nazis were not the kind of people he could sympathize with or
even "understand." He emphasized that he could have stayed home
since he was father of three children and was 35 years old. That was
more than enough to get him a deferment. But he thought about the
parents of the boys who were serving in the armed forces. What must
they think when they saw him on the screen, apparently very young
and healthy and enjoying the fruits of the land while their sons were
on the firing line, some of them paying with their lives for what they
believed was a just cause.

He continued, "They would say, why doesn't that son of a bitch
go? My boy goes, but he doesn't go."

Fonda had discussed his enlistment with Frances before making
a final decision. She approved his taking that step. He did not think
that he was shrinking from his responsibilities as a father and as a
husband, since he had left his family financially secure.

Fonda's existence as an enlisted man was not the usual one
the average sailor encountered. He was, after all, a national celebrity,
a stage and screen star. He was invited to attend many social functions
by the officers and despite his desire to avoid them he could not in
good conscience turn the invitations down. That was not good form.
Despite working as a photographer and supervising a radio show he
was still able to go through basic training.

Back home, his children Jane and Peter waited hopefully for
mail from their father, but very few letters from him came their
way. Years later both Jane and Peter told interviewers that their
father had many shortcomings as a parent. He was accused of never
communicating with them and not sharing enough of his time with
them when they were very young. When he was told what they had
said Fonda snapped back and retorted:

"It gets boring to hear them say they missed Daddy when they
were young. So I should apologize because a world war came along
and I had to go away or because I had to work while the kids were
in a beautiful farmhouse out in Brentwood with their friends and
horses. That's a crock."

But it was not all that much of a crock. For whatever reasons,
he left to go off to war when his two children were too young to understand what it was all about. Unreasonable? Perhaps, but it was a
very human reaction on their part. They did believe that he had deserted them. Jane expressed her feelings quite openly as a child,
but Peter, the more reticent, kept whatever he felt to himself.

Chapter IX
Back Home Again

The war was finally over and the men were now returning home to take up their peacetime pursuits. That is, most of the veterans with some rare exceptions. Fonda and Stewart were among the few who had no burning desire to start acting again. Stewart who had served in the Air Force in Europe rented his house during the time he was away at war. When he came back he was confronted with a tenant whose lease still had many months to run. Fonda asked Stewart to come and live in his guest house. He was to stay on there for the next five months. Both men spent their time either giving parties or being invited to them. After a night on the town they came back to Fonda's house and played dozens of jazz records and drank beer until the early hours of the morning.

Fonda and Stewart had been discharged from the service in September. They did not resume their acting careers until the following June. The first film in which Fonda played was **My Darling Clementine**. As usual, it was directed by John Ford.

While he was still under contract to Fox, Fonda was now able to get out of it. The time he was in the service was, according to a precedent established in the courts, to be counted as part of the time he still owned the company.

Olivia de Havilland had started a suit against Warner Brothers. The studio had attempted to add a few more months of the life of her contract. But the court ruled that she was now a free agent. That case established a precedent that now served the interests of Fonda, Stewart and other actors. In the case of Stewart his contract had expired. But Mayer, the Czar of the Studio, begged him while he wept copious tears to continue working for his studio. It was said that the act he put on would have made a Laurence Olivier green with envy. But while Stewart was about to agree to work for him, his agent Leland Hayward was not too impressed with his performance. He advised his client to stand firm and continue to be a freelance actor.

Fonda faced a different problem. After his discharge from the Navy his contract had one more year to go. He still owed three more pictures to Zanuck. When the producer tried to get him to sign another contract. He discovered that even an actor knows where his best interests are. Fonda would only agree to work in pictures over a period of three years. In the end he only worked in two of them. They were **My Darling Clementine** and **Daisy Kenyon**. He also did a picture for RKO in 1947 and appeared in **The Long Night, Fort Apache** and **The Fugitive.** He also made a picture with Jimmy Stewart called **Miracles Can Happen.** But before he was to start working in a third picture for Zanuck, a once-in-a-lifetime opportunity came his way. He received an offer to play the role of Mister Roberts in a work of the same name. It proved to be one of the great turning points in his career. From the time he first appeared in the play, the name Fonda became permanently associated with the role. There were many actors who have since played the title role but it was and still is Henry Fonda who was able to fuse his own personality with that of the character he portrayed so perfectly so that he continued to be regarded as a real-life Mister Roberts.

In the meantime his children were still enjoying their rustic-type of life on the "Spread" in Brentwood. Jane recently said that "the way I was affected by the movies was that my father brought it home with him, not the business end, and not the movie star angle, not the glamour, none of that, because he separated that very well. But he did look the way he looked in the movies. And he brought home the people he was in pictures with. John Wayne, John Ford, Ward Bond and Jimmy Stewart—they were the company at home.

"They would play a game called pitch and sit around this big table with a chandelier above it that had a great big covered wagon wheel with lights hanging over it. And they wore cowboy hats with holsters, and they would take the guns out and put them on the table, and they'd sit around and play cards, and it was right out of any of the movies. We didn't need to see the movies."

When Fonda was told how she had described life at the Brentwood farm he said that her imagination had run riot:

"It didn't happen frequently." he said. "In fact it only happened once. It was a benefit party and someone took photographs and I still have the pictures. It was a single event, not a way of living. When a legend grows up around a man, there is often no means of pruning it, even within the family."

After his return from the war when Fonda was hoping to go back to Broadway, his children were more circumspect in their behavior. They were not, for the moment at least, making any serious problems for him.

Brooke Hayward in her book **Haywire** tells about her own family and informs us that life with her own father and others was not very calm. The Haywards lived a distance away from the Fondas. The children saw each other frequently and were close friends. Margaret Sullavan, the mother of that clan, had become an actress of some renown. Her acting in John Van Druten's **The Voice of the Turtle** had made her a star on Broadway overnight. She had been astute enough to invest $3,000 in the production and was able to reap a harvest of dollars as a result. Despite her achievements as an actress she was not a very happy woman. And there was no logical reason why she felt that way. She had a husband who was very successful. And she had three beautiful and highly gifted children. Yet, she found life to be a bore. Despite her emotional outbursts at the slightest provocation, most of the people who knew her regarded her with affection. Carl Van Druten, an individual generally not given to excessive sentimentalities, said that she was a woman who "had a simplicity, an almost embarrassing directness and friendliness that have nothing of the theater gush about her."

On the other hand Josh Logan said, "I believe that she was essentially selfish. She never loved Fonda as much as (his) 'other wives.'"

But let us go back to Sullavan and her career in the theater. The play grossed three million dollars. Her investment had paid off handsomely. After acting in the play for a year she had to leave because of ill health and returned to California where she promptly divorced Hayward. She was awarded custody of the children; Hayward in turn wasting very little time, proposed marriage to Nancy Hawks who had divorced Howard Hawks, the director. A few years later Nancy shed Hayward and was awarded custody of their daughter.

The children of those rapidly dissolving marriages were emotionally disturbed because of the lack of stability in the households. To them it was like a game of musical chairs. They did not know who was going to replace their father or their mother the next time around. But in time they managed to adjust to the change in their life styles. There were some deep emotional scars however.

Fortunately for both Jane and Peter, life at the Fonda house was more stable; both Frances and Henry saw to it by simply staying married. Jane, who was a perceptive child, did recognize the differences in being raised by wealthy and famous parents. As she said, "If you have glamorous parents you have to live differently than the girl or boy next door."

Jane was going to the Brentwood School and was considered a good student, but a mischievous one. The school's student body included the son of Laurence Olivier, Gary Cooper's daughter (she is now married to concert pianist Byron Janis), Claude Rains' daughter and other offspring of similar exalted parentage.

Jane was occasionally invited to the parties that were given by the local nouveau riche. The other children were bedecked with expensive finery. She generally wore very plain clothes. She could never understand why the other children lived differently than she did.

Even when she was still in her teens she found it hard to indulge in small talk. She generally breathed a sigh of relief when her parents told her that it was time to leave and go home.

Jane admitted in her later years that she felt more at ease in the company of her brother Peter and with the many animals, including chickens, that abounded on the family estate. She enjoyed horseback riding and unlike the other Hollywood youngsters who were always dressed in fashionable riding habits, she wore blue jeans, a large hat and spurred boots. She was far ahead of her time. Today, jeans are considered quite fashionable.

Jane still idolized her father and tried to emulate him in every thing he did. She was a tomboy and waged many a fight with her schoolmates and the boys at the local riding stables. She also suffered some injuries. In one fight her arm was broken. She also sustained a fractured wrist while roller-skating in the hall of her house.

Life as a whole was comfortable for both children. Frances was a devoted mother. The children did complain years later that their father seemed to be incapable of showing them any affection; he was too remote.

There was at least one explanation for Fonda's lack of patience with his children during their early years. He was working for a man whom he found to be irritating, and his problems were reflected in his conduct toward his children. Colonel Zanuck, an officer who had never participated in a battle during the war had come back to Hollywood to take up his duties as commandant of the studio. He was now trying to intimidate Fonda and the other actors who were working for him. But as we know Fonda was not the kind of man to be frightened by the likes of a Zanuck. He had emerged victorious in his contract difficulties with the Czar and was now more than eager to start rehearsing in Tom Heggen and Josh Logan's play **Mister Roberts.**

Mister Roberts: Henry Fonda discussing scenes with Josh Logan.

Chapter X
A New York Play Opening

Josh Logan was vacationing in Cuba and enjoying the sights of Havana. He was reading Tom Heggen's novel about life aboard a Navy cargo ship during the war and was so impressed with it that he decided to acquire the rights to the book. He believed that it had distinct dramatic possibilities and that a play could be written based on the author's experiences aboard the vessel. When he was told that Leland Hayward had acquired the rights to the book he was greatly disappointed. Hayward had been quite ill in Honolulu with a pancreas problem, and was slowly recuperating from its debilitating effects. There were no direct telephonic communications between Havana and Honolulu. Logan solved that problem by flying to Miami where he was able to telephone the agent-producer and discuss the project with him.

In the meantime Heggen had written his play based on his novel. Logan was able to lay his hands on it and saw that it lacked sufficient dramatic treatment. He met with Heggen and discussed the play at his home in New York. The two men decided to rewrite it together. It took three months to write the first act. They were able to finish the second act in one night.

A day after they had finished writing the play, Logan read the script to Hayward. The producer expressed his enthusiasm about the play and said it was "the greatest one that had ever been written." The sceptical Heggen said, "But what about Aristophanes?" And Hayward, not a bit taken aback by the remark said:

"Aristophanes could never have written as good a play as yours." And a few days later Logan began casting **Mister Roberts.**

The war was over and there were many soldiers who had read the novel. Many of them were firmly convinced that they were good actors. They lined up at the stage door one morning--800 strong. They were allowed to enter the Alvin Theater in groups of 20 where they stood in a semicircle as both Logan and Heggen walked past them, looking at each man and trying to ascertain if he was right for the parts. Hayward also helped select the cast. Maynard Morris, Hayward's casting director and stage manager, Billy Hammerstein, son of the famous Oscar, and his assistant, Ruth Mitchell, were also asked to give their choice for the roles.

The main character parts--Doc, the Captain, Lieutenant Pulver and Roberts--had as yet not been assigned to any of the actors. Logan however had already made his own choice some time ago. He was not quite ready to reveal whom he preferred for the Roberts role.

But Heggen told Logan that he had one actor in mind when he was writing the book.

He said, "Henry Fonda is the right actor for the role."

Logan knew that Fonda was about to start working in a picture. He was also aware that the actor was in New York and would remain in the city for a few days. Fonda was not at liberty, but Logan asked him to read the script nevertheless. He told Fonda that he knew he had already committed himself to make a picture. He also asked him to consider playing the part of Roberts. Fonda liked the idea, but Logan started to have second thoughts about casting his old friend in the play. Heggen had decided on Fonda who was tall and handsome. But the character was described in the novel as short and rather shy. It was quite clear that Fonda certainly did not look the part physically. Logan, who wasn't entirely sold on Fonda got in touch with David Wayne, a well-known legitimate actor. He at least looked like the character in the book. Logan, who is a sensitive man knew how Wayne would feel about being a second choice for the role. He assured him that he had always been his first choice. Fonda, he told him, was still tied up with a picture project in Hollywood. But Wayne, who had always admired Fonda, said:

"I have no objection to being the second choice to Fonda."

Tom Heggen was in the room when Logan read the play to Wayne and Fonda. He had hardly finished the reading when Wayne got out of his chair and ran out of the room. No one there could understand what prompted him to act in that way. Fonda also was puzzled by Wayne's action. Logan, who was troubled by the unexpected behavior turned to his friend and said, "Hank, I'm really sorry you won't be able to play Roberts."

"On the contrary Josh, I'm going to play the role," he answered.

"What about the picture you have committed yourself to make?"

"That can be handled."

"How?" Logan asked.

"Lew Wasserman, my agent, is a very clever chap. I'll let him know that I want out on that picture 'cause I'm going to be doing Doug Roberts."

Heggen and Logan were now deliriously happy. With Fonda agreeing to play the leading role, they knew that they had a very valuable property on their hands.

A few minutes later the telephone rang; Wayne was on the other end of the wire. Before Logan could say a word, Wayne said, "Hank Fonda should play Roberts, not me, but I would like to do Pulver. I'm not telling you. I'm demanding that you cast me in that role."

The next character to be cast was that of Doc. It called for a droll kind of man. Logan and Heggen auditioned many actors. None of them seemed right for the part. Then they saw Robert Keith amble down the aisle of the theater and they knew immediately that he would be perfect for the role. Heggen motioned Logan to sign him up.

Hedda Harrington was in the theater when her brother was proposed for the captain. That role called for a martinet who could convincingly intimidate the kind-hearted Roberts and the other members of the crew. An actor playing that role would have to show a certain amount of insensitivity and at the same time make the audience believe that he was a dullard.

Nedda Logan for some reason was troubled because her brother was going to be chosen for the part. But her advice not to engage him was disregarded. Harrington was hired to play the part of the captain. He read the play and impressed Logan who said that his interpretation was "marvelous" and "brilliant."

At the first day's rehearsal the cast read the lines aloud. Many of the actors were in high spirits, laughing, applauding and even crying at the more poignant moments. Logan decided to have his actors move about the stage as they read the lines for the first time. It was an unusual procedure at that time. A director usually has his actors learn and perfect their lines before they move around the stage. But Logan believed that the cast would render a more spontaneous reading if he did not do anything to inhibit them.

The rehearsal stage was quite limited in its space and the cast felt cramped. Logan suggested that Fonda walk in front of a desk and sit in a position so that the other actors could be easily seen by the audience. When Fonda received the instructions he looked very sharply at Logan. The director, who could read his friend's thoughts, knew only too well what he was going to hear.

Fonda: "Didn't you tell me to move after the line?"

Logan: "Yes, but I'm sure it will be okay eventually. If you do it for me now it would be of real help."

After hearing that the unreconstructed rebel grunted, "I'm not trying to help you. I'm trying to play 'Mister Roberts.' "

"Roberts wouldn't move an inch on that line. Let me tell you, Logan, this is not a Princeton Triangle Show. This is Broadway. We're going to face a New York audience."

"I realize that, Hank," Logan retorted, "but I know New York. I've done a lot of shows since I handed you that cake of ice. So if you don't mind let's stop haggling and go on with the rehearsal."

"Listen Josh, have you any idea what the character Roberts is all about," asked Fonda.

"Do I understand him?" Josh snorted. "Why, you son of a bitch, I wrote it. I know that Tom Heggen wrote the book but I had to write all of Roberts' lines because he hardly said anything in the novel. Listen here, Fonda, I can discuss that character for the next month."

With a strong dose of sarcasm in his voice Fonda snarled, "I would like to hear you. I would be interested to discover if you really know what you are talking about."

Deciding that Fonda had said more than enough, Logan now asked him to come to his apartment and spend the rest of the evening talking about the treatment of the play.

When the rehearsal was over Fonda went to Logan's home. His wife Nedda greeted him and then tiptoed out of the apartment. She had ordered a dinner to be sent up for her husband and her guest. And for the next few hours the two men ate, argued and ate again. And after they had had their fill of food they walked into another room and started the discussion all over again. At certain moments during the evening the argument threatened to flare up into a battle royal, but Logan took over before Fonda had a chance to become too surly. He explained Roberts' childhood, and his young adulthood in detail and told him about the experiences Roberts had had as a student in medical school. And how he felt about being assigned to the despised ship. And how he reacted to the crew, to the stupid, dim-witted captain and to the war. Logan finally finished his discourse in human psychology and its application to the play by 11:30 P.M. Fonda by this time was sitting quietly like a schoolboy listening to his friend take the character apart. At last he ended the lecture with "And that's Roberts."

There wasn't a sound out of Fonda for a few minutes. He finally raised his lanky body out of the chair, looked sharply at Logan, and whispered, "I understand. Thank you." He grasped Logan's hand, held it for a few minutes and then swiftly walked out of the room.

Logan never encountered any more difficulties with Fonda. The actor became a meek Casper Milquetoast in deed and manner. He quietly accepted Logan's every suggestion as Gospel truth. In the process he gradually became Roberts, just as Tom Heggen and Logan had conceived him to be.

Reminded of that in later years Logan said that Fonda was never an opinionated man. With a kindly smile Logan says that Fonda would always take advice when it was offered and when he respected the person who gave it. But it sometimes takes time before he will accept it. He has, says Logan, "deep within him a small but inextinguishable flame that burns in worship of the art of the theater. He is one of the high priests of that art."

Logan went even further. "He is," he said, "the greatest actor in the world now. Olivier used to be the greatest but he is old and ailing now and not at his best; Fonda is now in his prime as a performer."

Praise of Fonda's acting came from many other persons other than his friend Logan. Fonda's peers say that his greatest moments in the theater occurred when he played in **Mister Roberts**. If one were to judge him at that time and be swayed by the reactions of the audience it must be admitted that he had indeed reached the apex of his career.

The men and women who were in the Alvin Theater on opening night were stunned not only by the impact the play made on them but by the masterful performances given by Fonda and the other members of the cast. There was not a sound between the laughs. The performers sensed the response they were receiving from the audience. In the last act when Lieutenant Pulver says to the captain, "What's all this crap about no movie tonight?" the men and women in the theater gave the actors a ringing approval. And when the final curtain was rung down everyone in the house stood up and cheered, applauding both the actors and the authors of the play.

During that first performance Logan and his wife, Nedda, stood behind the boxes and looked down nervously at the audience. Both husband and wife were keyed up. Many thoughts ran through their minds. Was the play really that good? Would the critics like it? There was no need to be concerned.

Fonda knew that he had given a superb performance that night. If he had had any doubts at all the reviews in the newspapers quickly reassured him, but he still wasn't completely satisfied. After the first night he began to refine his interpretation of "Roberts" more and more. Fonda scorned the ideas propagated by the followers of the so-called "Method" school of acting and its self-appointed gurus. Logan, who had been to Moscow when he was still with the University Players, had discussed the art of acting and staging with the great Stanislavsky and had taken what the master had to say very seriously. The Russian ridiculed what he called the practitioners of "The Method." Stanislavsky told Logan that "The Method" was not a static concept. It was always in the process of change. And was only to be utilized in the bathroom, the back porch or deep in the woods where one could make all the racket and all the mistakes one wanted in order to find out what could be helpful. "The Method," Stanislavsky explained, should not be an end in itself. It becomes "self" instead of art. One must, he said, always experiment and leave oneself open to change. Create a method of your own, he advised Logan.

Since those early days Logan often discussed his meetings with Stanislavsky with Fonda and other actors. Fonda found himself in total agreement with Logan's ideas about the local "Method" people. While he was working on the Doug Roberts' role he used his own method. He had his way of getting inside a character. He calls it "babying up" a role.

The "babying up" period was very difficult for him. He was usually irritable, argumentative and questioned everything the director told him. It was very hard on the other members of the cast. His wife and children also had to bear the brunt of his anger during the gestation period. Fortunately for them they were hundreds of miles away from him in California during the **Mister Roberts** rehearsals.

But rehearsals of a play were not necessary to create problems between husband and wife. There had been very serious differences between Fonda and Frances before he had left his home in Brentwood to travel East. Frances was aware that there was a basic lack of understanding between herself and her husband. She had finally reached a state where she had actually walked out on him for a short time. Her health was of great concern not only to her but to Fonda. She had been operated upon for a suspected cancer. Both she and Fonda believed at the time that her ailment was terminal, and that she had only five years to live. That troubled him during the "Roberts" rehearsals.

The public, now interested in this rising star, knew very little about his private life. A feature writer of the New York **Times** who interviewed him revealed how Fonda had first met his wife in London. She wrote that he had been happy in his married life and quoted him as saying that he had been "most fortunate as an actor." He told her how he had been introduced to a young girl whom he had married. That was all. The writer omitted mentioning the fact that he was now the father of two children and that his marriage was now in tatters.

There were moments when Frances' illness did prey on his mind. But she was still over 3,000 miles away in California and he was completely preoccupied with the role he was playing in **Mister Roberts.** All of New York knew that a very unusual actor was now appearing in an outstanding play. New Yorkers couldn't avoid seeing his name on the marquees of the local movie houses where **On Our Merry Way** and **Fort Apache** were being exhibited. The latter picture, directed by John Ford, had been one of the pictures he had played in before leaving Hollywood for the East.

The "Golden State" had become increasingly distant. He was now telling everyone that the seasonal changes in the metropolis were preferred to the more even kind of climate in California. He scoffed at the actors and actresses who had never appeared on a Broadway stage. The experience, he said, was absolutely necessary for any actor who wanted to learn his craft.

During a rather lengthy interview with a reporter he spoke about his constant strivings to improve his characterization of the role he played in **Mister Roberts.** He acknowledged that many friends had told him that he was getting better and better all the time. Then he talked about George M. Cohan and said that he had often mentioned what he called "the improvements" an actor was constantly indulging himself in during the run of a play. Cohan was a star, a director, a playwright and a professional flag-waver. He could always be depended upon to wave the flag when an audience's attention was lagging. One play which was a smash hit on Broadway had become rather ragged after 50 performances. Cohan decided that something had to be done about it. He ordered a special rehearsal to be held, saying that it was necessary because the "wrong improvements" had crept into the actor's performances. Fonda said that Cohan wanted to eliminate them. They occur, Fonda explained, when an actor puts in bits of stage business to get a more spontaneous reaction from an audience and, in the process, the staging becomes quite distorted and the work loses whatever meaning it had.

Fonda also believed that there are certain subtleties an actor will use, which are the right kind of improvements. "It takes a long time to get to the basic roots of a character," he said. It is never dull to continually refine a role. Playing in a work gives an actor the opportunity to develop more substance as time goes on."

It was while Fonda was trying his best to discover what motivated the character **Mister Roberts** that he was told that Frances and the children had started to make the necessary arrangements to leave Brentwood and travel East.

Chapter XI
The Fonda Family Travels East

While he was living in New York, Fonda was a houseguest of Joshua Logan. The apartment in River House on East 52nd Street is very spacious and tastefully appointed. It is still occupied by Logan and his wife Nedda. On one of the walls in the living room there is a very fine still life. It is thoroughly professional in its execution and was painted by Henry Fonda.

The main reason the family had remained in California was to have the children complete their school term. Now that term was ended. Before they arrived in New York, Fonda found a furnished house in Greenwich, Connecticut for them to live in. There were a number of reasons why he wanted to have them live in the suburb. The chief reason was that the schools there were considered to be among the best in the country. It was also within easy commuting to New York.

It was Frances, however, who really wanted to live there. During the 1950's Greenwich's population was almost exclusively white, Protestant and wealthy. There was not a Jew nor a black in the area. Greenwich was not an ordinary suburb. There were many large estates and no slums. Nor was there any place that could be the farthest stretch of the imagination be thought to be "the wrong side of the railroad tracks."

The offsprings of the rich were enrolled in such schools as the Greenwich Academy, the Brunswick School, the Greenwich Country Day School and Rosemary Hall. And for those who were religious, there was Christ Church, Round Hill and the Community Church. And as in all such communities there were a number of exclusive country clubs. Round Hill, the Field Club and the Greenwich Country Club were where the wealthy and the snobbish socialize.

Peter was enrolled in the Brunswick School, an old and hallowed institution. The building looked like many of the centuries' old private schools that are still found in England. In fact, this 19th century stone building looked as though it had been transported stone by stone from the mother country.

Peter attracted the other students' attention when he showed up at school dressed in Western boots, jeans and a multi-colored jacket. Most of the pupils were far more properly dressed. Peter, at that time, was frail in appearance and quite shy.

Jane was enrolled in the nearby Greenwich Academy—a girls' school. That school was far more old-fashioned than Peter's. The students, like their European counterparts, had to wear uniforms.

They were also required to wear brown oxfords. Their skirts barely touched the floor. There was also a strict rule against perfume or make-up. A school song which all the girls had to sing in the assembly on Mondays and Thursdays went like this:

> "What gifts are these that thou dost impart
> To those who ask for thee?
> A joyous mind, an eager heart
> A spirit fair and free."

Fonda was too involved in his art to play the role of a loving parent. He left the care of his children to his wife and to their schools where he had enrolled them. It was the unpretentious Frances who was in a broad sense both mother and father to her children during the first few years they were living in Greenwich. She took a deep interest in their studies and visited the schools frequently to discuss their progress.

Alfred Everett, the director of one of the schools, said that he enjoyed talking with her. He described her as a very attractive woman, genuine and apparently devoted to Jane and Peter. He also said that she seemed in good health and didn't show any signs of depression.

It took some time before Fonda went to see the teachers of his children. He visited one of the schools on "Father's Day," a day set aside by the school principal in order to give the parents an opportunity to find out how their offspring were adjusting to their environment. The teachers discovered soon enough that Fonda was not an advocate of progressive education. He believed in the old-fashioned disciplines.

Peter liked to recite a poem entitled "Aladdin." It begins, "When I was a beggarly boy and lived in a cellar damp." He also wanted to take part in the annual school play and was being seriously considered for a role. Frances who knew her husband all too well warned the director that Peter must not be made to play the part of a girl. Fonda, she said, would object violently. The director took her advice and had Peter play an Indian. The boy wore the garb of a redskin and even had his face painted; he was handed a tomahawk. A gentle boy, he was now playing a role that was out of character for him. He had one complaint, however. He had not been given the chance to lurk in the woods like Indians generally did. His father, on the other hand, did not like the idea of his son acting at all. He had seen to it that both Jane and Peter stayed away from the Hollywood scene because he did not want them to become professional actors.

Hollywood had, and probably still does, have more than its fair share of broken marriages. One would therefore surmise that the children of such broken homes would become emotionally disoriented. But having a new parent every year or two appeared to have no disastrous effect on them. They accepted losing one parent and acquiring a new one as if it were normal. Greenwich and similar communities also had its share of divorced parents. But in the East for some unknown reasons the effect on the children appeared to be more traumatic.

One of Peter's closest friends lived with his mother. The father

had left a long time ago. When the students were learning about the
Biblical flood and Noah's Ark the boy announced that his mother's
new friend had brought some color slides of his boat to show him.
He also said this man was going to be his new father.

Peter, who at the time had had only one set of parents, couldn't
understand what the boy was saying. He asked him whether his mother
had ever been married. "My mother," said Peter, "was married years
before I was born."

Both Peter and Jane were still longing for their old friends
the Haywards who had been left behind in California. But shortly
after they were enrolled in the two schools the Haywards arrived
in town. Sullavan brought her three children East with her. Her choice
of Greenwich may have been because the Fondas were there.

Jane, as her friend Brooke Hayward describes her, was a bit
of a hoyden. Both girls were "kicked out of the Brownies" because
of an infraction of the rules. It seems that Jane and Brooke discovered
one classroom diversion—tossing spitballs at each other. They became
quite skilled at it and rarely missed their target, which sometimes
included the teachers. Their unruly behavior was brought to the attention of the principal who accused them of being "anarchistic and
natural ringleaders," Brooke, in her book about her family, said that
the two girls may have been responsible for an elderly teacher's heart
attack. Another teacher had a nervous breakdown.

Jane liked living in the East but her younger brother longed
to be back in California. He expressed his dislike of the East and
scrawled "I hate the East" all over the walls of his home. His father,
finding such actions too much for him to tolerate, exploded, some
say violently and ordered Peter to wipe off the graffiti. At that period
in his life Peter was considered to be a problem child. Frances, his
father and even his grandmother were quite concerned about him.
Today, Peter admits that he was a difficult child who sometimes
lied.

Between a young boy who was uncontrollable, an unhappy wife,
and a father who was far too heavily involved with his work to spend
enough time with his family, it was not too long before the neighbors
became aware that all was not going well with the Fondas.

Fonda was not the kind of man who would confide to a friend
what was troubling him, or take the neighbors into his confidence.
He maintained a reserved manner, polite enough, but distant. But
Frances, who had been raised in a Greenwich kind of environment
was far more at ease with the local people. They found her gregarious,
expensively dressed and high strung, but friendly.

There were some belated attempts on Fonda's part to assume
some of the obligations of parenthood. He knew at that time that
his marriage was in trouble, and he believed that by exerting more
effort as a family man he might patch up the differences that existed between his brood, his wife and other relatives. He taught his
son how to swim and took both Jane and Peter to the city museums.
Peter's friend, Ronnie Neilsen was usually invited to come along with
them. Ronnie recalled that Jane was more the tomboy than a typical
"Junior Miss."

In the meantime Frances tried to hide her depression by making an extra effort at being a good neighbor. The local people accepted her on her own terms, but they still could not accept Fonda. After his tremendous success in **Mister Roberts** he became an easily recognized public figure. Men and women stopped him on the streets and asked for his autograph. Newspapers published stories about his home life and career. He was portrayed as being the same kind of man they were seeing on stage and in the movies. In fact, he was now regarded as the model American male, honest, virtuous and, like Caesar's wife, beyond reproach. A man who perfectly epitomized everything admirable in the American character.

Jane Fonda discovered that her father was still regarded as Mister America when she was touring with a show in Texas. She was then in the forefront of the anti-war movement. A local sheriff berated her and said, "Your father is a wonderful man. He always was one of my idols. How could he have bred a daughter like you!"

During the time when Fonda was playing in **Mister Roberts** he made no bones about his enjoyment of the adulation he was receiving from his colleagues and fellow Americans. His friend, Josh Logan, who was also basking in the success often made it a point to walk into the star's dressing room just before the evening's performance and affectionately blurt out, "You son of a bitch!" It was, of course, a variation of "I love you."

Logan admits today that there had been occasional "ripples" between them. One such "ripple" occurred when Logan decided that his friend's under-acting was having too much influence on the other members of the cast. The other actors decided to emulate him and after the play had been running for a few months, weaknesses developed, and Logan ordered a rehearsal. During the rehearsal he tried to correct the bad habits that the actors had picked up. Fonda did not like the idea of being criticized obliquely. "It's no longer my play," he shouted. And Logan responded with, "You superior bastard, the play happens to be mine."

Fonda had obviously been under the delusion that the play was his to do with as he pleased. No one had dared call him to account. But now Logan was doing just that.

The movie director, Henry Hathaway, an old friend of Fonda's who had worked with him on a number of pictures, said that Hank ran the company "like a hard-driving infantry officer commanding combat troops." He also said that he 'was in New York when my film was being shot.' For a bit part in the picture I was using one of the actors from the cast of the play. It worked out fine because the man could shoot with me during the day and do his performance with Fonda at night. He had only one line to say every night. But one matinee day I inadvertently kept the man overtime, and Hank called me in utter fury. He really raised hell. He threatened me to have me fined and the actor fired and kicked out of the union. He said I was irresponsible and uncaring and everything else he could think of. But then the following week he called me and we had dinner together. He never mentioned one word of our battle. But what a temper!"

As we have already indicated the lack of communication between the husband and wife which had been so much in evidence during their California days reached its climax about two years after they had come East. Frances now believed that she was a discarded wife because Fonda was spending most of his time in New York. She was becoming more depressed and now spoke openly about commiting suicide. Yet there was no history of mental illness in the Seymour family to explain why she felt that way.

Her remarks about doing away with herself were no idle threats. She revealed what was on her mind to a friend and said that she suspected that her husband was interested in another woman. At one point she confided that if she were committed to a mental institution it might stop him from shedding her to marry the woman. As if her problems with Fonda were not enough, the tormented woman's daughter Pam, Brokaw's child, who had been married for a year gave birth to a child that lived for two hours. Frances suggested that her daughter should go to Europe and try to forget what had happened. Shortly after the child's sudden death Pam dissolved her marriage. By that time Frances knew that her marriage was about over. All that was lacking to finalize it were the divorce papers.

The couple was now living apart. Fonda had his flat on East 64th Street in New York. The columnists in the daily tabloids were having a field day writing items about the actor escorting Susan Blanchard, who was only twenty-one years old at the time, around town. The new flame in Fonda's life was the child of Dorothy Blanchard, now the second wife of Oscar Hammerstein II. It had begun one afternoon when Susan walked into the theater where **Mister Roberts** was playing, to see her stepbrother, Billy Hammerstein, an assistant stage manager. After she was introduced to Fonda she knew that she could fall in love with him. But Fonda did not react to her immediately. He later became more interested in the young woman. She was very attractive and had certain elan and a generosity of spirit. She admired the people of the theater. That combination was just what Fonda was seeking. They were now seen everywhere; their relationship was now an open secret.

Back in Greenwich, Frances was becoming more aware of what was happening. Once she was certain that her suspicions were correct it became only a matter of time before her distraught state of mind would lead to a nervous breakdown.

Frances, who apparently held the family purse strings, was now intent on getting all she could from her errant husband. That is exactly what she succeeded in doing. But stripping him of most of his assets did not ease her mental anguish. A friend suggested that she see a psychiatrist, and she did--once. After that aborted attempt to get professional help she became more irrational. She told everyone what a sorry mess she had made of her marriage. Her mental state became worse and she was finally admitted to a sanitorium in Stockbridge, Massachusetts. While there, she came to the conclusion that there was no hope of a reconciliation with her husband. With a sudden feeling of despair she tossed her wedding ring out the window. It was obviously a symbolic gesture that her marriage had come to an end.

During her stay at the sanitorium her friend, Eulalia Chapin sent her a printed prayer of Saint Francis of Assisi. Eulalia was trying in her own way to help a friend in distress.
It read:

"Lord, make me an instrument of your peace;
Where there is hatred, let me sow love;
Where there is injury, pardon;
Where there is doubt, faith;
For it is in giving that we receive.
It is the pardoning that we are pardoned."

But that message fell on deaf ears. Frances was now more disturbed than ever before. Her money did not help her find peace of mind. She had had a bad marriage with Brokaw and had hoped that her second one would be successful. But now she knew that she had been cast aside. She knew that Fonda who was considered one of the most gifted actors in the country had found being married to her a trial. But she also knew, being an intelligent woman, that there are and have been many talented men who had lived out their lives with commonplace women and yet had been able to find some measure of contentment, even happiness with them.

Some of her close friends knew what was happening to her and they tried to ease her pain. But there was very little that they could do.

After leaving the Stockbridge sanitorium, Frances had herself committed to the Craig House Sanitorium in Beacon, New York. Several weeks passed, and it seemed to the staff that she was gaining some control over her emotions; one of the nurses said that she was now well on her way to a complete recovery. Her behavior was normal in every respect. She was mentally alert and cheerful. But well hidden from them was her plan to do away with herself. The doctors never realized how close she was to ending her life.

On the fatal day she played bridge with her doctor. After the game was over she retired to her room. During the night of Friday, April 14, 1950, she wrote two letters. One was to her nurse, Amy Gray. She was not to go into her bathroom, but she was to get in touch with Dr. Bennett. The second note was addressed to the doctor and said, "Very sorry, but this is the best way out." After she had written the two letters she taped them to her bathroom door.

When Miss Gray walked into her room at precisely 6:30 A.M. carrying a glass of orange juice she saw that the bed hadn't been slept in. Her suspicions were confirmed after she had read the note. Realizing that the sight that would meet her eyes when she opened that door would be too horrible for her to stand she ran out of the room and summoned Dr. Bennett. He asked a colleague to go with him to the patient's room. The two men walked to the bathroom. They opened the door and were shocked by what they saw: Frances Fonda had cut her throat with a razor blade.

Chapter XII
The Children of the Tragedy

Fonda was playing in **Mister Roberts** when the suicide occurred. He was told what had happened just before he walked on stage that night. As Logan recently revealed, "Despite this very painful day he went on with the scheduled performance. Not by word or deed did he show the emotional stress he was under."

Word of their mother's suicide was kept from the children. Brooke Hayward's mother, Margaret Sullavan, had discussed Frances' death with Mrs. Seymour, the Fonda children's grandmother.

Should they be told how their mother had died? They decided that Mrs. Seymour, the self-appointed censor, would see that no newspapers or magazines would be delivered to the house or the Sullavan home. Shortly after Frances had committed suicide all subscriptions were cancelled. The two children were told that their mother had had a fatal heart attack.

Everyone in Greenwich tried to cooperate with both families. At the Greenwich Academy the entire student body and faculty were cautioned by Miss Campbell, the principal, not to tell either Peter or Jane how their mother had died. Jane learned what had really happened quite by accident; her friend Brooke was looking through a movie magazine and noticed that the entire story of the suicide had been printed in it. Brooke turned the page quickly, but not quickly enough apparently. Jane saw the caption, and turned back the page and learned what had happened. After she had read the story she turned away and did not speak for the next few hours.

Years later, when Jane was a mature woman of 40, she spoke to a writer about that period of her life. When she was asked how she had felt after reading how her mother had died, she said, "My personality was fixed by that time, stamped with the happiness of my earliest childhood so that I was not hideously scarred." But when one of her schoolmates at Emma Willard was asked how Jane had reacted she told a different story. She remembered the "wildness, the despair" that Jane was feeling. She "went beserk. She screamed and broke things."

Jane, trying to explain why her mother had done away with herself said, "My mother was outgoing, gregarious, a woman with lots of potential and no way of expressing it. She could have been a great businesswoman. She lived in a time and in a society that placed primary emphasis on youth and beauty. When that deserted her, she had nothing; she had no substructure for support."

Today, she does not blame either her mother or her father for what happened. "If you live in a society that represses generosity, courage and social responsibility, and fosters competition this is what you get, competition," she says.

But that was a woman now past 40 explaining her reactions. She was only sixteen when her mother committed suicide. And the bitterness she felt toward her father may have had its origin in the way her mother had died and what she thought was the cause of the tragedy.

After his wife's suicide there were the usual last minute funeral arrangements to be taken care of. As Frances had requested, her body was cremated. The remains were taken to the Seymour Cemetery in Ogdenburg, New York. On the day of the funeral while the two were riding in a car with Grandmother Sophie Seymour, she asked Fonda again and again why her daughter had taken her own life. She did not get any response from him, nor had she really expected any. In her heart she knew the answer. She knew that Frances had been rejected by her son-in-law and for that reason life had become a burden to her. Whatever plans Fonda had about his children's future would probably be countermanded by Sophie Seymour and her family. She knew that Jane and Peter could be permanently scarred by the tragedy.

Peter discovered how his mother had died years later when he was in Rome with his father. He was perusing a magazine while waiting to have his hair cut and read the entire tragic story about his mother's death.

Chapter XIII
The Aftermath

Frances' suicide naturally enough had cast a deep pall on the Fonda household. A day after her death, Mr. Everett, the headmaster of the Brunswick School, accompanied by Edna Hale, a fifth grade teacher, came to the house on Sherwood Avenue. The headmaster was welcomed by Fonda and his son. They guided Everett into the living room while Sophie Seymour motioned Miss Hale to follow her to another room.

Fonda, Peter and the headmaster found it difficult to carry on a conversation. Desperately trying to "break the ice" the headmaster, who knew that Peter was interested in weapons began to talk to him about them; the subject was quickly exhausted. Everett looked around the room and noticed a painting on the wall. He assumed that it had been painted by a professional artist and was surprised when Fonda told him that Peter had done it. That broke the ice. Everett started to talk about art and artists and just before he left the house, he suggested that Peter return to school the next day. Fonda agreed.

Jane and Peter were back at school the following day. It didn't take long before the other students began making snide remarks about Fonda and Susan Blanchard. Jane in particular was incensed by the slanderous remarks. She said that it was besmirching the reputation of a respectable young woman. Helen Wallace, a devoted friend of the family assured her that her father would never have anything to do with an immoral woman.

Fonda was still reacting to the effects of the tragedy. He gave the impression of a man in a daze; he was depressed and friends were becoming concerned about his well-being. He had very little to say even when he was with Susan.

The two tried to find some diversion to keep their minds off the suicide. They accepted many invitations to visit friends and go to a number of parties, and Fonda, who could always be counted upon to lift the spirits of his friends with his Elmer act and his mimicry usually sat in a corner with Susan and gazed vacantly at a wall.

Frances' will was read a few weeks after she died. The world now learned how bitter her feelings had been towards her husband. She had had the will drawn up a half-year before her death. Her mother was awarded life occupancy of the house she had bought for her in Los Angeles. After her death it would belong to Peter and Jane.

Grandmother Seymour also received her daughter's grand piano and other valuables. In addition, she willed 60 percent of the dividends from a trust fund to her for the remainder of her life. Jane and Peter were to receive the remaining 40 percent when they reached the age of 25. The estate on Fonda Island was awarded to her son.

The entire estate amounted to $650,000. It was not quite as large as most of her friends thought it would be, but it was substantial enough. Her husband was left nothing. Connecticut law states that a deceased spouse automatically leave one-third of the estate to the survivor. Fonda didn't try to contest the will. He accepted his wife's decision even before the will had been probated. Despite his own desire to leave well enough alone, the lawyers managed to keep a large sum of money for their services.

There was the sum of $75,086 banked jointly in the couple's name: Fonda received half the amount; the remainder went to the children. But as if fate had ordained that salt should be rubbed into open wounds, he was forced to petition a California court to order that he be appointed the executor of his son's inheritance. In a last thrust of the knife Frances had stipulated that her mother, not her husband, be her children's guardian.

Time usually is the healer. But the scars still remain. For Fonda the scars caused by the tragedy remained with him for the rest of his life. The suicide and the way it happened proved to be a devastating trauma to Fonda. Susan tried unsuccessfully to help him through that trying time.

Life must go on. Fonda and Susan were married at her parents' home. The ceremony unlike that in which he married Frances at the fashionable Park Avenue church was a simple one. Susan's mother and stepfather, a number of relatives and a few close friends of the groom attended. It was performed by Dr. Everett Clincy, the President of the National Council of Christians and Jews. Susan's parents left their home in Bucks County, Pennsylvania, right after the ceremony to attend the wedding of author John Steinbeck to Elaine Scott, the former wife of screen actor Zachary Scott. It was that writer's third marriage.

After the ceremony the Fondas set out on a honeymoon in the Virgin Islands and while they were gone Peter was involved in a near-tragedy.

A week after the wedding he was asked by his friends Reed Armstrong and Avery to come to the Rock Hill estate in Ossining, New York. Avery's grandfather Kress was the owner of the estate.

John Reed, the Kress' chauffeur, was instructed to drive the boys from Greenwich to Ossining about 45 miles away. On a dreary Sunday morning the boys walked to the shooting range to try their skill at target practice. Peter, who always found guns fascinating, was handling a Civil War relic, a family heirloom of sorts. Certain that the pistol was not loaded he pressed the barrel to his stomach and while he was using his right hand to break open the weapon the gun suddenly went off. A bullet pierced his liver and damaged one of his kidneys.

Peter was only ten years old at the time. When he discussed it years later he revealed that his life had had no meaning for him at the time and that he had tried to do away with himself. Apparently though he had said that in order to inflict some pain on his father. Some time later he was interviewed by **Playboy** magazine and he said, "I'm not sure if I was really trying to kill myself or not, but I do recall that after I shot myself I didn't want to die. I was conscious after I shot myself. I was also very scared...."

A small amount of blood seeped from his wound. But with two organs damaged it was evident that internal hemorrhages were occurring and that Peter's life was at stake.

If it had not been for the chauffeur's presence of mind, Peter might have died. With very little time to spare, Reed broke every speed law in the books as he drove him to the hospital. Peter is grateful to the black chauffeur to this day and still remembers vividly what had happened to him years ago.

"They were giving me shots for gangrene and shock and pain and I was beginning to get a little dopey, but I remember that they didn't know what to do at first. There was just one physician who was very skillful in operating on bullet wounds and he wasn't around when we arrived at the hospital. After some frantic telephone calls he was located. I remember looking at the floor and seeing all those legs passing by. They belonged, I later learned, to the doctors and nurses. After a few minutes I saw a pair of legs with hunting boots on the feet. The boots were very muddy. I was told that those legs belonged to the surgeon who operated on me."

The doctor was Charles Sweet, a physician and surgeon at the prison hospital where he had many occasions to operate on the convicts who had been gunshot victims.

Fonda was contacted on his honeymoon island and told the frightening news. St. John's Island was almost inaccessible. It had no telephones or airfields. Fonda was told that a Coast Guard vessel would stand by to take him to the nearest land where he could take a plane to the mainland and from there to Ossining.

After the plane arrived in New York he drove to the hospital. Peter had, as yet, not been operated upon. The surgeon told Fonda that an immediate operation was necessary in order to save the boy's life. The ten-year-old boy had lost a great deal of blood and was given three transfusions. After surgery he was taken to the intensive care room, where Fonda saw him.

What must Fonda have been thinking about as he saw his young son struggle for his life? He had lost his wife only a year ago; was he to blame? Could he have been more patient and understanding of her problems? And now, here was his son: Two deaths in one year? The thought made his head reel.

The boy however was very young and he had, the surgeon assured Fonda, a fierce desire to live. As Dr. Sweet said, "He had a wonderful and unexpected recovery."

During these troubled days, friends of the Fondas helped all they could. Among them was Fonda's former wife, Margaret Sullavan. When Peter was still hospitalized she served as the family chauffeur, driving the Fondas and Sophie to the hospital in Ossining. At long last Peter was declared fit to go home.

After convalescing for a time Peter went back to school. He was now the most celebrated student at Brunswick. While he was still in the hospital the director of the school had made daily announcements about Peter's condition. When he finally made his appearance at the school he was hailed the conquering hero. Strangely enough the accident tended to change his character. No longer did he act like a rebel. He became, much to the amazement of his teachers, a model student. All this happened while Fonda was still acting in **Mister Roberts.**

Fonda set himself up with his new wife and his children in another house. Jane found her stepmother more than agreeable, saying it felt like having a family again. She also found a new friend in Susan. The very beautiful young wife was admired by the young girl who, at that time, believed that she herself was an ugly duckling.

Mister Roberts: Henry Fonda with Director Josh Logan (standing).

Chapter XIV
Problems Within the Family

Everything eventually ends. The Broadway production of **Mister Roberts** was about to lower its last curtain on one of the longest runs in the history of the American theater. But it would not be the last time Fonda would play the title role. He was scheduled to tour with the play. But first there were some serious problems to solve that affected his children.

Before he could reach any conclusion about their education he would have to consult Sophie Seymour and other members of her family. They had made it quite clear that they believed themselves to be more fit than he to guide the future of the youngsters. A number of conferences were held with the Seymours. Fonda, and his wife Susan, and his own sister took part in them. The discussions were acrimonious. Frances' sister and her husband were not pleasant to Fonda. When Jane and Peter told them that they loved Susan and intended to address her as "Mother" the Seymours were outraged. They said some things that in a calmer moment they never would have said.

An agreement was reached. Jane was to go to the Willard School in Troy, New York, and Peter was to be dispatched to Fay in Southborough, Massachusetts. And so, what seemed for a time to have been a rebirth of a family unit was now in the process of disintegrating. To all intents and purposes the Fondas were now on their own.

Fonda was touring in **Mister Roberts**. One of the openings was in Los Angeles. But prior to that, he played in San Francisco. Josh Logan, who had written the play in collaboration with Tom Heggen and who had also directed it, found that the cast was acting like a troup of sleepwalkers on stage. There seemed to be no life in their acting. And the cause of it, Logan knew, was his star. He could not fault him for his own acting. He was letter perfect. But his way of understating his lines had affected the other actors. And to Logan's horror they were actually exaggerating his style on stage. Where ebullience was necessary, they were "bland" and "smug." Logan knew that if the actors performed that way in Los Angeles the hypocritical movie star audience would laugh them off the stage. He rehearsed the actors once again and tried to "bring back the wild comedy." He was not aware of the effect that that was having on Fonda.

He contacted Fonda the night before the play was to open in Los Angeles and told him that he wasn't satisfied with the way the actors were interpreting their parts and that there wasn't enough time left to change their erring ways. At that point Fonda exclaimed,

"Thank God for that." Logan was flabbergasted. He didn't know what to make of that remark.

He said, "Didn't you want me to bring back its original spirit?"

"No," said Fonda. "I don't feel it's my play anymore."

Logan's patience was now worn thin. He responded with, "No, you son of a bitch, it's mine!"

The next day Fonda vented his anger at Logan to Hayward. He warned the agent that "if that goddamned Logan directs the picture I won't play in it."

Once Logan heard that remark from Hayward he became even more incensed about the chutzpah that the actor displayed. He said what he had to say about Fonda to Hayward and left in a huff.

Fonda played **Mister Roberts** seventeen hundred times during a four-year period. He continued to insist that he enjoyed the last time he played the role as much as he had the first time. He also insisted that his acting was better in that last performance than it had been at the play's opening.

When an interviewer questioned that remark he said that Logan who directed the play would tell everyone the same thing.

"I don't have to say it. Anybody else who saw it—and lots of people did dozens of times—said that it just gets better all the time."

He once spoke about the many replacements for the roles that had to be made because the young actors who were playing them left for better opportunities. Whenever an actor was being replaced the stage manager would rehearse him and then Logan would walk into the theater for the last two rehearsals and have the cast go through their paces. But after watching Fonda and Bob Keith he would look on with puzzled amazement and then say, "Bastards, I don't know what you do, but you just get better!"

Fonda was always pleased when he received those compliments because his ego demanded such praise and because he was the perfectionist he had always been, he still entertained doubts about how good he was. His reward for such dedicated concentration to improve his skill was not motivated by a desire to make more money but for the recognition he received from his fellow actors and the theatergoers.

The world, as Shakespeare wrote, is a stage. And an actor, especially a person like Fonda, was not only called upon to show his skill as a thespian but now with his wife dead and a new wife in tow, he also had to undertake the role of a concerned parent. The friends who were close to him during the time the children were growing up attest to his interest and concern for their well-being.

Jane was still a student at the Willard School, and there she applied herself seriously to her studies. She was also capable of being mischievous and on frequent occasions would spill lighter fuel in the corridor leading to the room where the students were living and putting a match to it. She knew that the flames would die out before any real harm was done. She knew that the students would now be careful not to incur her anger.

Jane was very lonesome while she was a student at Willard; she could not make any close friends there. But her restlessness was alleviated to some extent when she went to see her stepmother. The two women visited Peter at Fay and assured him that they loved him. He was in real need of affection from his family.

At that time Peter was small and frail-looking. His teachers said that he had an enormous ego and was insecure, but they conceded that he had a good sense of humor.

After Peter had been at Fay for a few years his father was working in **Point of No Return,** a play based on a novel by John Marquand. Fonda managed to find some free time to visit his children. As usual, he was not pleased with the play and showed his dissatisfaction. It was a popular success nevertheless.

In reminiscing about the plays in which he had acted he said that he "didn't enjoy working in that one." While the play was not a simple task to fathom it was "not rewarding" for him. He once told an interviewer that he never let down on a role. He took special pains to make the audience believe that he was having lots of fun with it, but he did not like the role of Charles Gray who had worked as a struggling bank executive striving to reach the top in the institution. He had no deep interest in his daily work and now was trying to find a way out. The man who was publicizing the play and its cast was being driven to distraction because Fonda was not cooperating with the press. When one journalist asked what he thought of the play he said it was terrible.

He said, "I can't discuss the character. There is no character. Write anything you want about it, but keep away from the theater." He also said that it wasn't worth the price of admission. Despite all that negative publicity theater-goers kept on buying tickets.

Chapter XV
Mister Roberts Again

Seven years had passed since Fonda had acted in a movie. Back in 1947 he played in **Miracles Can Happen** with Jimmy Stewart, Paulette Goddard, band leader Harry James, Fred MacMurray and Burgess Meredith. It was a stellar cast wasted on a mediocre film. Its title had been changed to **On Our Merry Way** but it did nothing for it; to quote John Springer, Fonda's press agent and friend, "It was hopelessly hokey and submerged the talents involved."

During that same year he also played in John Ford's **Fort Apache.** It was one of that director's better efforts. In it an army colonel whose name was Thursday arrives at Fort Apache to take up his duties at the fort. He was a typical army martinet who was very opinionated and refused to heed suggestions given to him by the seasoned veterans. As a result of his bad judgment he was resented by everyone under his command. He was also saddled with a daughter who bore the unlikely name of Philadelphia Thursday and created problems for him.

Critic Bosley Crowther of the **New York Times** said that it was a picture with "a new and maturing viewpoint upon one aspect of the American Indians wars. For here it is not the 'heathen redskin' who is the villain but the hard-bitten army colonel, blind through ignorance, fiercely stubborn and stiff with galantry."

Despite those fine notices Fonda still longed to be back on the New York stage. He left for the big metropolis to play in the original production of **Mister Roberts.** The play, ran on Broadway for several years and then toured the country; in fact there were quite a number of Roberts' companies touring at the same time. During that time Logan and Heggen had been working on a screen version of the play. Before Heggen died the two men talked about its screen treatment in great detail. In those days before Hollywood's permissive era it was considered necessary to eliminate some of the stage's pungent dialogue and substitute lines that were less offensive. Logan and his actors in the touring company tried out the new lines and studied what effect they would have on the audience. It was important to take special note of which laughs were lost in the process and at the same time to avoid tampering with the basic spirit of the play.

The screen treatment was now complete. The new version was first staged in San Francisco and shortly thereafter in Los Angeles. Fonda did not approve of the changed dialogue. He lost his temper and vowed that he would never act in the movie as long as Logan was associated with the production.

Leland Hayward knew that Fonda was a stubborn man; he also

knew that he meant what he said. Taking him at his word he started to look around for another actor to play Doug Roberts. Logan, who had always admired Marlon Brando, approached him and asked whether he would play the part. Logan knew that Brando had signed up to play in **The Egyptian** for 20th Century-Fox. He also knew that the actor did not like the script. Brando assured him that he would find a way to get out of that contract. Hayward felt that with Brando in the starring role, the movie would be what the trade calls "a block-buster."

Some of the actors in the stage production told Logan that the reason Fonda did not want to play the title role was that he believed he was too old for the part; he was 45 years old at the time. Roberts was supposed to be 24. But Fonda now wanted to play Doc. When Logan heard that, he knew that he was once again in his friend's good graces. He was more optimistic now about the movie project. To hear him tell it he was now "sitting on a pink cloud." But powerful signals now warned that his ship was about to pass through very danger-ous waters. Logan had hoped all along that he would direct the film. But Lew Wasserman, the demon movie agent, shattered those hopes. He walked into Logan's office one day wearing a conservative black suit, a black tie and shoes to match and announced, "He likes it."

"Who is he?" Logan asked.

"Why, don't you know! It's none other than John Ford—John Ford likes **Mister Roberts**. He is willing to direct the picture. Congratu-lations."

Wasserman continued: "Believe me, this is the greatest break you've had since I first became your agent. Ford is a great genius around here, and with his name the picture will coin millions of dollars."

Logan felt crushed by the news. He felt that he was the logical choice to direct the picture. He had, after all, written the play, pre-pared the movie script and directed the stage production. Now it was being taken away from him.

"But, but," he muttered. "I thought it was understood."

Wasserman gazed at him with a benign expression and said, "You'd be fine, also, Josh. I told everybody connected with this produc-tion that you are just right for the job. But Ford is extra special. He's one of the greats in this business. By the way, Leland Hayward told me to offer you a bigger percentage of the picture if you'll go along with us about having Ford direct. You'll be getting one-fourth of the blockbuster. Can anything be sweeter than that!"

Logan felt like Caesar after being bloodied by Brutus. His troubles had begun when Fonda first threatened to run out on him in San Fran-cisco. And then his friend Leland, who apparently was putting dollars ahead of friendship made his move. And now Ford came into the picture to finish off Logan.

Ford laid down one condition before accepting the job. The brawling Irishman said that he would not direct the picture unless Fonda was hired to play the lead role.

Ford had come to New York from West Point where he had been directing Tyrone Power and Maureen O'Hara in **The Long Gray**

Line. Although he had come ostensibly to see Fonda play in **Mister Roberts** at the Alvin Theater, he spent most of the evening at a nearby bar where he imbibed his fill of whiskey. By the time he had had enough the show was over. He walked into the now darkened theater and went backstage to Fonda's dressing room. The two men talked about the old days in Hollywood where they had worked together in a number of pictures.

Fonda's dresser told Logan that when the actor had asked Ford whether he had enjoyed the play, Ford said that he hadn't seen it. "Why," he asked, "should I look at that homosexual play?" And when the members of the cast had been told what he had said they took an instant dislike to the man.

Logan, on the other hand, was unable to understand why Ford had made that insulting remark. The play was really concerned with the trials and tribulations of a sex-starved crew who were aching for the sight of an attractive female.

Logan now decided to beard the lion in his den. He asked Hayward why he insisted that Ford direct the picture since he had obviously overlooked the basic points of the play. He said that he was the logical choice to direct it. But Hayward, who was never at a loss for words, explained what had made him chose Ford in the first place. "Well frankly Josh it's the money," he admitted. "Ford is money in the bank. He is our solid guarantee that a picture will sell well at the box office. Let's look at this honestly. You haven't been near pictures in 17 years since you made **Met My Love Again**. And you weren't even the director; you were the co-director. You're strictly a man of the theater. The best, let me assure you. The very best, but can you guarantee how big a movie you'd bring in?"

Logan reminded Hayward about his frequently voiced expectations to direct **Rear Window** based on William Irish's novel as a kind of warm-up before he undertook to direct **Mister Roberts**. He had every reason to believe that Hayward would use him in both pictures. Now he learned better. Hayward came back with more unexpected news. He told Logan that he was about to sell the rights to the Irish novel to Hitchcock because the latter wanted to direct a picture based on the book. Hayward's excuse was the usual one, more money for him. He had worked out a deal whereby he would be paid for the rights to the book and make far more money than by producing the picture.

Logan was practically near the end of his patience with his alleged good friend. He tried to hold on to his emotions as Hayward continued to rationalize why he was letting him down. He told Logan that he had no cause to complain since he was willing to give him one-fourth of the gross intake of the **Mister Roberts** film. He also said that he would protect his interests and see to it that Logan would get an honest deal from the movie company.

"Brando," he said, "will be a sure-fire guarantee that the picture will be a success." He promised to get the star to work in the picture. Brando had already committed himself to act in **The Egyptian** for Zanuck, but Brando was doomed to be disappointed. After he broke his contract with Zanuck he was left out on a limb by Hayward. Logan said it was a clear case of a doublecrosser doublecrossing everyone else in order to get Ford to direct the picture on his terms. And they included having Fonda play the title role. By then Fonda was more than willing to act in the movie, but he never anticipated the problems that would be coming up—due to Ford's strange behavior during the time he directed the movie. To put it mildly Ford committed every crime in the book when he took charge of the project.

Fonda, Cagney, Jack Lemmon and the aging William Powell were in the studio when the first segments were being screened. Logan was also invited to witness what the director had done to his work. After seeing the results of Ford's directing, he suddenly had an impulse to tiptoe out of the projection room and disappear. Instead he sought out Hayward and stared at him. Hayward, Logan said, looked like a man who had just been dug up from a cemetery plot. His complexion was a ghastly green.

There was murder in Logan's eyes. His rage was not only directed at Hayward for allowing Ford and the others to ruin his play, but to Nugent, the former movie critic, who had, he later said, "used some shopworn Hollywood tricks by lifting perfectly good dialogue and then changing it just enough to make everyone think it was an original script written by a master writer.

Logan reluctantly accepted Hayward's invitation to have dinner with him at his home. For the rest of the night the two men ate their meal and discussed the sad state of the picture and what could be done to save it. Logan minced no words and said that the story line was ridiculous in its new version. The prison-like ship now looked like a cruise boat bound for days of fun in the Caribbean Sea. Ford had changed the entire plot. The men on the ship now acted like a gang of happy hooligans. Logan asked Hayward what he believed was a very pertinant question, "If they were so beaten down and abominably treated by the captain, why did Mister Roberts practically sell himself to get the captain to grant the sailors some liberty? And what sense did it make to see the abused sailors swimming around like a school of contented dolphins, screaming and shouting at each other and generally behaving like ghetto youngsters on a holiday?" Logan had much more to say about the Ford treatment of his play. "Why," he wanted to know, "did Ford make the captain as played by Cagney, act like a good-natured, well intentioned slob who was so solicitous about his men's welfare? Without a villain as the captain was described to be in the play, there was no sense to the story. And where there was no story there was no picture. And as for Ward Bond who played the tough guy, why," he asked, "did he act like an over-aged bovine pouring out the milk of human kindness to one and all?"

Logan wasn't through with Hayward. He said, "That wonderful scene when Doc talks to Roberts about the captain's name-signing contest. Why did the director kill that one? It was horrible. And the nurses' scene. This," he shouted to Hayward, "is not a picture. It's nothing more than a rape!"

He then leveled a finger at Hayward and snarled. "You, Hayward, allowed him to get away with it. You are solely responsible for this crime."

Hayward by now was completely overcome with remorse. He

was silent for a few moments and then found his voice at last and spoke up, "It is true," he murmured. "You are right. But you can't realize what I had to go through all those weeks on that damn island.

"On the very first day of filming I happened to see Ford slashing out all those great jokes between the enlisted men. I couldn't stand by and see him doing that. So I asked him what had happened to the jokes and he shouted, 'Don't annoy me, Asshole. Just get lost.' And then I witnessed the battle being filmed in a peculiar effect. Fonda, who was used to the laughter and action and the excitement of the play was now aware of what was happening. The scene was unbelievable. What do you think occurred after that?"

"Fonda spat in your face," Logan surmised.

"That would have been welcome. But it was worse than that. Fonda was in his cabin with some other people in the cast. He was feeling relaxed and having a drink. Ford walked in on the boys and asked Fonda what he thought of the day's shooting. Without mincing any words he said, 'I think it was shit.' The irascible director wouldn't take that sort of a remark lightly. He leaped forward and punched Fonda in the jaw. The force of the blow sent Fonda reeling across the room."

"Fonda is a younger man," Logan said. "He is quite capable of murdering Ford. The director is way past his prime."

"I know, I know," said Hayward. "He is much stronger. A couple of chaps seized Fonda and begged him to desist and not hit the old man."

It was typical of Ford to react to criticism in that way. Ford always made a point of humiliating anyone who offered a suggestion.

Tyrone Power, the most gentle of men, once approached him with an idea that called for the actor to smoke a corn-cob pipe. He had been portraying an old man in the picture. Ford gave him a stoney stare and then shouted, "Everyone sit down and listen. I would like to hear more from this thinking actor."

After the brawl with Fonda, things went from bad to worse. The next day Ford told Fonda that he was sorry and then turned away from him. It was not a very convincing apology; Fonda would have nothing to do with the director from then on. Ford, still angry, was ready to wage another fight with Fonda again. It was the turning point in the relations between the two men. Many of their friends were surprised by what had happened. The old friendship had soured for good. It was a far cry from the day when Fonda, very elated, learned that his old friend was going to direct the picture.

Talking about those long gone by days recently Fonda said, "It began like a dream come true. Years had passed since I had worked with Pappy. I felt he was the perfect choice for the job. He had served in the Navy. He was a fabulous location man who especially knew how to direct men. In fact I, along with most of the others in Hollywood, considered him one of the best directors in the business. I knew that after our many years of working together he had a deep affection for me as well as for Duke (Wayne) and Ward Bond. But I felt rather disturbed at the changes he was making in the script, and I lay awake nights hoping that Pappy would not change it too much since the

Mister Roberts: David Wayne as Pulver and Fonda.

Mister Roberts: William Harrigan and Fonda.

original version had been so successful as a stage play. But I had forgotten that Ford was "an egomaniac as well."

The alleged "egomaniac" as we know now was working havoc with the picture. After the aborted battle, both men lost their enthusiasm for the entire project. Ford became increasingly erratic and shot scenes that had no relations to the story line. For example, at one point he had the men diving into the sea dressed in weird-looking bathing suits. And there were some natives hanging on the side of the vessel while others were nearby in their war canoes. And in another scene they were climbing the ropes onto the deck. For a teaser he included a scene in which the native girls sauntered across the deck shaking their derrieres suggestively.

By that time everyone connected with the picture was afraid to ask Ford what he was really up to. After all, the acknowledged genius in Hollywood should not be asked any questions. It would be considered sacrilegious to cast any doubts about so awesome a talent.

There was still more to the sorry tale. Eight days later in Hawaii, Ford went completely beserk. He let everything go haywire and then asked his old drinking buddy Ward Bond to take over the director's chores. Ford began to drink heavily; his normal intact of whiskey was usually far more than the average man imbibes in a week. He became a recluse and hid himself on his boat "The Araber" and continued to drink himself into a stupor. He sent word to everyone that he didn't want to be disturbed and he stopped eating. Matters were going from worse to worse. Hayward knew that his production was going down the drain and was seriously thinking of scrapping the entire project. The cast was vacationing in luxury at the Edgewater Hotel. The actors were hoping to get the good news that Ford had finally stopped drinking; five more days would go by before Ford decided that he had had his fill of liquor.

Jack Warner was finally told what was happening. In his customary fashion he hastened to fire Ford and replace him with his good friend Mervyn LeRoy. By that time the cast had departed from Hawaii for Hollywood to complete their work. Ford now had a ruptured gall bladder and was carted away post-haste to St. John's Hospital where he had it removed.

LeRoy read the Nugent script while Hayward sought more help from Logan. The now thoroughly cynical Logan knew that even a good friend could betray him when lucre was involved. For the next few weeks he devoted all of his time snipping pieces of film here and there and matching them up with some of the others. He also used closeups and had a prompter read the lines offcamera to the actors. He tried to salvage the swimming sequences which he believed were important even though they seemed to contradict the basic concept of the story line about sailor's lives aboard what was to all intents and purposes a floating prison ship with a tyrannical captain ruling his men without compassion. He worked closely with LeRoy and the cast for a few days. It was like a jig-saw puzzle. He also reshot the last scene where Ensign Pulver knocks on the captain's door and demands that a movie be shown that night.

Lemmon, who was grateful to Ford because he had engaged him for the role also had something to say about the distortions in the script. He said that the most jarring scene in the picture was caused by Ford's insistence that the famous nurse scene be rewritten. Instead of having one nurse as in the play, Ford insisted on using six more. The original scene made sense. It called for only one nurse being lured into Pulver's bunk. He had been sex-starved and wanted a night in bed with her. While she was on her way to his bunk she sees Roberts and flirts with him. Pulver almost loses her. The comedy develops as the crew finds out that there is a woman aboard. In no time at all the entire ship's complement crowds on deck. Some of the men hang from ladders. And then we have that line that always brought down the house, "Got $100 bucks that she's the one with the birthmark on her ass." When the girl hears that remark she runs away. The crew's hungry expectations are frustrated and poor Pulver is once again doomed to lead a monastic life for another year. We see the girl leave the boat. When she lands on the island she tells the nurses to pull down the shades when they are in the shower room. She had put two and two together and come up with the right answer. The crew had been having some vicarious thrills watching the girls bathing naked. The sailors are now thrown into a fit of despair; the shades have been pulled down. They leave their quarters and as the scene draws to a close, Doug Roberts picks up a pair of binoculars and slowly puts them to his eyes.

That scene, with all of its humor and poignancy was thrown out of kilter when, instead of having one nurse aboard the ship there were six of them sauntering all over the boat. "That distortion ruined the 'sexual intimacy' of the entire episode," according to Logan.

Jack Warner was persuaded to have the scene reshot, and he agreed to have only one nurse in it. But two days later after he had arrived at that decision he changed his mind. He said that the nurse scene must include all the women because "it was one of the only full scenes that had been shot out-of-doors in the calm, beautiful Pacific Ocean with an island showing." He also said that he had been impressed with the natural beauty of the tropical fauna, the blue sky and the rolling ocean. He also insisted that the scene must be included. It was quite evident to Logan and Fonda that Warner was solely motivated by a desire to put more sex into the picture.

Having six attractive women instead of one, plus dozens of native girls swaying their torsos around would certainly attract more patrons and help fill the company's coffers. The Czar of the Warner Studio had delivered his "ukase" and it had to be obeyed. More women were used in the scene.

Editing of the film was finally completed by Logan. Fonda said that the Doug Roberts role had been ruined by Ford, LeRoy and Jack Warner. He made no bones about being disappointed with his work in the picture.

While Logan revealed what had happened during the shooting Fonda soft-peddled Ford's responsibility for the fiasco. He said that Ford was replaced as the director because he had had a gall bladder attack and been confined to a hospital for eight weeks. Hayward could not afford to hold up the production for that length of time. That was why he had had to hire LeRoy to finish the job. That was truth in part. Fonda admitted that Ford's irascible nature had made it almost impossible for anyone to work with him. But there was another side to the episode: Hayward would have fired Ford even if he had been a healthy man.

Fonda said that LeRoy was confronted with a very difficult task when he took over as the director. He explained, "It's like a cook taking over a souffle from another cook; it's pretty delicate. But that is just what Melvyn did, and that's why Ford was no longer directing the picture."

When Fonda was asked by a reporter why Logan had not been used to direct the picture in the first place he said that everyone including himself had expected that he would be the one to handle the job. But, he added, Josh was on to something else and Hayward was ready to start shooting the film. "Logan," he said, "told Hayward to go ahead without him."

There is very convincing evidence to the contrary. The fact of the matter was that Logan was shoved aside by Hayward for purely monetary reasons.

Logan later said that his only true revenge for the shabby treatment he had been accorded was "alleviated somewhat by fate in the person of the 'walking monster' in the form of Ford. The bickering between the star and the director undoubtedly flawed Fonda's performance, and he must have felt it deeply."

For many years Fonda never said a word to Logan about his differences with Ford. But Logan "knew all along how he felt" and was certain that Fonda "knew what they both felt."

Fonda had undergone an artistic defeat. He gave what he knew, down deep in his heart, was a mediocre performance. He honestly believed that the picture was not up to the high standards he had always set for himself.

Ford has since gone to meet his maker, and while Fonda had always held him in very high regard as a director there was no chance of renewing their long friendship.

Mister Roberts was released during July, 1965, and was immediately acclaimed a masterpiece by the critics and the public. It grossed $5.8 million a year after it was first shown. The only member of the cast whose reputation was enhanced as an actor was Jack Lemmon who won an "Oscar" for his portrayal of Ensign Pulver. Ford, who had so eagerly looked forward to directing the film refused to even talk about it with his friends. He was not pleased when he learned that it was a box-office success. He also made it quite clear that his friendship with Fonda was over. Fonda, who had every reason for feeling that he was the aggrieved party also knew that his "love affair" (with Ford) "was over."

Ford always had a fierce hatred for any form of injustice, especially when it was perpetrated against the American Indian. He frequently voiced his hatred for those who persecuted any minority. Yet he displayed little sympathy for the working actors. His career ended not in a blaze of glory but in a sputter. There is no doubt that in the far beyond where he now exists he hears his favorite song "Shall We Gather at the River" being rendered by a host of angels.

Chapter XVI
Working in Rome

Fonda was still working in the film version of **Mister Roberts** when he accepted Dino De Laurentiis' offer to go to Rome and play in his film **War and Peace.** At that time his son Peter was still a student at the Westminster School in Simburg, Connecticut, and Jane was in her last year at Emma Willard in Troy, New York.

Westminster was the preferred choice of many of the successful Broadway actors who wanted their sons to receive the best education. At one time it was all theater there. Talented students had the opportunity to write and produce plays of good quality. One of the students whose father taught there wrote and produced a number of plays that were staged on Broadway.

By the time Peter was at Westminster the school had undergone a radical change. Professor Milliken, the headmaster, was a rigid Calvinist. Sports were encouraged and the liberal arts were downgraded. Peter, who was still small in size, found it difficult to cope with the tougher boys.

The teachers were a rugged lot. Discipline was strictly enforced. And upper-classmen often took full advantage of their priviledges to inflict corporal punishment on the younger students. An infraction of the rules usually resulted in a paddling that was enthusiastically applied to the derrieres of the victims by both the older boys and the teachers.

Peter, who by nature was a non-conformist, was the recipient of many a paddling. His difficulties started the first year at Westminster. He was punished for smoking, for not being neat enough, and for other alleged wrong-doings. To make matters worse he cried whenever he was beaten. That didn't sit too well with the older boys.

Peter felt that he was being sadly neglected by his father although Fonda did write many letters to the teachers asking how his son was adjusting to life there. The letters, according to the members of the faculty, were lucid, quite eloquent and showed a real interest in his son's welfare. The teachers were impressed with the father. But the same could not be said for Peter.

Fonda did visit his son on rare occasions. Yet, when he did come he appeared to be incapable of communicating with anyone, let alone his son. He arrived at the school on "Parents' Day," ate a hearty dinner at the group table and never uttered a sound. When one of the other parents sitting near him asked whether he wanted a second helping he grunted, "No." That was the sum total of his conversation that day.

Towards the end of Peter's first year at Westminster and Jane's final one at Emma Willard, Fonda decided to take both of his children to Rome. Five years had gone by since the death of their mother. Yet, Peter still didn't know how she had died.

Fonda's attempts to assume the role of a concerned and understanding father did not come off too well. Jane later said that the summer she spent in Rome was a bore. She said, "We lived on an estate outside the city and I had nothing to do except eat dozens of figs, gain weight and watch Gina Lollobrigida, who lived close by, with my binoculars."

Peter took to drinking gallons of wine and learning about sex for the first time in his young life. He was fifteen years old when he was walking past St. Peter's where he was accosted by a United States Air Attache and his wife. They suggested that he should go to their apartment. When he arrived, they introduced him to the mysteries of sex. That episode apparently made a great impression on him if one were to judge his reactions to it.

"It blew my life out!" he said.

While Peter was having his traumas in Rome and Jane was being bored to death because of her aimless existence there, Fonda was being beset with his own problems of trying to cope with producer De Laurentiis who had engaged him to play the role of Pierre in the film **War and Peace.**

The Tolstoy novel is justly thought to be one of the great classics of world literature, along with Cervantes' **Don Quixote,** Dostoyevsky's **Crime and Punishment** and Dante's **Divine Comedy.** Only a man with a super-ego like the producer's would dare tamper with the work, but that was exactly what he did.

Director King Vidor and Fonda were the kind of men who respected the art of a great writer. They wanted to film the masterpiece and do full justice to its quality. Vidor in his desire to have the picture truly reflect the author's thoughts even assisted in writing the movie script. But De Laurentiis had ideas of his own about how the book should be treated. He was determined to produce a typical Hollywood blockbuster that would reap millions of dollars for him.

"Art," he said, "was for absent-minded professors who lived in ivory towers." "The average moviegoer," he said, "wants to be entertained. And a film in his opinion should include plenty of sex, gory battle scenes and soap-opera type romance." If the director gave him that kind of a picture it would not only play well in Peoria but in the European counterparts of that town as well.

Fonda, as one critic wrote, was apparently the only person connected with the film who had actually read the book.

Pierre, as Tolstoy depicted him, was a huge figure of a man, moon-faced, a bumbler with "two left-feet." He was a decent human being and was constantly tortured by what he saw about him. He always asked questions like, "Why are we here? What really constitutes happiness? And is there a purpose in human suffering?"

Pierre as many readers of the novel knew is Tolstoy himself—a great writer who had witnessed death at first hand when he was an army officer. Fonda had studied the character of Pierre intending to enact the role honestly. Fonda wanted to wear glasses just as he did. When De Laurentiis saw him in spectacles he told Vidor to see to it that Fonda "take off those glasses."

Fonda had a great deal to say about De Laurentiis after he had finished working in the picture.

"Having already got some of the scenes we'd shot within the scene where I am seen taking my glasses off, so it didn't look like suddenly I have glasses and suddenly I don't." It raised some difficulties for him when he tried to cope with the producer's changes of mind. Fonda later confessed that he had been surprised when Vidor first approached him and said that he would be perfect for the role of Pierre. He wanted to know why a man hailing from Omaha, Nebraska, could be expected to act the role of a Russian. It was he thought, like trying to mix pure corn with 100-proof Vodka and some borsht and bliniki. But after he had read the Irvin Shaw script he said that it was just "too good to walk away from. It was a challenge."

The arguments between the producer and the star continued during the entire time the picture was being made. King Vidor, who had had such problems with other producers and emotional actors before tried to act like a peacemaker. Fonda whose temper would flare up easily enough warned Vidor that he could "be a mean son-of-a-bitch." And he meant it.

Vidor tried to pour oil on the troubled waters. He insisted on driving Fonda to the studio every day. During the 45 minute drive he talked about the movie and sympathized with the trials and tribulations the star was encountering from the producer. It worked for an hour or two. But a few hours later De Laurentiis and Fonda were at each other's throats again.

Even a trivial incident appeared to arouse Fonda. When the script called for a Borzoi in one particular scene, Fonda demanded that the animal be removed. It was. When De Laurentiis made an appearance on the set Fonda deferred to his wishes and played Pierre as ordered. But when he wasn't there he would revert to his original conception of the character and play the role he had conceived it to be. It took some time before Fonda learned that De Laurentiis really wanted to have two Hollywood glamour boys play the roles of Pierre and Prince Andrew. Neither Fonda nor Mel Ferrer could be classed as that kind of a personality.

Years later when Fonda was still ridiculing the antics of the producer he said, "He might just as well have had a Rock Hudson instead of Mel Ferrer and me; that's just what he wanted, attractive leading men. The character I was trying to portray was quite different from De Laurentiis' conception of it. So it didn't come out as much of a character as I would have liked. I would have liked to wear padding under my wardrobe and have my hair combed forward. I couldn't get away with that."

To make matters worse Fonda had many arguments with the sound engineer. He said that Fonda was whispering his lines and he was unable to pick them up.

King Vidor who was having his own difficulties with the star also shouted "Speak a bit louder." He expected an outburst from Fonda but the actor remained strangely silent. When the two men were at dinner one night Fonda came up with a suggestion. He thought that some of the lines should be spoken in Russian. It made no sense to Vidor. He laughed and said nothing. The idea was stillborn.

The more discerning movie buffs who knew their Tolstoy said that Audrey Hepburn's Natasha was superb. She looked the part of the lovely naive girl who had the "irresistable radiance of youth," as described in the novel. Fonda's Pierre was just passable; to many moviegoers he seemed to be more the Nebraskan cornhusker than the sensitive Russian. They also said that his nasal enunciation of the lines did not lend conviction to the role. Fonda remained in Rome until the picture was completed, but he sent Jane and Peter home when the summer was over. Jane matriculated at Vassar College with her childhood friend Brooke Hayward in the fall.

Chapter XVII
Back Home

Vassar was a vast change from Emma Willard. The college occupies a large area of land a few miles from the old Dutch town of Poughkeepsie, New York. It is within commuting distance of the big city. Back in 1955 when Jane first matriculated there it was the kind of place where, as one writer put it, "Young women of privilege and intelligence were dispatched in order to acquire a formal education and be polished off with a bit of sophisticated cultural overlay. It was all done in order to prepare the young ladies for marriage, motherhood and menopause."

Vassar was a highly regarded educational institution of higher learning, nevertheless, and also provided its students with the added advantage of meeting boys in their own social class who were studying at Ivy League schools. The Women's Lib movement and its concentration on careers for women rather than marriage was more than a decade in the future. The main purpose of the girls' parents was to have their children find fulfillment in marriage, one that would also include financial security.

Fonda had by some kind of osmosis instilled in his daughter a love for the theater. But she was also a Seymour and they adhered to certain standards of conduct. Marriage and monogamy were basic in their scheme of things. Fonda, as we know, concurred with those standards, but ironically enough his life style was not setting a very good example for his children. When they were older he admitted that he had "come from a background of a happily married family." He said that he was "ashamed it was not that way with me."

Jane's life at Vassar was far more relaxed than the regimen she had had to endure at Emma Willard. She was free to do what she wanted during weekends. She could leave the campus, date young men or go to see her stepmother and her sister Amy in New York. She hardly had a care in the world. Her father was aware of the kind of a life she was living at Vassar and did not approve of it. Nor was he happy when he heard about Peter's troubles at the Westminster School.

When Fonda returned to New York, his state of mind could only be described as one of silent rage. He attempted to reach out to his children but did not have the emotional resources to do it effectively. He knew that something would have to be done to control and if possible guide them. He suddenly decided that he would rent a house on Cape Cod and have them live with him for the summer season. It was there that Jane told him that she was interested in acting. She had previously acted in a play with her father at the Omaha Playhouse and had impressed the local citizens with her talent.

Despite all the praise she had received at that time she still lacked confidence and did not believe that she had any ability as an actress. Her father, always the reticent one, did not try very hard to encourage her. He did express some gratification about her abilities, but basically his attitude was that of a man who really did not take his daughter's strivings very seriously.

Recalling his own early years of hardship and heartbreak when he was struggling for some recognition in New York, he wanted to spare his children a similar experience. He really did his best to discourage Jane from becoming a professional actress, but he did not have any effect on her especially when she was praised by her college friends. She took their opinions seriously. When she was on the Cape she finally decided to test herself and try her hand at acting with a seasoned tour of artists. At first Fonda discouraged her, but after giving it some further thought he asked the directors of the Dennis Playhouse where he had begun in 1928 to give her some work. The first role she played was that of a maid in a Restoration comedy. Her performance had the audience sit up and take notice. She proved to her father that she had a real stage presence. Fonda naturally enough, was proud of her. Years after her debut Jane quoting a friend who had overhead Fonda muttering half aloud, "If you were any other SOB you'd say get that girl into the theater, and don't use a ship to get her there."

Towards the end of the summer Fonda was asked to play the lead role in **The Male Animal.** Jane was also a member of the cast. When it was first proposed that she be in the play she demurred. She believed that nepotism had something to do with her being picked to play the ingenue part, but the lure of the theater was now too much for her to resist, and she accepted the offer. It was, she said later on, one of the best weeks of her life.

It was during that summer that Day Tuttle, the director of the Mount Kisco Playhouse happened to come across a news item which said that Fonda was acting in a play in Dennis. He decided to go to the Cape and see his friend. After he had settled down in the hotel with his wife he took a walk around the playhouse grounds. He heard himself being hailed, it was Hank Fonda. "Hey Day, you old good-for-nothing," he was shouting, "what are you doing here?"

The two men renewed their friendship and Tuttle now says that Fonda made his stay in Dennis a very pleasant one for both him and his wife. He also saw Jane's performance and said, "We were thrilled with Fonda's and Jane's acting." And speaking of his friend he also said, "He is a remarkable human being and always ready to do what one asks of him. He's also an actor of superb talent." Tuttle went as far as to compare him to a saint.

Because he considered him that kind of a man Tuttle could not understand why Fonda's private life had been so tragic. He recalled that Margaret Sullavan whom he and his wife knew was truly a fine human being. In having that opinion he was at odds with Logan. That marriage had only lasted two months. Later, he had been invited to the wedding of Fonda and Frances Seymour Brokaw. He really thought that that marriage would last for a lifetime. It was, he said, a perfect choice of a wife for Fonda to have made. Tuttle said that he couldn't understand what had gone wrong. Fonda apparently could not be permanently married to any woman. Tuttle also deplored what was happening to Fonda's children because of the actor's unsettled life. He still insisted that Fonda was one of the kindest men he had ever known.

Similar opinions about Fonda were also expressed by many of his friends. Most of them hastened to add that his character defied understanding. His old friend John Swope said that his relationship with each woman goes through a strange metamorphosis. It starts in high gear and ends in a silence on his part that is almost impenetrable. Swope also said that he can break off a long-time relationship with a woman or a man with the same feeling a surgeon displays after he has cut out an organ. For a man who was supposed to be sensitive he showed a curious insensitivity at times.

It took Jane many years before she was able to comprehend what was wrong and what was right with her father. She remembered seeing a highly-respected actor perform in a play. He had impressed her with his artistry, and yet, while he reminded her of her father there was a difference. She could not put her finger on what was puzzling her. It finally struck her that Fonda's acting was indeed different. And it was because there was always an undercurrent of melancholy in his makeup. It came through to the audience. She reasoned that if the characteristics in his personality had vanished, all that remained would have been a one-dimensional actor who would be adequate, not great. If that underlying depressive feeling in his makeup was in a strong sense responsible for the success he had achieved in his profession it was apparently also making his life barely tolerable. It spoiled every relationship he had ever had with a woman.

Fonda had left his wife alone in New York and had gone off to Rome to act in **War and Peace.** He found some solace during his stay in the Eternal City with Afdera Franchetti, a native of Venice. The rather fey young woman could never make up her mind whether she was a Baroness or a Countess. She was addressed by both titles. Afdera knew that Fonda was married, but that did not deter her from pursuing and eventually snaring her quarry. Afdera was only 24 years old when she was first introduced to Fonda. She was a tall, svelte-looking Italian beauty with burnished dark hair, penetrating eyes who was said to bear a striking resemblance to Frances.

Back in New York, Susan, who had been subjected to the usual silent treatment by her husband during the last years of her marriage heard tales about his liaison with another woman. Her marriage had been disintegrating for some time. It had been doomed from the beginning. Her mother, Mrs. Oscar Hammerstein, was probably right when she said that her daughter "was much too young when she married Fonda." She also said that "Susan had expected her marriage to be like the one between Oscar and myself. We always held hands together.

And because of what she saw in her home she had romantic ideas about marriage in general. Fonda was engrossed in his work, and he was very remote. She had always been left alone. . . . She was alone." And being left alone so much of the time and subjected to those silent moods of his coupled with the gossip she was hearing about his affair with a new woman in Rome brought her to a definite decision. She would seek a divorce.

After she had confirmed the rumors she left for Reno where she sued Fonda for a divorce. The couple's adopted child Amy was to remain in her custody.

It was a friendly parting. Fonda did not raise any objections about the property settlement. Her grounds for divorce were the usual ones. She claimed that he "had caused her intense mental pain." Her anguish was obvious. But she could console herself with the knowledge that every woman he had been married to had also received the silent treatment.

In a very brief telephone conversation with the writers Susan was asked to say something about her marriage. And she said, "I prefer not to. I am leading a peaceful life now and I would like to keep it that way."

Amy, Fonda's adopted daughter who is a clinical psychologist, also complained about her father's remoteness. When Mrs. Hammerstein was asked what Amy's current relations with her father were she said, "I think things are all right now between her and her father. I think he had been a bit remote with her."

Mister Roberts: Fonda Gives Ensign Pulver (David Wayne) the word.

Mister Roberts: Destroying Palm Tree.

Chapter XVIII
A New Wife

And so, for the second time Jane and Peter were to acquire a stepmother. Fonda had already been married three times. It could be surmised that the staid citizens of Omaha, his home town, would be shocked by such goings-on. On the contrary. They were more inclined to make allowances for his propensity to rid himself of his wives. They still regarded him as one of their most distinguished fellow-townsmen and tended to condone his weaknesses. They generally believed that Fonda was a decent man who loved his children and who believed in the old and traditional standards they lived by.

Jane desperately wanted to agree with those opinions. But there were many moments when she had some doubts about them. She tried to adopt an objective attitude towards him and was able to succeed to some extent. But it was really too much to ask of Peter who was bearing the brunt of his father's rather irregular lifestyle. He was not allowed to forget that Fonda had been married many times. The students and some members of the Westminster School faculty saw to that.

Peter's most malignant persecutor was a "master" who because of a physical infirmity had been called "The Gimp" by the students. One afternoon he accosted Peter in one of the corridors of the school building and berated him for being late to chapel. The teacher had obviously been drinking and could hardly control his body movements. He warned Peter that if it happened again he would not get off easily. There would be no coddling him just because he was the son of a famous actor. Punishment, in accordance of the school's Calvinistic principles, included being wacked repeatedly on the buttocks. The teacher accused Peter of being an atheist. That was just too much for the boy to take. He told "The Gimp" that he was closer to God than he was. The teacher shouted some expletives at him. One word led to another. When it appeared that "The Gimp" was about to assault Peter physically, another member of the faculty tried to stop the oncoming fight. "The Gimp" continued to hurl insults at Peter. He shouted, "Anybody who has been married all those times has got to be a son-of-a-bitch." When he heard it, Peter punched the teacher in the face. The latter returned the blow. Being the heavier and stronger of the two he was bound to prevail over the frail-looking young boy. At that point the other teacher seized hold of the enraged "Gimp" and guided him away from the scene.

Fonda was told what had happened. He felt guilty about having indirectly been the cause of his son's problems at school. He wrote

124

a long letter to the headmaster in which he admitted that his too frequent marriages had been creating hardships for his son. He also said that it was unfair for Peter to be held accountable for his messy private life.

The faculty at the school agreed. They looked into the teacher's past behavior and found that he had been involved in many arguments and fracases with other students. They discharged him.

Fonda was now about to marry for the fourth time. Jane, who was still at Vassar College, was invited to the ceremony along with the groom's sister Jayne and her spouse John Schoentgen. The latter two had travelled all the way from California to attend the wedding. The ceremony was conducted by a local jurist in the East 74th Street townhouse. It was the first marriage for the Italian noblewoman.

Fonda was no longer the starving young actor who had lived in a decrepit looking railroad flat. He was now earning thousands of dollars a week. And his new wife planned to employ all of her ingenuity in devising ways to spend it. She engaged two Italian servants who had formerly been in the employ of a foreign diplomat, and shortly thereafter she was all over the town buying expensive furniture to replace the old in the townhouse. After the rooms had been completely remodeled and furnished she invited hordes of her fellow-countrymen to be her guests there. Fonda groaned when he saw the bills, but he paid them. Did he have any choice? Afdera bought the most expensive high-fashion clothes and insisted that her husband should accompany her to all the posh places where she danced the nights away.

The very expensive furniture underwent a beating when her free-loading friends, always in high spirits, rampaged through the rooms wrecking everything that stood in their way. Leland Hayward described one such wild night, "For dessert they had ice cream and chocolate sauce. There was some dancing, and all of a sudden those nutty Italians started to throw ice cream and sauce on the walls. I thought Hank would commit murder, but he just stood there and smiled pretending to enjoy it."

During a brief period of time Afdera managed to exert dominance over the household. Every one of her whims became an order that had to be satisfied. In the process she managed to arouse the hostility of both Jane and Peter.

The countess was the kind of woman who acted on impulse without taking time to weigh the consequences of her actions. Fonda's two children found it hard to tolerate her behavior. The fact that their father had married a girl who was only 24 years old amused and annoyed them. At the rate he was going, they said, his eleventh wife would "probably be in diapers."

Jane and Peter felt especially angry when they saw their father indulge his wife in every one of her foibles. In contrast Susan, his third wife, had been a wife and gentle woman; Jane couldn't carry on an intelligent conversation with Afdera. Her command of English was limited. Fonda who was an unbending disciplinarian with both his children made all kinds of allowances for his new wife. Ironic, but true.

In time, Fonda realized that his wife's unpredictable ways and super-swinger kind of a life was not conducive for his peace of mind. Jane and Peter now returned to school. They were both very disturbed. A few weeks later Fonda was told that Jane was behaving irrationally. She had been asked to turn in an examination paper and instead gave her teacher some blank pages filled with doodles. She also left the campus one weekend without informing her faculty chairman that she had gone out on a lark. When she returned to the college she expressed her regret to her faculty counselor. Jane now tells us that "Before I got a chance to say I was sorry, he said he understood that my father had just married for the fourth time and that I was emotionally upset. I wasn't really. I'd just gone away with a boy for the weekend."

Peter took his father's fourth marriage more seriously. He returned to Westminster and started to swallow phenobarbital pills as if they were delectable Swiss chocolates. He was becoming increasingly restless and was disliked by the other students. He was also involved in a number of fights with the other students. On one occasion, when he and some of his classmates were on a bus on their way to a Harry Belafonte concert he saw some oddly dressed blacks on a street corner. He made some unflattering remarks to them. The blacks responded by throwing rocks at the bus. When the students returned to Westminster they were taken to task by the headmaster. An investigation to determine the responsibility for the incident was conducted and the faculty members questioned every boy in turn. Peter escaped blame and the faculty issued a statement which said that the school itself was to blame for not inculcating in the student body an attitude that every citizen regardless of origin, creed or color was to be considered an equal and treated with proper respect. It was emphasized that those principles had been embodied in the Constitution.

After that incident Peter wanted to leave the school for good. He felt a strong urge to confide to someone what was troubling him. His father and his current stepmother were honeymooning in Europe, but Jane was still at Vassar. He telephoned her and she drove down in her stationwagon to Westminster. A few days later the two were off to Omaha to visit their Aunt Harriet and Uncle Jack. The couple were no-nonsense Midwesterners. They heard what Peter had to say and then practically ordered him back to school. Peter still believes that his relatives considered him a mountebank and a fabricator. He also had reasons to believe that they were certain he would wind up in an institution for the mentally disturbed.

After some urging by his relatives Peter consented to see Dr. William Thompson, the chairman of the liberal arts department at the local university. The dean was a trained psychologist. He had Peter undergo some tests. Thompson was impressed with the results. Fonda talked to Dr. Thompson after the tests had been conducted and was pleasantly surprised to learn that his son had an I.Q. of 160. Dr. Thompson suggested that Peter should be a college sophomore. He was "too intelligent to remain in a secondary school," he said.

There was now the problem of getting enough credentials to

enable Peter to matriculate at a college. He had not graduated from
high school. Arrangements were made to enroll him at Brownwell
Hall, an all-girls school that was run by Episcopalians. In four months
Peter earned enough credits to enable him to matriculate at Omaha
University. He was now under the personal supervision of Dean Thomp-
son.

Jane also had her share of problems. Even a father whose time
was completely taken up with his profession could not help but be
aware that his daughter was in need of help and advice. Two months
after he had married the fair Afdera, Jane left Vassar for good and
traveled to Omaha to see her brother. She had tried to study piano
at the Mannes School in New York but gave it up after she had taken
a few lessons. She had also registered as a student at the Berlitz
School and studied both Italian and French for a short time. And since
she had a certain flair for painting, she went to the Art Students
League again for a short time. At nineteen Jane was at sea drifting
and apparently did not know how to organize her life in a more productive way. She asked her father whether he would approve her living
in Paris; he told her that she was old enough to make up her own
mind.

Jane left for Paris with the full knowledge that the town had
provided inspiration to many American expatriates including such
men of letters like Ernest Hemingway, F. Scott Fitzgerald and musicians like Aaron Copeland and many others. A few weeks after she
had arrived she enrolled as a student at the Academie Grande Chau-
miete and the Academie Julian, both well-known art schools. She
dropped out of them soon enough and spent most of her time either
sleeping late or going to the antique shops on the Left Bank and also
gallavanting around the city with a group of swingers. It was at that
time that she was introduced to the flamboyant Russian film producer-
director Roger Vadim Plemianikov—a man who had long since dropped
his last name because his friends and acquaintances were unable to
pronounce it. Vadim, a former actor and newspaperman had produced
a picture that was entitled **And God Created Woman.** His wife, Brigitte
Bardot played the female lead. The picture startled the rather staid
generation of the 1950's but it was an instantaneous success nevertheless. Vadim eventually discarded Bardot and was seen around Paris
with his new protegee, Annette Stroyberg who was heavy with child
as the saying goes. Vadim's mistress who had been displaying the
proof of his affection for all to see gave birth to a baby the day following Jane's meeting him at Maxim's Restaurant. Jane left Paris a few
days after meeting the man who was destined to become her husband.

While Jane was having her fling in Paris, her father was having
his troubles back home. He had been going through his own purgatory
for many months. It was being caused by his having to act in **Two
for the Seesaw.**

Fonda had invested $20,000 of his own money in the production,
which entitled him to 25 percent of the profits. The plot of the play
was a simple one. A man just past his prime of life who had been
a fairly successful lawyer back home arrived in New York from Omaha.

His marriage was about to end in a divorce. He meets a young girl quite by accident. She lived in one of the outlying boroughs of the city. He falls in love with her. The plot concentrates on his attempts to cope with the situation he finds himself in.

From a financial standpoint Fonda had a great deal to gain if the play proved to be a success. He was to receive $2,500 a week which would be counted against 15 percent of the gross receipts. That would go on for six months. He was also insured for $225,000 during the run of the play.

But things never went easy for Henry Fonda. He read the play and let everyone know that he was not satisfied with the character of Jerry Ryan, the role he was to play. It was, he said, not a well-developed character. He also said that William Gibson who had written the play had given him a one dimensional role to work on and that Gittle Mosca, who was to be played by Anne Bancroft would over-shadow him on stage.

Gibson was greatly disturbed by Fonda's criticism. It had taken him twenty years to have one of his plays produced on Broadway and he did not want to see his efforts go up in smoke. Since Fonda was the star and could not be replaced, Gibson had to go along with his wishes and start rewriting parts of the play.

It is ironic to note that the playwright who did not want Fonda to work in his play in the first place because he said he was too old to play the role of a lover of a young girl now had to bow to his wishes.

Gibson had asked Richard Widmark to play the part. When that actor told him that he had another commitment he turned to Paul Newman, Richard Basehart, Jack Palance, Larry Nelson, Eli Wallach, Don Murray and Fritz Weaver in that order and was turned down by all of them for one reason or another. Fonda therefore was the last choice for the role.

There were many "angels" around who were now more than eager to invest their money in a play that starred Fonda. Everything seemed to be ready to go. Gibson now had his star, and Fonda, who had always hungered for another chance to return to the legitimate stage, should have been more than pleased now. But he did not like the dialogue that Gibson had written for him. Whatever lines Gibson wrote had to be revised in order to appease him and he was never satisfied with them.

Fonda arrived in New York during the summer. He asked Gibson and an unknown actress who was being considered for the female lead to come to his townhouse on East 74th Street. There, the actress read her lines. Fonda without any further ado forgot about auditioning Julie Harris, Kim Stanley, Lee Grant and Gwen Verdon who has also hoped to work in the play. He told Gibson that the actress was his only choice for the part. Her name was Anne Bancroft.

The actress was signed at a salary of $550 a week. There was a stipulation in her contract that if she did not measure up to what Fonda expected of her she could be let go after a week or two of out-of-town tryouts.

Fonda was now definitely in the driver's seat. All of the important leading men on Broadway had refused to work in the play. The producers were left with Fonda and he knew it. The entire production would have to be closed down if he decided he did not want to work in it.

Fonda was now trying to grow into the part, but it seemed hopeless. When some of the people who were associated with the production told him that all was going well he merely grunted and said that the male role just wasn't right for him. "Ryan," he said, "just isn't the kind of character I can get my teeth into." What he really meant was that Gittle Mosca was a flesh and blood person and that Bancroft would dominate the stage.

Gibson, who was trying to go along with his wishes, was now facing a dilemma. The question he asked himself was whether he really was convinced that changes in the dialogue were necessary.

In his diary Gibson reveals how much he had had to endure trying to cope with Fonda and his demands. He wrote, "In my view Hank's style which I respected, and that of the role in those attributes where it had my respect were not compatible. Their marriage was one to which I had given a reluctant blessing on the brink."

He could have said it more clearly. He didn't think that Fonda was the right actor for the role and had only accepted him because he was the only star around who was at liberty at the time the casting was in progress.

Gibson must have believed that a very harsh judge had just passed sentence condemning him to be enslaved to write endless lines forever. The sequence ran like this--Fonda asked for changes in the dialogue. Gibson rewrote the lines. Fonda read his latest efforts and said he did not like the new ones. Gibson wrote some more dialogue. And once again Fonda expressed his opinion that it would not do. If one was to believe that Gibson was being subjected to cruel and inhuman punishment because he had inflicted a character like Ryan on a poor inoffensive actor it was clear to those who knew Fonda that he was also having a difficult time of it. He lay awake nights trying to find some way to get inside the character with whom he was not in sympathetic accord.

The two men spent day after day reading and re-reading the lines Gibson was writing, but Fonda continued to disapprove of them. By the time Gibson had completed his last rewrite he must have felt that he had been working on at least a half dozen plays. Fonda said that he could not speak a single word on stage unless he felt comfortable with the lines. Unfortunately for the playwright there were very few lines which he liked.

The director, Arthur Penn, a modest young man and a follower of Lee Strasberg and his method also had his differences with Fonda. The star scoffed at "The Method." Penn, who was a close friend of the playwright, did not help matters too much. It seemed to Fonda that Strasberg, the High Lama of all "Method" disciples was ganging up on him. Anne Bancroft had studied at the Actors Studio, the Strasberg citadel. Penn was also a "Method" director, and Gibson was probably an advocate of that school of acting. Fonda who had been told by Josh Logan who years earlier had sat at the feet of the great Stanis-

lavsky in Moscow that the Russian master thought that actors had
to find their own method and not be imitative of any set pattern
called "The Method." And now to his chagrin Fonda was surrounded
by men who he knew did not really understand what the Russian had
stood for. He now felt like an outsider especially after Penn undertook
to coach Bancroft—help which she happily accepted since it was being
offered by the self-annointed professor of "The Method."

Despite the fact that Fonda was now going along a different
road both Penn and Bancroft knew that here was a man who commanded
and deserved respect because when he walked on stage he took possession of it.

Fonda continued to differ with both of them and kept on saying
that the character Ryan was still alien to him. "It simply isn't right,"
he said to Penn. "It doesn't work for me at all. And I can't explain
why it doesn't. I wish I could."

The company had now been in rehearsal for over three weeks
and still the star had a feeling that the play lacked something. It
was now the end of November and well into the Broadway season.
In an effort to create a more agreeable atmosphere among the actors
and especially for Fonda the belabored playwright came up with what
he hoped would be an acceptable peace offering. He gave Fonda a
bottle of Jack Daniels. A bottle of bourbon, Fonda's favorite liquor,
may have been better appreciated. Fonda acknowledged the gift with
a nod of his head. That was the prelude to still another rehearsal
before an audience of fellow professionals. Fonda, to hear Gibson
tell it, "seemed to shrink into the background," a sure sign that he
was finding the situation he was in too much for him to bear.

About a week later the show opened at the Shubert Theater
in Washington D.C. The cast had dinner together before curtain time.
Fonda was asked to join the other actors but declined the invitation.

After relaxing in his room he arrived at the theater in a despondent mood. He heard his cue and walked on stage and for the remainder
of the evening he appeared to act like a sleepwalker or perhaps like
a man who was trying to erase reality from his mind and lose himself
in some never-never land.

Surprisingly enough, the Washington critics liked what they
saw. They suggested some minor changes in the play script. Gibson,
who by this time had long since lost count of the rewrites he had
done, proceeded to write some additional dialogue. He knew that
nothing he would put down on paper would satisfy Fonda.

"Hank," he later revealed in his book, "could not play what I
wrote and I could not write what he played."

Fonda continued to struggle with the part. Despite the fact
that his new wife Afdera was with him in his hotel suite where he
was busily engaged spouting his new lines out loud it did not help
put him in a better frame of mind. Gibson was now avoiding him as
much as he could. The strain had become too much for the two men.

When **Variety,** the theatrical trade publication, published some
flowery stories about Bancroft and negative lines about Fonda and
the play, the actor decided that it would be in the best interests of

the production and himself to quit. Fred Coe, the producer, believed that Fonda had been miscast. The situation had now reached a crisis stage. It seemed to the cast, the playwright and the financial sponsors that the time had come to recognize failure and start curtailing their losses and close down the project. But that did not happen. Gibson, regaining his confidence, started to rewrite the first act just before the play was to open in Philadelphia. It opened at the Forest Theater. The critics were more than kind. Despite that encouraging note Fonda still behaved like a man who had been sentenced to a long term in prison by a relentless judge. Gibson recalled watching men in danger of being killed who had displayed a more cheerful demeanor than the unhappy actor. He said, "I thought the price his soul was paying for this piece of entertainment was exorbitant for anything short of paradise, and his stamina (under such stress) was quite laudable."

When someone wanted to know whether Fonda had finally overcome the problems he had encountered trying to work out the Ryan characterization he said, "No. I still have the feeling that Ryan's complexities still puzzle me. I can't get the feel of the character."

Chapter XIX
Success

The night the play opened on Broadway at the Booth Theater found Gibson still slaving away changing the lines and red-pencilling others. The chill wind emanating from Fonda was making the harassed playwright more nervous than he had ever been since production started. He knew that the payoff was now. If the critics for his work found it wanting it would finish off his budding career in the theater. He had had to wait 20 years to have one of his plays produced on Broadway and now it was all hanging in the balance.

To the surprise of the star, the cast and everyone else connected with the production, the audience found what was happening on the stage much to its pleasure. The applause at the end of the third act was ear-shattering. And when the curtain finally was rung down, the entire company knew that it had a hit on its hands. The actors and the producers were ecstatic. That is, everyone except Fonda. The star of the show had been invited to come to an after-the-show dinner along with the rest of the cast. He turned it down and went home to brood. His reverie was broken when Fred Coe called him on the telephone to tell him that all of the reviews were favorable.

Brooks Atkinson, the King of the New York drama critics, wrote, "What he (Fonda) does not say in the dialogue he says with the silent eloquence of a fine actor. . .soft, shining, acting."

The public read the reviews and reacted in a predictable fashion. On the following morning a long line of theatergoers were standing three deep to buy tickets. The play ran on and on. It became one of the most successful Broadway productions. But that did not make Fonda feel any better. He was not impressed with the public's acceptance of the play nor of his acting.

His troubled state of mind was now affecting his health. He was laid low with an attack of influenza and was confined to bed for a week. But like the long-suffering Job in the Bible he accepted his fate stoically and continued to labor away trying to perfect his acting. Friends tried to console him. They told him that his acting was beyond reproach and that the audiences were enjoying his work. He reacted as expected. He had always been uncomfortable with those individuals who praised him and through the years he had developed an immunity to flattery. Despite their assurances he deprecated his own efforts and the play as well. The $4,000 a week he was now getting plus proceeds from his initial investment did not make him any happier. Fonda was becoming more irritated with his fey and

132

Fonda and his fourth wife, Countess Afdera Franchetti, at the New York premiere of "Twelve Angry Men."

ethereal wife because of her free-spending ways. She was now given the usual Fonda treatment—silence.

A friend who was asked why Fonda was so irritable said he was unhappy because he was associated with the play. "Hank," he said, "finds solace in work, a great deal of work." And when he finds himself playing a role that does not sit well with him he becomes dour.

Chapter XX
Henry, Jane and Peter

Paris had been a great disappointment for Jane. She had hoped to lead a productive life there and instead had spent all of her time in useless pursuits. Fonda was told what was happening to her in Paris and summoned her home. After she arrived in New York she ensconced herself in her father's townhouse. Shortly after that she began to solicit advertisements from the publishers for the local office of the **Paris Review.**

Jane was completely unaware that she was a very striking-looking young woman. A friend suggested that she model clothes for the magazine he was working for. Jane thought it was a good idea and began to apply herself diligently to her new career. James Franciscus, a young actor of talent served as her male escort for a brief period of that time.

By applying herself to long hours of work she hoped to please her father. He would now begin to believe that she was trying to make a useful life for herself. He was impressed but never said a word that would indicate to her that he approved of what she was doing. When she tried to get a response from him or when she attempted to discuss her work he reacted negatively. She longed to hear some words of encouragement from him but none was forthcoming. Fonda had a great deal on his mind. That could perhaps explain why he was so impatient when she tried to talk to him.

In a way it was her father's current activities that led Jane to turn to the theater. To relieve his sense of frustration caused by his playing in **Two for the Seasaw,** Fonda decided to accept a role in the movie, **Stage Struck.** Susan Strasberg was to be his co-star in the picture. The young actress had achieved a modicum of fame after making her debut in the Broadway production of **The Diary of Anne Frank.** She was known in theater circles because she was the daughter of Lee Strasberg. It was at that time that Jane became acquainted with Susan and at long last reached a firm decision to become a professional actress.

Stage Struck had first been produced in 1933 with Katharine Hepburn as its star. Its remake was decided upon by one of the bright Hollywood executives who believed that it was just the right kind of a vehicle for Susan. Fonda had been drawn into the co-starring role with Susan because of his friendship with Sidney Lumet who was going to direct the picture.

The plot at best was a hackneyed one. It was a story about a young and ruthlessly ambitious actress who used all of her feminine wiles to win a place for herself in the Broadway theatrical jungle. Similar plots had been used in pictures countless times before.

Stage Struck just as Fonda had feared, received very bad reviews. A.J. Weller of the **New York Times,** while conceding that Susan Strasberg was competent as a determined Eva Lovelace, had very little praise for either performer. He found Susan to be "petite and fragile and sometimes pallid in a role that seems to call for fire, not mere smouldering. Henry Fonda is largely a placid type as the producer who discovers his heart can be reached by love as well as the theater."

Jane by that time was a good friend of Susan's. Fonda, who still had no regard for the Method school of acting respected his young co-star and saw to it that she met his daughter. The two girls became fast friends. During the next few weeks Jane also got to know many of Susan's friends in the theater. Although she found many of them fascinating she was also repelled by their fanatical pursuit of fame at any cost.

She said, "I didn't like what I saw, what the acting profession does to people who go into the theater. All the young actresses I've met are obcessed with the theater. They think and talk only about one thing. Nothing else matters to them. It's terribly unhealthy to sacrifice everything--family, children--for a goal. I hope I never get that way. I don't believe in concentrating your life in terms of one profession, no matter what it is." She changed her mind in the next few weeks.

Fonda still hoped to escape for a time from **Two for the Seesaw** and that summer was able to leave for Hollywood to play in a movie. It was a Western with the unlikely title of **Warlock.** Fonda thought it was a welcome change from working in a play he didn't like.

Bosley Crowther of the **New York Times** wrote that **Warlock** was "good, gripping Western fare."

Fonda rented a cottage in Malibu, a short distance away from Los Angeles and had his children and his wife Afdera stay there for a few months. About a mile down the beach were Lee Strasberg, his wife, Paula and his daughter Susan and son John. The latter two were contemporaries of his own children. Paula was in California to coach Marilyn Monroe who was playing in the movie **Some Like It Hot.** Both families frequently visited. Fonda arranged barbeques for the Strasbergs and they in turn did the same for his family. The two girls had a great amount of time on their hands and would talk about life and their careers for hours on end. Susan asked Jane why she hadn't become an actress. Jane did not respond at first. But in her many visits to the Strasbergs she met dozens of actors, directors and producers and listened to all they had to say about the theater and the movies. She found their conversation interesting and was also attracted to the informality and warmth she witnessed at the Strasberg household--a contrast to what she saw at home.

During one such visit she met the director, Mervyn LeRoy who was there with his two children, Linda and Warner. The LeRoys also asked her why she had not worked in the profession after she had performed so well at the Dennis Playhouse in Cape Cod. Jane told

them that she didn't feel she had enough talent to warrant her becoming
a professional. And once again she repeated what she had said to
her friends. The high standards that had been set by her father made
it difficult for her to be less than perfect. LeRoy said that her remarks
were amusing. He told her that those fears were groundless. Then
he asked her if she would be interested in playing Jimmie Stewart's
daughter in a picture about the F.B.I. Jane now realized that LeRoy
was not being facetious, that he was serious about having her act
in the movie. Jane was frightened at first. Would she be able to do
full justice to the part? Later that day she spoke to her father about
it. He told her that "there must be something better for you than
play the part of Jimmie Stewart's daughter in that movie."

The following day she was at the Strasberg cottage and talked
about the offer with Marty Fried, a highly-regarded director. He
also wanted to know why she hadn't made a career for herself in the
theater, since she appeared to possess the basic attributes including
youth, beauty, vivacity and a distinct flair for acting. And once more
she repeated her refrain. She was Fonda's daughter, one of America's
great actors, and she believed that she could not live up to what would
be expected of her.

Jane knew that living a purposeless life was not for her. She
felt that the time had come to stop using her father's fame as an
excuse not to work in the theater. One day she announced, "Dad,
I think I'd like to study with Mr. Strasberg."

In recalling what happened when Strasberg interviewed her
for the first time Jane said, "He talked to me as if he were interested
in me, not because I was Henry Fonda's daughter." That was her impression of the man; Strasberg later confessed that it was the frightened
expression in her eyes that intrigued him. "It was," he said, "fear
pure and simple." The panic she felt was probably caused by her
being subjected so minutely to an examination by a man who was
the acknowledged teacher of many of the most eminent artists in
the theater. He accepted her as a student and as a result her enthusiasm
was shot skyward.

In the fall of 1958 Jane made her first appearance at the Studio
work room with her friends Susan Strasberg and Marty Fried. The
latter two had come along to bolster her courage.

A student who was there that day said there was every indication
that she was unsure of herself. Still, one could sense that there was
something special about the girl. She did bear an almost uncanny
physical resemblance to her father.

Jane applied herself to her work at the Actors Studio very diligently. It was now clear enough despite her father's sceptical attitude
towards her that she would not repeat her former abortive attempts
at learning foreign languages and music and take what she was doing
seriously. Her father still continued to scoff about her work and The
Method. He did not believe that Strasberg served a useful purpose
in the theater. Jane later admitted that she was very sensitive to
her father's criticism of Strasberg and the Actors Studio. She would
come home after a day there, her spirits high and her heart full of

hope with a definite feeling that now at last she had found what she wanted to do with her life. But when she tried to tell Fonda what had happened that day at the studio he would snort and shout, "Shut up. I don't want to hear about it." But when he was asked later on by an interviewer why he had reacted so sharply he said, "I don't understand. I came home from a visit to the dentist and was toasting my teeth with scotch. Maybe I do things I'm not aware of that may mean something to other people. I don't know what she means when she says the 'curtain is going down.' It may be I'm trying to hide my emotions, and it is a curtain coming down."

When he was told that Jane was only trying to get to him he exclaimed, "She does get to me."

However, he also made a point of saying that he was not a demonstrative man and that he knew his daughter was more outgoing. And so there it was again--that Henry Fonda trait. He felt deeply about his daughter's aspirations and welfare but found it impossible to show his feelings.

Jane kept brooding about his not being sympathetic with her problems. She received encouragement from her friends and acquaintances but not from a father whom she loved and whose opinions she respected. His seemingly indifferent attitude only served to increase her feelings that she was being rejected. But now she was totally committed to becoming an actress and nothing her father could say would discourage her from making a career for herself. Lee Strasberg was in effect assuming the role of her surrogate father and encouraging her to apply herself to her art.

It was Strasberg who kept assuring her that she had much to offer the theater. But his confidence in her talent gave her a sense of worth. She was completely convinced of his sincerity and his honest desire to help her. She knew that he had nothing to gain by flattering her. Moreover as a friend and teacher he sensed in Jane Fonda the qualities that destined her for great things in the theater and movies.

Now that she had decided to break loose from her father she left his townhouse. She had been friendly with Susan Stein, the daughter of a former ophthalmologist and the Czar of the Music Corporation of America, one of the most important talent agencies in the country. Susan was now in New York and she suggested to Jane that they share an apartment; Jane readily agreed. Jenny Lee, a friend, also shared the small duplex apartment which was a few blocks away from Fonda's house. Before moving however, Jane who had been raised to observe the proprieties asked and received her father's permission to move out of his house.

Shortly after she had moved into her new home she was introduced to Ray Powers, a young agent who was associated with Famous Artists, a talent agency. She engaged him as her agent although she could easily have been accepted by the Music Corporation of America since Susan Stein's father was the head of that agency. Fonda, however, was a client there and Ray Powers later explained, "I found out soon enough that Fonda didn't take her acting at all seriously. He thought it was something she did to keep her busy and did not encourage her at all."

Fonda continued to caution her about the hazards of the acting profession, the demands it made, and the years of work and risks. Even when she was growing more involved in her career he kept on insisting that the path to stardom was strewn with bitterness and hardship. The critics, he said, would demand more from her than from any other young actress because she was his daughter. Fonda did not really intend to break her spirit; his only purpose, was to prepare her for the disappointments she would encounter in the years to come.

It was at that time that Josh Logan learned that Jane was attending classes at the Actors Studio. His wife Nedda had been urging her to become a fulltime actress for years, but her suggestions had fallen on deaf ears. Logan, who had faith in his goddaughter's abilities now was considering her for a part in a picture he planned to produce. The movie was a romantic little story about a young man in love with a girl. The characters were upperclass. Logan said that Jane, who was a Seymour, and Beatty, who was the scion of an old Virginian family, were perfect for the roles.

After Logan asked her to accept the part she sought her father's advice, but he again gave her no definite answer. She would, he told her, have to decide for herself whether she really wanted to be a movie actress. However, privately he told Logan that he approved of the idea of having his friend guide her professional life.

That role would have been the beginning of a career in films for her. But Logan had a change of heart; he became concerned about the two young thespians' box office appeal. It then occurred to him that Vivien Leigh and Clark Gable would attract more people to the movie houses, and when they had both turned him down, Logan decided to put the project on ice. He did promise however to find another vehicle for Jane.

While waiting for his promise to come through, Jane went to the Eileen Ford Model Agency and asked to be booked for assignments. The agency's head now says that she found Jane to be something special. Despite her obvious attractiveness Jane was surprised to find that many people liked her and that magazine editors wanted to have her on their publications' covers. Soon several national magazines had used her picture on their covers and in a short period of time she became known as one of the most wanted high-fashion models in town. But she still had her heart set on working as an actress and she continued to go to the Actors Studio. Her fellow students there still recall that she worked harder than anyone else.

Jane's big acting opportunity was not long in coming. Logan was asked to produce **The Homecoming**—a picture that was based on the Broadway play, **Tall Story**. He offered Jane a leading role in the picture. It had been adapted by Howard Lindsay and Russell Crouse from a novel by Howard Nemerov. The plot was all about college basketball and the corrupting influence exerted by professional gamblers. Jane, as one would expect, was extremely nervous about her latest debut. That feeling of not being good enough still persisted and as a result she had a mild case of insomnia and nightmares. The dreams were always the same. She had had similar ones when she

felt rejected as a child. She also had a severe case of boils—a phenomenon that always occurred when she was under stress. It wasn't too
difficult to understand her feelings of inadequacy.

She explained that "there is a great deal of difference between
being raised in a theatrical family when someone (her father) is doing
great things and doing something yourself."

She admitted that when Logan had offered her the part in the
picture she started to have grave doubts about being suited for the
role.

With still a few weeks to go before starting to work in the picture,
her agent, Ray Powers, had her appear in **The Moon's Blue** at a New
Jersey theater. She was badly miscast and Jane knew that she was
not very good in the part. An experience of that kind would not have
bolstered the self-confidence of a more mature actress; it didn't
do her any good.

Logan was still telling Fonda that his daughter was destined
to be a star. Fonda wanted to believe it because he knew how frustrated
she would be if she was not successful. He was in a despondent mood
at the time; he had gone back to Hollywood to star in a television
series called **The Deputy** after being assured that it would be a superior
kind of Western. It was the usual potboiler that had been produced
dozens of times in the movies. The scripts were amateurish and the
directing left much to be desired. A perfectionist like Fonda found
it hard to take. When the series was finally cancelled out two years
later Fonda vowed that he would never act again in another television
series.

Fonda's melancholy state of mind wasn't helped any when he
was told that Peter, now 19, and in his second year at the university
was still having problems. Peter was living with his aunt and uncle
and was behaving like a rebel. He still resented his father. "I was
programmed to be a Boy Scout," he confessed years later. "That's
all my old man wanted me to be." His troubles, he said, weren't all
that unusual. He admitted that his life had been a comfortable one
because his father was wealthy and famous. But he resented the fact
that while his father had made life easier for him, he hardly saw
him. He also said that he was amazed when he and Jane had first
learned that the so-called perfectionist wasn't all that perfect.

There had been times when Fonda tried to act like a concerned
parent to Jane, Peter and his adopted daughter Amy. Jane recently
said that when she was a very young child he would enter her room
just before he left for the studio and sing the following ditty:

"My doggie's name is guess
My doggie's name is guess
He wags his tail, for yes, yes"

After singing that doggerel he smiled and left the room.

Amy recently said that he would make a statement and it sounded like a kind of declaration. "There was no easy give and take between
him and any of his children. He used to scare me. He directed us
a lot."

While all of his children say that relations between them and their father had improved during his later years, there are still memories that continue to haunt them.

Life for Peter in Omaha was becoming more intolerable. He was at constant loggerheads with his professors, and he was always up to some mischief after school hours. At one point he went so far as to get some of the other students to put a fake bomb in the local Greyhound Bus Terminal. After placing it there Peter telephoned the local police and warned them that it was about to go off. Peter and his friends stood a short distance away from the terminal and watched the police look for the device. That incident made headlines in all of the Omaha newspapers.

Peter was also involved in a more serious escapade when he was a student in Omaha. His aunt kept urging him to date some of the local girls. Being a dutiful nephew he did as she asked. One of the girls became pregnant, and Peter raised $500 to pay for her trip to Puerto Rico where she had an abortion. He raised the money by selling his shotgun.

Although Fonda was still irritated with his son's carryings-on he was now becoming more sensitive to the needs of his daughter Jane. He was well aware that she still did not have any confidence in her talents as an actress, so he advised her not to pay any attention to those individuals who were saying that he had been responsible for her being chosen for the part in the movie, **The Homecoming.** He advised her to have faith in Logan's judgment and to heed what he told her. He also cautioned her to be more relaxed in front of the camera.

All neophyte actors know that the camera is always working at filming whatever is in front of it all the time. Their natural impulse is to do something—anything to fill up time. Fonda, because of his experience as a screen actor knew that the camera could be very intimidating to the novice. He told his daughter to act natural when she was acting in a picture.

Jane also discovered that "The Method" could not be adhered to completely and that her techniques as an actress would become more polished if she took her work seriously. In time she began to profit from her father's advice.

Jane knew that the picture she was working in was not very good and thought it was because of her amateur performance although others said that she was not at fault. She was playing the part of a basketball hero's girl friend and was doing well with the role. She convinced Logan that timing was good and that she had a distinct flair for comedy. Perkins was just not right for the part of a basketball star; he was too clumsy on the court and the moviegoers were bound to laugh at his efforts. The crew was not at all reticent in expressing their opinion about the film. The actor heard what they were saying, which did not help make them perform better. Jane had no way of knowing that the crew's remarks were not directed at her.

Logan admits now that the picture was not one of his best efforts. He blames himself for not doing a better job as a director, but one

fact stands out in his mind: "Jane's acting," he says, "was impressive."
He also said that even at that time she was one of the best actresses
he had ever worked with.

Jane was now on her way to real achievement, both on the stage
and in the movies. She would now be able to meet her father on her
own terms and not be plagued continually with guilt feelings and
resentments. She was also enjoying a sense of financial independence.
Besides getting a salary from Logan, who had her under contract,
she was also receiving a stipend from a trust fund that her mother
had established for her. She bought a cooperative apartment on West
54th Street, a few steps away from fashionable Fifth Avenue.

Life was now treating her quite well. But a financial matter
arose which marred her relations with Logan. The producer, director-
writer was paying Jane $10,000 a year. For that he had the right
to farm her out to other producers and receive more money than
he was handing her. The practice is a usual one in the entertainment
business.

Up to that time Jane had complete trust and confidence in
Logan. But that feeling evaporated in part after he loaned her out
to play in **Tall Story** and **There Was a Little Girl**, two plays that were
instant flops. She felt that he had shown bad judgment in getting
her to play in both works. And her trust in his judgment received
an added blow when she was loaned out to Charles Feldman to work
in his film, **Walk on the Wild Side.** It had been adapted from Nelson
Algren's novel.

She had been rather dubious about accepting the role after
Tall Story. A young director, Andreas Voutsinas who, according to
her friend Timmy Everett, was showing her how to gain more confidence had gone along with her to Hollywood. He was to be her coach,
but her friends say that he was more than a coach; he was her lover,
confidant and advisor and during that time she never made a move
without consulting him.

Changes in her personality became apparent to all who knew
her. She was becoming more outspoken and did not hesitate to give
her opinion about artistic and political matters; only two years earlier,
Hedda Hopper, the gossip columnist, wrote that Jane was a nice girl
who apparently felt ill at ease in Hollywood. But she informed her
many readers that Jane had changed considerably. She was now a
tall, well-poised young woman who was quite soignee and who said
that she had no intention of getting married. She set the columnist
back on her heels when she told her that marriage was an archaic
institution and should be eliminated forever.

That interview was syndicated to many newspapers all over
the country. Hedda, who was later to achieve a great deal of notoriety
when she became one of the leaders of the wolf pack who hunted
down alleged Reds during the time of Joe McCarthy, wrote that Jane's
ideas smacked of dangerous radicalism.

By that time Andreas Voutsinas was totally in command of
Jane's career. Everyone who worked with her knew it. One of the
crew on the set said that she was playing a whore so realistically

because Voutsinas was teaching her how prostitutes worked at their business.

One scene called for Jane to fight Sheery O'Neill. Jane inflicted a bloody nose and major bruises on Sheery.

Jane also had her problems with the director and script writer. The part, she complained, was not big enough. But she was later to confess that the role of Kitty Twist "was wonderful." The part was that of a hard-core ghetto kid who ran away from an orphanage and a reform school and committed every crime in the book.

While Jane was pleased with her acting, critic Bosley Crowther of the **New York Times,** wrote "that cornball from cheap romantic fiction, the prostitute with a heart of gold staggers through **Walk on the Wild Side** and she has no more substantiality in this instance than she had in the works of the old dime novelists.

"Everything in this picture. . .produced from the novel by Nelson Algren which it doesn't resemble in the least, smacks of sentimentality and social naivete. It is incredible that anything as foolish would be made in this day and age.

"Lawrence Harvey is barely one-dimensional and Barbara Stanwyck is like something out of mothballs. Jane Fonda is elaborately saucy and shrill (a poor exposure of a highly touted talent). And Edward Dmytrik's direction makes you wonder whether he read the script before he started shooting. It he did he should have yelled."

Critic Paul V. Beckley of the now defunct **New York Herald Tribune,** found "Jane" to be "a bouncy, wiggly, bratty little thief and prostitute (who) **seems more like** a Nelson Algren character than anyone else in the picture."

Jane still insists that she enjoyed working in the film. She claims that she fought with the director and tried to get him to adhere to the novel which she had read. She still says that it was due to Voutsinas' help that she was able to function.

During that period of her life Fonda made no secret of the fact that he disapproved of her liaison with Voutsinas. He discussed the affair many times with his close friends. In reading the newspapers he frequently came across many stories about his inadequacies as a father and how it had affected his daughter. Jane had talked about her desire to see a psychoanalyst. Fonda said that there was no need to waste her money that way. She told the newspaper reporters that she had to undergo analysis because her father had driven her to it. In fact, she said, he would also benefit if he underwent analysis. He should have had the good sense to do it 40 years ago. It would have helped him considerably.

Despite her state of mind Jane was offered many roles. During the time she was working in one feature she was offered a part in **The Chapman Report,** a story about the strange kind of life the ladies in the suburbs were leading. She was also offered a part in Garson Kanin stage play, **Sunday in New York.** She turned the offer down and accepted the film assignment.

Jane had decided to play in the picture after she had been told that George Cukor would be directing it. He was considered to be the best women's director in Hollywood. The critics said that his reputation was well-deserved. Cukor asked her to come to his house to talk about the role. When she arrived he told her that she would be playing the part of a frigid woman.

It was at that time that she made some harsh remarks about Logan. He had demanded $100,000 to release her from her contract. When Fonda, who was in Europe working on **The Longest Day** was told what Jane was saying about his friend, he expressed his displeasure about her trumpeting her grievances about his old friend. He also made it quite clear that he did not like Voutsinas and did not approve her way of life.

Fonda was now in high dudgeon. He had been plagued with the problems that his children were creating. His son Peter who was now in his junior year at the university had suddenly decided to drop out of college and leave for New York to take up an acting career.

After Peter had spent a summer with a New York State stock company, acting and painting scenery he wanted to take time out to rethink his next move. One day he walked into his father's house in Manhattan and told him that he intended to stay in the city and try for a part in a Broadway play.

It was during that summer that tragedy took its toll in his life. His great love, Bridget Hayward, committed suicide. He was devastated when he heard the news. In his misery he looked for some sympathy from his father. But Fonda did not respond in the way he had hoped. He invited his son to have a drink, and he spoke about his poor bereaved friend Leland; he did not have a word to say to his son.

Completely at a loss on how to cope with his tragedy, Peter left for Omaha to see the psychiatrist who had been treating him for the past three years. He remained in Omaha for the next few months and when he returned to New York he got a part in a play entitled **Blood, Sweat and Stanley Poole**. Success of a kind came at last to Peter Fonda. Although the play was found to be less than satisfactory by the critics, he was commended for his acting.

A week later Peter married Susan Brewer, a student at Sarah Lawrence College. With his new start in life and a career in the theater in prospect, Peter hoped that his father would at last give him some words of encouragement—or at the very least respect his determination to lead a kind of life that would be approved even by the good citizens of Omaha. But that did not happen. Fonda expressed his doubts about a success that had come too easily and about Peter's transformation into a serious-minded young man.

Fonda now felt a lack of fulfillment in his own work. He had been active on the stage and in the movies for a quarter of a century. During that time there had been several roles that were impressive even to his discerning judgment. But the parts he was now playing were nothing more than a dull succession of boring chores. Roles like Mister Roberts were not offered frequently. After he had finished what was only a bit role in the film **The Longest Day** he came back to New York hoping to find a good part for a change. He waited in vain, and when nothing happened he decided to accept a role in Garson

Kanin's play **A Gift of Time,** a rather morbid story about a man suffering from terminal cancer.

The Broadway audiences did not like it. Most of the theatergoers did not relish seeing a man slowly dying on stage, nor was the play a particular good one. Fonda was praised by the critics but that did not give him any satisfaction; he now decided to change his agents. Instead of being represented by the giant Music Corporation of America he had now signed up with Ashley Famous. That agency advised him to spend his time alternating between acting in pictures and on the stage. Disregarding that advice he accepted a role in **A Gift of Time.** The play, as his agents had predicted, expired.

Fonda's contract with Ashley Famous called for him to play in **Spencer's Mountain.** He was criticized for agreeing to do that film because it was not up to the standard he had set for himself. But he was aware that an actor has to play in all kinds of films, good and bad, or else be ignored by the producers when future roles were available.

Fonda had become more cynical about the tastes of the public; therefore he decided to play in **Spencer's Mountain.** He knew that it would be a money-maker. He told Ashley Famous that the script was adulterated tripe that would set the art of picture-making back at least 25 years.

It was during the shooting of the picture that Maureen O'Hara, his co-star, arranged for her daughter to play a minor role in it. The girl arrived late at the studio. Not wishing to disturb the rest of the cast she sat down quietly and waited to be called. Fonda who was in the throes of terminating his marriage to his fourth wife saw the young woman and was attracted to her. O'Hara caught that certain look in his eyes and knew that he was thinking of dating the girl. She looked at him and asked what he was thinking about. He told her that he wanted to date the girl. "She is my daughter," said O'Hara, "and you can just forget all about her."

Jane knew by that time that the Afdera-Fonda marriage was nearing its predestined end. All the telltale signs were there. The restless eyes, the prolonged silences, the calculated exclusion of his fourth wife from his activities. And knowing about his propensity for marrying younger women and doing it so frequently Jane and Peter were amazed when he faulted them for their way of life. His son Peter, who saw the contradictions in his father's constant avowals about the sanctity of marriage and his frequent changes of wives, said that the difference between him and his father was that Fonda sent his young "chick" home every night. He also said that "the outrageous examples he set for us in lieu of what he himself did blew our minds!"

Jane continued to criticize the way her father conducted his life for all to hear but Fonda decided to control his anger. Instead of responding to her remarks, he told reporters that he was happy about his daughter's success as an actress and, without blinking an eye, he declared that she was a better artist than he was.

In private however he appeared to be a man who was suffering

because of his children's verbal onslaughts against him. He was referring
to newspaper headlines which revealed his failures as a father and
in which he was portrayed as a fraud and an unfeeling parent. As
if that was not enough he had to suffer the pains of a man who was
a dedicated artist because he was playing in a picture like **Spencer's
Mountain.** If he had ever entertained any doubts about the quality
of the feature the critics enlightened him about it soon enough.

Judith Crist, the eminent critic, said that it was nothing more
than a "pointless package of piety and prurience that had been concocted and that everyone who had been connected with its creation
and exhibition ought to be strung up—or at best be made to sit through
it with their eyes open." But on the other hand **Variety,** the Bible
of the entertainment world, found Fonda's acting to "have real dignity
and depth."

It now appeared that fate was measuring out even more bitter
pills for him to swallow. Edward Albee, one of Broadway's more talented playwrights, had sent his work **Who's Afraid of Virginia Woolf**
to him when he was in California. Fonda was in his agent's office
when he picked up a New York newspaper and read that the Albee
play had opened up on Broadway the night before. He turned to his
agent and said, "I've always enjoyed reading his short stories."

"That writer," said the agent, "was trying to get you to do his
play but we thought it would be a better deal for you to play in the
film so we turned it down."

Fonda turned pale. The shock of being told that Albee had wanted
him and that Ashley Famous had not cleared it with him was just
too much for him to take.

"In Heaven's name," he gasped, "why did you turn it down without
clearing it with me?"

"There's really nothing to this work of his," said the agent. "It
is just a shouting match between a virago of a female and her professor
husband. It won't go on Broadway."

How wrong he was. It was both a critical and financial success,
and he had been kept from playing a role that might have been com-
pared with his past triumphs in the theater. Jimmy Stewart, Josh
Logan and his daughter Jane, who had seen the play, told him that
he would have been perfect in the part of the harrassed professor.
He knew that one of the great opportunities in the theater had been
lost to him because of the Philistine-like attitude of his Hollywood
agent.

Later, Albee, who had really wanted to have Fonda play the
part of the professor said that for once in his life he had actually
visualized Fonda in the role while he was working on the play. He
had not known that his letter had never been handed to him. He believed
that the actor had been rude in not acknowledging its receipt.

Fonda's missed chance to play the professor continued to haunt
him. When he returned to New York he saw the work. Perhaps it served
some kind of a psychological need for him to witness at first hand
what he had missed. He may have hoped that the actor playing the
part wasn't doing a good job. But in all honesty he could not say that.
He did say that Arthur Hill was superb in the role.

More disappointments were to follow. There were some serious discussions about having him play the part in the film version with Bette Davis as the harridan, but that was not to be. Elizabeth Taylor and her husband Richard Burton were awarded the parts.

If money is a consolation Fonda should have been pleased to have played in **Spencer's Mountain.** The film was an instant success at the box office.

After that Fonda played in a succession of pictures, some passable, a few that were good and others—the least said the better.

In 1962 he played in **Advise and Consent.** The tall, balding Otto Preminger who looked like a Prussian army officer and behaved like an army officer on the set directed the picture. The cast included a stellar array of actors: Charles Laughton, Don Murray, Walter Pidgeon, Peter Lawford, Gene Tierney, Franchot Tone, Lew Ayres, Burgess Meredith and George Grizzard. While Fonda received top billing in the film, his part was not all that important. Drury, a political conservative had written what he knew was a best-selling novel about some flawed Washington politicians. Fonda played the part of a controversial nominee for Secretary of State, a character who was rather one-dimensional in the novel. The film treatment was diminished to the extent that he ceased to be believable.

Both the novel and the film was meant to enlighten the public on the way their leaders behaved. What appeared to be idealism was only a mirage that had been conjured up by the movers and shakers of the government. Drury's novel was a roman-a-clef. The characters in the book were supposed to be easily recognized as true-to-life people. It is a surefire method of selling books, and it has been done many times. Jacqueline Susann in **Valley of the Dolls** and Gore Vidal in his play **The Best Man** took their characters from real life. Gore Vidal in his play had easily recognized public figures such as Harry Truman, Adlai Stevenson and Richard M. Nixon as the main protagonists. The characters were well delineated. But the same could not be said of **Advise and Consent** as a novel and as a movie.

The situations in which the politicians maneuvered in the Preminger version of life in Washington D.C. seemed to be strangely unreal. The critics said that there were two conflicting plots in the picture, the idealism of some officials and the implied sexual deviation of a Senator. The director had thus created two main themes, one working against the other and in the process managed to confuse the audiences. The picture ended on a bland note.

The actors struggled through their parts with an intensity worthy of better things without any conviction that it was worth the effort. Fonda's Leffinwell was not one of his better efforts. The only actor in the film who brought more than a puzzled conception to his role was George Grizzard who was "splendid" according to the critics.

The year 1962 had Fonda acting in films that had more characters than a mammoth Russian novel. He did a cameo part in **The Longest Day,** a quasi-documentary that was supposed to be a true depiction of the cross-Channel invasion of France during the second World War.

The other cameo role he worked at was in the super-colossal film, **How the West Was Won**. This overpowering production had Henry Hathaway, John Ford and George Marshall as its directors. There was plenty to look at but very little story line in that feature. Every cliche that had ever been used in a Western was to be found in it. Fonda's bit part was that of a buffalo hunter. He did not look the part. One writer described his appearance as that of a 19th century hippie replete with flowing locks and a drooping moustache.

The **New York Times'** Bosley Crowther wrote that "everything is a dutiful duplication of something you have already seen in one to a thousand Western movies in the last 60 years." He suggested that the title should be changed to **How the West Was Done to Death.**

How did Fonda justify his acceptance of that minor role in a bad picture. In speaking about his work in both blockbusters he said, "I'm glad I was asked to do them because it's important to be in these pictures. These are big box office successes and everybody in them is given credit for that success whether you're in a cameo part or not. You've got to do many box office pictures—good or bad—in order to be able to afford the luxury of doing the pictures you enjoy doing like **Twelve Angry Men** which was not box office."

He had said all that before. He did work in better parts in two political films, **The Best Man,** directed by Franklin Schafner and **Fail Safe,** directed by his friend Sidney Lumet whose abilities as a director he had always admired.

That picture ran into some problems even before shooting had begun. There were rumors that the administration in Washington did not look with favor at a picture that foretold what would happen to mankind in the advent of a nuclear holocaust. Fonda later said that he knew from certain unimpeachable sources that the rumor was true, but it seemed to be a rather strange coincidence that many of the movie companies who were trying to get the film rights suddenly decided to stop bidding for them and act as if the book had become a contagious disease.

Max W. Youngstein and Sidney Lumet were not that easily scared off by the frowns of the Washington power brokers. They acquired the rights to the book, but they still had a problem that they could not have expected.

Stanley Kubrick, a native of the Bronx in New York and a very successful film producer who operated in England was about to produce and direct a picture that was based on Peter George's novel, **Red Alert**. The subject of the book was similar to that of **Fail Safe**. He started a suit for plagiarism against the authors. The suit was settled in a friendly way by Columbia Pictures—the same company that was about to release both films. It was agreed that Kubrick's picture **Dr. Strangelove** would be the first release by Columbia.

Fonda who had previously played the part of a well-meaning candidate for the Presidency two years before and also a controversial Secretary of State was chosen to play the President in **Fail Safe**. The role called for him to do all his acting in confined quarters. It was the second time he had had to act in cramped quarters, but in

Twelve Angry Men he had some freedom of movement. That helped to some extent offset the basically static qualities of the picture. In **Fail Safe,** however, he had to sit on a chair with a telephone receiver cupped to his ear and carry on a life and death conversation with the Soviet Premier. Despite that handicap and with the help of Lumet's direction, he was able to hold the audience enthralled with his performance.

The scene where Fonda as President does his utmost to convince the Soviet leader that the plane attack against his country had not been intentional is nerve-shattering in its impact on the moviegoers. "Henry Fonda," one critic wrote, "as President in the film makes sane government seem possible and makes credible the melodramatic telephone conversation with the Russian Premier."

And not lagging very much behind in its praise **Time** Magazine said, "Fonda speaks steadily and carefully, in a voice that is intense but curiously flat, as though every word were crushed by a burden of significance too great to bear. And as the voice drones on and on pleading and reasoning and pleading the figure of the actor swells and charges with tension and importance. The presence of the man becomes the person of mankind and his voice, the voice of the species, pleading for its life. The whole history seems consumated in an instant. Armageddon talks in a telephone booth."

Fonda the actor in the year 1964 also had less heady roles to play beside that of a President trying to save the world from a nuclear holocaust. He acted in a picture that was a dozen levels lower in taste. It was **Sex and the Single Girl.** The title seemed to guarantee a success at the box office. To Fonda's credit it must be admitted he did struggle valiantly against the blandishments of Warner Brothers and Richard Quine. He finally sucumbed to the pressure after being told by Joseph Heller, author of **Catch 22** that he was to write the script. The original non-novel was concocted by Helen Gurley Brown, the wife of the successful producer of **Jaws.** While the book was not highly regarded by the critics, the adaptation was even worse. It had no relation to what the author had written. Only the title was used. Fonda now admits that he had been conned by the director of the picture and its producer.

Said Fonda, "I don't hesitate for one minute to say this about Richard Quine because I'm angry with him. He didn't do one thing to make it better, and as a matter of fact he did a lot of things to make it worse. I don't like his humor and I won't work with him again."

The picture struck a very sour note with most of the reviewers. Judith Crist who could demolish any film with a few well-chosen words, wrote that "**Sex and the Single Girl** is enough to put one off sex, single girls and the movies for the season."

And Howard Thomson not to be outdone by his colleague sentenced Natalie Wood and Tony Curtis to what could only be considered to be a permanent purgatory for bad acting. He also said the "Fonda and Lauren Bacall as Curtis' scrappy neighbors, supply real spice and fun, especially Miss Bacall who has the wittiest lines and all but pierces the picture with her buzz-saw growl.

"**Sex and the Single Girl**? Fooey. Three cheers for the old folks at home."

Despite the universal panning the picture received from the critics and despite Fonda's complaints that his artistic integrity had been sullied because of his association with the picture he still could console himself with the fact that he was very well paid for his efforts.

Chapter XXI
A Year of Struggle and Some Success

Life for Henry Fonda as he approached his 60th birthday still had a degree of uncertainty mixed with a desire to regulate his personal life. His many failed marriages (he had just divorced his fourth wife Afdera) did not lend peace of mind. Nor did his children's strident complaints about his short-comings as a father.

Jane's liaison with Voutsinas who he said was an adventurer pained him. Despite his dislike of the man, Jane made it quite evident that she had no intentions of breaking off her relations with him. Her former lover, Timmy Everett was deeply hurt after he had been cast aside by her. One night he burst into her apartment, hoping that there would be a renewal of their former relationship. But when he saw Voutsinas there he ran into the kitchen, took a knife out of a drawer and slashed his wrists. When Jane saw what he had done she wrapped his hands in a towel and rushed him to Roosevelt Hospital.

After that disturbing episode Jane left New York for Hollywood. In that dream city by the Pacific she worked in a movie that had been adapted from a play by Tennessee Williams. It was a bad picture.

She also continued to shock her father because of her outlandish way of life. She told a reporter that her father's many marriages had not set a good example for her. She also said that Fonda was still in the process of finding himself and that he apparently wasn't doing very well in the quest. She also had much to say about Peter. She accused him of worshiping money for its own sake. And she accused him of being a neurotic, a young man who, like his father, was trying to find out who he really was.

The battling Fondas were at it again. Peter bristled with anger when he learned what his sister had said about him. During an interview with the press he said that his sister was living with a leech.

Voutsinas convinced Jane to play in **The Fun Couple**. The play's opening was attended by many of Jane's friends and fellow-students at the Actors Studio. The audience could not restrain itself that night. They roared with laughter, shouted words of derision and booed the actors on stage. The critics agreed with their reactions to the play.

Richard Watts, Jr. of the **New York Post** wrote, "The incredible thing about the play is that two such talented young performers as Jane Fonda and Bradford Dillman were willing to appear in the title roles. Even the sight of Miss Fonda in a bikini doesn't rescue **The Fun Couple** from being an epic bore."

Voutsinas, Jane's friends said, was less than forthright when he involved her in that disaster. They said that he should have known that the play was not up to professional standards and that he was really motivated by his desire to be involved in a Broadway production.

It was now apparent to Jane that Voutsinas had outlived his usefulness to her and she terminated her relationship with him. Fonda now hoped that she would settle down to a more conventional kind of a life. But Jane had ideas of her own.

She had first met Roger Vadim Plemianikov at Maxim's in Paris as we know. During the years after she had returned to the United States Vadim acquired three wives. There was Bardot whom he had molded as an actress. And there was Annette Stroyberg who bore his child while he was still married to Bardot. That understanding wife even offered to be the godmother of that child. And now there was Catherine Deneuve, a very stunning-looking 18-year-old who had become his friend. They were married and in gratitude she also presented him with a child.

Vadim was about to finish off his marriage to Deneuve when Jane met him again in Paris. He asked her to have lunch with him and when she accepted his invitation the two discussed the possibility of her play in **La Ronde,** a picture he wanted to direct.

Jane now found herself attracted to the man and his ideas. She knew that he was hedonistic and that he had had many wives and mistresses, yet longed to settle down to live with a wife and have a home of his own.

A man who was now approaching his 40th year, Vadim clearly felt a need to live with Jane. He knew that she could help revive his fading film career. He had had a number of failures recently and was in desperate need of someone who could assist him financially. Jane was an actress of great appeal and could be, in his estimation, an ideal helpmate.

When his journalist friends asked him why he had been attracted to her he said that he had always been partial to vulnerable women. And Jane, he was shrewd enough to recognize, was very vulnerable. She was very unhappy and longed for peace and contentment. She wanted to believe that she was beautiful; yet she wasn't quite certain that her friends were telling her the truth about herself.

It was at the beginning of their liaison that she began to take potshots at her brother and father again. When she was asked whether she planned to appear in a play with them, she said that Peter who had played in four pictures had not been able to find himself either as an actor or as a man. And besides she could not tolerate either her father or brother unless they agreed to work in television with her. She explained that it only took two weeks to produce a television play and that was about as long as she could stand working with either of them.

After venting her spleen at both men she went back to Paris to take up her life with Vadim. The couple went to Russia and when she returned to Paris she said that the people in that country had been grossly maligned by a biased press.

During the next few months Jane occupied herself renovating an old French farmhouse which dated back to 1830. But before she had finished with her task, she was called back to Hollywood to play in a film entitled **Cat Ballou** which was based on Roy Chansor's novel. The picture was an overwhelming success at the box office. And it definitely confirmed that Jane was a light comedian of no mean talent. It also established Lee Marvin as a star.

Jane purchased a modest size house in Malibu and set up home with Vadim. Gossip columnist Hedda Hopper, who was a self-appointed moralist, announced in her syndicated column that Jane was now living in sin with Roger Vadim. Fonda read the item but he had already learned that his daughter had a new man in tow. He was anxious to see for himself what kind of a man she was living with. He was certain that he would not like him. The oft-married actor knew all about Vadim's many affairs and marriages and believed that it did not augur well for his daughter.

And as if that was not disturbing enough there was Peter who was passing through another crisis in his life. His best friend Stormy MacDonald, heir to the Zenith Radio Corporation fortune committed suicide. Peter was in Tucson when he killed himself. He had always admired Stormy—a friend who was always advising Peter to be true to himself.

The local police found a large amount of marijuana in the house. Peter, who was deep into the counter-culture of the young, had first tried the drug when he was in London. He was sharply questioned by a coroner's jury and was declared not guilty of any complicity in the tragedy. But the newspaper stories about Peter and his affection for marijuana had been grossly exaggerated, and his relations with Stormy did not go un-noticed by his father.

Peter previously had to face up to the suicides of his mother, Bridget Hayward, a girl he had been passionately in love with, and now Stormy. The result was a trauma that affected him for many years. He later said that there was hardly a time when he did not think about his mother and how she had died, and what had happened to Bridget and his beloved friend Stormy.

Fonda who knew what his son was going through, was deeply troubled about Peter's state of mind. He now believed that his own life had been a failure. His children still resented him; he could not in good conscience approve the way his daughter was living. Yet, that did not deter him from telephoning her one day and ask her whether she would welcome him if he would visit her in Malibu.

Jane still remembers the first time her father saw Vadim. He had arrived at her home with some pre-conceived ideas about him. Everything he had been told confirmed his opinion that he was an unsavory individual. But to Fonda's surprise, instead of finding a place where Roman-type orgies were the rule, he saw his daughter dressed in blue jeans working in her kitchen while Vadim was squatting on the beach fishing. Fonda, who enjoyed that sport decided then and there that he may have misjudged the Frenchman.

Actually, it was Vadim who liked Fonda when he first saw him. He made Jane see that her father was a man who had had a very troubled private life. He advised her to try to understand rather than condemn him for what she said were his indiscretions. "A mature person," Vadim said, "should not be self-righteous. Human beings are prone to make their mistakes and they all have their foibles." He impressed her with his advice. She began to adopt a more sympathetic attitude toward her father.

Fonda now 60 years old found to his surprise that he had a friend in Vadim. Roger could understand the older man because he was the father of several children himself and had had his full share of desirable women.

During that summer Vadim was able to cement his warm friendship with Fonda. Jane's own opinion, as we know had undergone a change. She had always loved her father, but now she was beginning to feel closer to him. In her desire to please him she decided to finalize her relations with Vadim and marry him. She was wise enough to know that her husband-to-be could never be married permanently to any woman.

Being married to someone seemed to be in the air for the Fondas. It was in 1965 that Henry Fonda was to find a wife for the fifth time.

Chapter XXII
Henry Fonda Takes a New Wife

Henry Fonda was still in a somber mood. And for good reason. His son Peter had barely escaped incarceration on a drug charge and for possible implication in the death of his friend Stormy, and Jane was still unfriendly. The bitter feelings his children expressed toward him in their public statements were depressing. There were days when he felt that life made no sense.

Professionally, he had achieved more than he had hoped for, but his personal life seemed bankrupt and devoid of any meaning. He frequently asked himself how a man who had been raised in a respectable middle-class family and who inwardly had always adhered to its code of behavior could make such a fiasco out of his married life.

There had been four marriages—all of them failures. And he was finding it increasingly difficult to excuse those failures. His children certainly did not condone his actions.

In reminiscing about his acting career and what it had done to his children he said, "Both Jane and Peter wanted their own identity as far back as I can remember. It was difficult because they followed Pa in the same profession. I didn't discourage them or lead them by the hand. I wasn't a good father. I knew they would like to feel they did it on their own.

"Children," he continued, "grow up the son and daughter of a movie star. A man who had to work where his job took him which could be in Missouri for 14 weeks. You don't take them with you because they are at school. It's not good, but you can't help it. Shall I say I'm sorry I'm an actor? I'll quit and become a shoe salesman. Of course not. So you don't apologize for it. You do the best you can when you are at home. The life of an actor is different so it's not an ideal home situation."

During the early years it was worse for the children because of the untimely death of their mother. The surrogate mothers weren't around very long. That state of affairs did not make for a stable emotional life for either Jane or Peter; Fonda was aware of that. And because he could not or would not do anything to ease their situation he became more despondent. But there was some light coming into his private and professional life. He was offered the male lead in **Generation,** a play by William Goodwin. Ironically enough, the theme of the work was the gap that exists between the younger and older generations. That was a subject that Fonda was thoroughly conversant with. While the critics found very little to be happy about after viewing the play, most of the theatergoers liked it. His role was radically different from those he had had in the theater or in the movies.

Fonda's image as an actor was that of a man who was endowed with youthful male verve. He was the male who was always being pursued by the female—in the movies. The public really believed that that was the way it happened in his private life as well.

The character he was portraying in the play was that of an understanding father of a daughter who was leading a Bohemian kind of existence in Greenwich Village. She wanted to marry a man which was natural enough. Except he didn't approve of him.

The play was amusing in spots. Audiences tended to overlook the work's shortcomings and appeared to enjoy it. One critic who had always admired Fonda as an actor wrote that he was not only a living testament to the stage but to all those "dreams of human perfection into which no conflict is ever allowed to enter."

Playing in a successful work pleased him. But there was also Shirlee who was becoming increasingly important to him. The two had been introduced to each other by a Hollywood press agent and had since become inseparable companions. Afdera had long since been forgotten. She had left for her native Italy to be comforted by her friends because of her failed marriage.

Shirlee, the new girl in his life, had worked as a model and an airline stewardess. While the two saw each other every day, Fonda saw to it that she was escorted back to her apartment after her date with him. At that late time in his life he was determined to observe the amenities.

Shirlee was apparently the kind of woman he needed. She had and still has a very pleasant disposition and is not given to the kind of tantrums he had had to put up with Margaret Sullavan. Unlike Afdera, Shirlee, was not addicted to the luxurious kind of a life although she did have a weakness for expensive clothes. Deeply affectionate, she once described her husband as "a warm sweet man." She always hovered over him and kept a close watch on what he ate. She made him take his vitamins and his morning glass of hot water and lemon.

Shirlee also introduced him to Yoga and made him exercise every day. She insisted that the Yoga stretch exercises had added a few inches to her height. Obviously Fonda who was six-feet one inch didn't need that.

Fonda was well passed middle age when he married Shirlee. But she never permitted him to talk about his advancing years. When he once bemoaned the fact that he was getting older she said, "Fonda, will you stop telling your age to everybody. After **Ash Wednesday** (a film he was working in with Liz Taylor) every woman will consider you a reborn Cassanova."

Fonda, whose health had taken a turn for the better because of his wife's care once exclaimed, "Shirlee I just can't help it. I feel so good, I feel like a contemporary of my son. I feel like a kid on a bicycle who says 'Look Mom, no hands.' "

Even before they were married Shirlee encouraged him to work at his painting. Through the years he had shown a marked talent in that art. She saw to it that he met Andrew Wyeth, the famous American artist. He looked at Fonda's paintings and said that they were thoroughly professional.

Life as a newly married man was serene at last for Fonda. But a minor incident occurred that almost caused a rupture in their relations. He was painting Shirlee's portrait; after many hours of posing she felt very tired. She tells what happened after that, "He never finished it, though. To this day the picture doesn't have a head. He was ruthless and made me sit for hours. I couldn't move. I couldn't even stretch. He got mad if I even breathed. I was ready to leave him if that was how he was going to treat me."

Fonda, who had not been aware how unreasonably he was behaving tried to explain why he had acted that way later on, "I get lost in my work. I forget that there's a real person sitting there."

Today, whenever Shirlee looks at that picture minus the head she smiles and says, "It's my own Dorian Gray."

And speaking about wives and their unpredictable reactions there was a very strange incident that related to Fonda's past that surprised Richard Burton. He was in Cortina, Italy when he received a telephone call from a woman who said that she was Mrs. Henry Fonda. The actor thought he was speaking to Shirlee. To his surprise it was none other than Afdera who had not been in contact with her former husband for ten years. She had been in prison for a brief period on a drug charge. She asked Burton whether he could help her effect a reconciliation with Fonda. Burton listened to her and at last said, "I believe that your former husband is happily married now." That ended that conversation.

After his success in **Generation, The Best Man,** and **Fail Safe** Fonda tried to forget that he had ever been associated with such films as **Sex and the Single Girl.** It had been a box office hit but an artistic black eye for him. To appease his troubled conscience that had been caused because he had accepted to play in the movie he tried to find a good play script that would, he hoped, be worthy of his interest. When Alfred DeLiagre, the Broadway producer, and actress Martha Scott, proposed that he join their repertory company—an enterprise similar to the one that Laurence Olivier and Tynan had organized in England, he accepted their invitation. The result was The Plumstead Playhouse in Mineola, Long Island. It was open for business in October 1968 with productions of Thornton Wilder's **Our Town** and Charles MacArthur and Ben Hecht's **The Front Page.** Both plays were revivals of Broadway hits.

Fonda played the lead role in **Our Town** and Robert Ryan, who was a star in his own right agreed to play a secondary part. Edith Oliver, a New York critic said that Fonda's acting was superb. The other critics found his performance equally noteworthy.

He was grateful to Ryan for having accepted the role of a minor reporter in **The Front Page.** And once again the critics waxed ecstatic about the acting of both men. The theater was sold out night after night, but due to the limited seating capacity they decided to close down the place for a time.

Shortly after the temporary shutdown of the theater, John Steinbeck, the renowned American writer, concocted a trifle titled **Sweet Thursday.** He wanted to have it adapted as a stage play and discussed the idea with Fonda who was a close friend. Fonda told him that he would be interested in playing in the film. But there was one hitch; he thought that it could be better as a musical. Shortly after that discussion Fonda started to take voice lessons.

Steinbeck was later to say that he hoped Fonda would never learn how to sing. He recalled that Walter Huston who could by no means have been considered a professional singer had nevertheless been able to give a superlative rendition of the "September Song" in the musical, **Knickerbocker Holiday.** He also recalled that Rex Harrison had given a good account of himself as a singer in **My Fair Lady.** He said that the less his friend knew about the techniques of singing the better it would be for the show.

The production was entitled **Pipe Dream.** The composer of the score was Richard Rodgers, and the lyricist was Oscar Hammerstein, but when Fonda auditioned for the role the two men turned him down cold. It was just as well it happened that way since the show proved to be a dismal failure and was closed down a few days after its Broadway opening.

After the **Pipe Dream** fiasco Steinbeck continued to insist that Fonda would have brought some kind of magic to the musical and that that would have guaranteed its success.

While the turndown by Messers. Rodgers and Hammerstein was disappointing to Fonda he managed to find some kind of solace when the prestigious and ultra-exclusive Holland Society whose membership was strictly limited to upper-class Americans of Dutch origin honored him at a special dinner. Among the invited guests were many celebrities, including John Steinbeck who got out of a sick bed to attend. Steinbeck died that year of a massive heart attack. Fonda, who was working in a film in California when Nat Benchley telephoned him to let him know what had happened, left for New York immediately to attend the funeral at St. James Episcopal Church on Madison Avenue.

As one of the deceased's closest friends, Fonda was asked to read excerpts from the works of Robert Louis Stevenson and Sir Thomas Mallory, Steinbeck's favorite authors. The latter's prose, Steinbeck once said, next to the Bible, had most influenced his own literary style. Fonda also read some lines from J.M. Synge's translation of Mallory's book that Steinbeck had picked up when he was in Dublin. It read, "If the bards are making lamentation or the green banks are moved by a little wind of summer you can hear the waters making a stir by the shores that are green and flowery. That's where I do be stretched out thinking of love, writing my songs, and herself that Heaven shows me though hidden in the earth I set my eyes on, and hear the way she feels my sighs and makes an answer to me.

"Alas, I hear her say, 'Why are you using yourself up before the time is come, and pouring out a stream of tears so sad and doleful.'

"You'd right to be glad rather, for in dying I won days that have no ending, and when you saw me shutting my eyes I was opening them on the light that is eternal."

Before leaving New York Fonda spoke to Steinbeck's wife, Elaine and tried to console her for her loss. Elaine gave him her husband's pearl studs. They were encased in a leather box which Steinbeck had made. When Fonda left her his eyes were filled with tears. He told her that while he was very grateful for the studs he really wanted the box.

On his return to Hollywood Fonda resumed his picture acting. He was playing in **Madigan** in which he had the role of a police commissioner. The critics reserved their special accolades for Fonda despite the fact that his was only a secondary role. Critic Andrew Sarris who was the kind of a reviewer who could be very caustic towards an actor who did not measure up to what he thought was a good performance wrote that "It was a pleasure to watch the trim, incisive underplaying of Henry Fonda and James Whitimore." He bemoaned the fact that the picture had not "measured up to them as a punchy, suspense thriller it tried to be." And **Time** Magazine said that Fonda was "at his uptight best as the up-from-the-ranks commissioner, so righteous as a cop on the beat that he sent back a butcher's Christmas turkey."

Fonda also worked in **The Boston Strangler** that year. It was based on the true story of a notorious killer who had stalked the streets of the historic city. The book on which the picture was based was written by Gerold Frank, a specialist in writing biographies about famous and infamous people. Unfortunately, the screen version of the book did not measure up to what the author was trying to tell his readers. The army of characters cluttered up the picture.

The film concentrated on the trail that had been left by the strangler, and tread rather gingerly on the perversions of the killer. While most of the critics said that the film had been done in good taste they agreed that it lacked the basic ingredients that had made the book interesting.

By 1969 just before Fonda was about to leave for New York to take on another stage role he was approached by Sergio Leone to work in a picture in which he would be called upon to play the part of a sadistically-inclined villain in a spaghetti Western movie.

The Italian director had always been a great admirer of American Westerns and had admitted that he had seen every one that had ever been produced. It was therefore practically in the cards that he would wind up as a movie director who would specialize in Westerns. After he had directed several of them he finally came up with a brilliant idea. He hired Clint Eastwood who had made a reputation for himself playing in the television series, **Rawhide**. He would be the hero in most of Leone's pictures.

The Leone films with Eastwood as star included every cliche that had ever been perpetrated on a helpless audience. In one of the pictures, **A Fire in the West** which Leone considered the high point in his flourishing career he cast Fonda as the bad man. Fonda, as we know, had been playing simon pure heroes ever since he had made his debut as a movie actor. Now, for the first time, he agreed to take on a role that was certain to shock many of his admirers. The moviegoers would probably not believe what they were seeing when

Mister Roberts: Henry Fonda stands up for the crew.

they saw their all-American favorite actor who had been suddenly transformed into a vicious killer.

Fonda described what had led up to his accepting the Leone offer. "The director," he said, "had sent the script to him from Italy." But when he read it he couldn't understand what he was looking at. The plot made no sense at all. He wired Leone and let him know that he wasn't interested in the role. That appeared to be the end of a budding friendship. But Leone was not easily discouraged. He took the first plane out of Italy bound for New York. He was accompanied by an English-speaking assistant. During the lenghty conference with Fonda, Leone asked him whether he had ever seen any of his pictures. When Fonda answered him in the negative he led him to a projection room where for three and a half hours he viewed **Fistful of Dollars, For a Few Dollars More** and part of **The Good, the Bad and the Ugly.**

Fonda found the films very amusing and entertaining. But he still was hesitant about working with Leone. He contacted his old friend Eli Wallach who had worked in one of Leone's pictures and asked him for advice.

"Don't miss it," Wallach said, "you'll love it." After that Fonda accepted the Italian director's offer.

His first thought was to change the color of his "baby blue eyes." Dark eyes, Fonda believed, would be far more appropriate for a villain. He went to an optometrist and had himself fitted with contact lenses. The lenses, he was told, would change the color of his eyes to a somber grey. He also started to grow a moustache in a style reminiscent of the kind John Wilkes Booth, Lincoln's assassin had affected.

When Leone took a look at the apparition he gasped and demanded that Fonda remove the contact lenses and shave off the moustache. "He wanted," Fonda said, "those 'baby blue eyes.' "

The picture begins with a pastoral scene. A happy farm family is preparing for a holiday. The father, his 18-year-old daughter, a 16-year-old son and a boy of seven or eight are piling up some food. There is an ominous silence. The father looks up and then suddenly drops to the earth. He is dead. Another shot is heard. The girl is killed. The 16-year-old boy who had gone to get a buggy and a horse because he is going to the station to pick up a relative is shot. The boy pivots off the buggy and falls to the ground. Then out of the house a youngster comes out carrying a few jugs of wine. He looks up and sees three wicked-looking characters with sidearms coming from five different directions towards him. The seven-year-old boy stands there with his dead father, his murdered sister and his dead brother looking up at Fonda, the leader of the gang.

One realized that Leone had anticipated the reaction the audience would have when they looked at the leader of the band. They were saying in effect, "Jesus Christ, that's Henry Fonda!" And that is exactly the reaction the audience had.

The story was unbelievable. It was certainly very campy and included every piece of screen business that had ever been used in an American-made Western.

Fonda went all-out in his portrayal of the relentless killer. He had not only ordered his band to cut the young boy down in cold blood but had his cut-throats kill everyone in sight throughout the picture. It was truly an astonishing sight to see the actor who had always played the role of a stalwart hero and man of peace now roaming all over the countryside with his gang bloodying up the terrain.

This actor was very definitely not a John Wayne type as one British critic wrote, "not the impulsive unthinking man of action, but an unassuming quiet man who tried to avoid bloodshed wherever it was possible, gunning down everybody within range of his gun."

Fonda was 64 years old when he played in the Leone picture. One would imagine that he would not feel very comfortable playing such a character. Surprisingly enough he appeared to enjoy his work in the picture. He said that it was perfectly right and proper for him to display his versatility by playing the role of a killer. The actor who had worked in such pictures as **The Young Mr. Lincoln,** certainly a very humane being suddenly was to be seen as a heartless sadist on the screen.

There were to be other similar roles for him to play. After he had had his fill of them he looked around for an antidote and found one. It was a chance to act in **Our Town** again with Mildred Natwick who had worked with him years ago. This time Fonda hoped to appear in William Saroyan's **The Time of Your Life** which Gene Kelly was to direct. Kelly had been the song and dance man in the original production. All was now set for the staging of the work. But for reasons that were never explained, Saroyan decided to withdraw the rights to the play. Fonda was very angry but there was nothing he could do to make the playwright change his mind.

Fonda's next choice was Steinbeck's **Of Mice and Men,** but there was a bit of a problem finding the right actor to play Lennie. They now decided to settle for **Our Town.**

While Fonda was working with the Plumstead Repertory Theater and acting in **Our Town,** Jane was getting ready to play in **They Shoot Horses, Don't They?** She had returned to the United States from France and had settled down with Vadim in Malibu again. She gave birth to her daughter whom she named Vanessa, honoring her good friend the British actress Vanessa Redgrave. Fonda also bought a house in Bel Air and was now spending most of his free time with Shirlee. His son had fathered two children and Fonda boasted to all his friends that he was a grandfather for the third time. Jane, he said, had made him very happy because she was showing that she had maternal feelings, an emotion that every woman should be proud of. He was gratified that she had had a change of heart about the institution of marriage and said that she was now a child he could be proud of. He also expressed a certain envy toward her outgoing kind of personality which was in such sharp contrast to his. He also commended her as a homemaker and hostess and expressed his amazement at her ability to create the kind of a home where her friends could come and enjoy themselves.

Fonda also expressed his pride in his son's film work. But he still disapproved of the way he lived. He had developed a special aversion for his friend Dennis Hooper, but Shirlee, who was far more tolerant, urged her husband to adopt a more sympathetic attitude toward Peter and his friends. While she could not in good conscience approve her stepson's values she sincerely liked the young man and did her best to understand him. She drew the line on his films and forbade Amy, Fonda's adopted daughter, to see them. They were, she said, too concentrated on the drug culture.

During his early days in Hollywood Fonda knew that his fellow-actors were shocked at Fatty Arbuckle's 1920 escapades with women and when a star like Wallace Reid died of an overdose of drugs it startled most of the thespians in those days of innocence. But now when Peter and his friends were producing pictures in Hollywood, its denizens were swallowing tranquillizers and sniffing cocaine freely. It had become an accepted way of life. Jane did not go for the drug culture but her brother experimented for a time with LSD. He claimed later on that it helped liberate him.

Fonda, as we know, was very much Middle America. He was still startled by the behavior of men like Roman Polanski, the latter's friend, Gutowski and Hollywood sex orgies. Polanski's film included scenes of witchcraft, incest and other bizarre practices all depicting the darker side of life. It was alleged that he even played out those roles in real life.

Fonda could not understand why Jane could be friendly with people of that kind. But he consoled himself with the thought that Jane and Peter were hard at work acting and directing good pictures. Peter and his friend Dennis Hooper who was married to Brooke Hayward, were working in **Easy Rider,** a film that was a searing indictment of American values. The movie was a triumph for Peter, Hooper and Jack Nicholson. It won first prize at the Cannes Film Festival and as one critic said, "It could have won first prize against even sterner competition."

Not to be outdone by her brother's success, Jane came up with **They Shoot Horses, Don't They?** The moviegoers viewing the picture saw the complete transformation of a young actress who had always been thought of as a bit of sexual fluff and now had become a dramatic actress of considerable depth of feeling. The Fonda talents were now manifesting themselves in the two offsprings of the superstar. Both Jane and Peter were in their own way following their father as serious artists who were completely dedicated to their art.

Chapter XXIII
More Problems

Fonda didn't know that his daughter Jane would be giving him many troubled moments in the future. The Vietnam War was very much in the news. And President Nixon, who had won the election because he promised to end the conflict with the help of Henry Kissinger, appeared to be doing all the wrong things to prolong the war. Jane's doubts about her country's values and her depressed state of mind were very much in evidence at that time. Susannah York and the other members of the cast of **They Shoot Horses, Don't They?** saw clearly how she felt. Her loss of faith in the values that she had been brought up to believe in and with what she heard from Vadim's friends in France—opinions about the war and the quagmire in Southeast Asia in which America had lost itself disturbed her.

Her commitment to the anti-war forces at first puzzled her father. Later it aroused his anger. Had he known that his daughter would be pilloried as a traitor he would have been even more concerned.

The continuing war was stirring up students at universities all over the country. Jane was now being drawn into an active protest against the policies of the government.

The brutal murder of her friends Sharon Tate and Abigail Folger by the Manson gang only increased her feeling of hatred of the violence she was witnessing in her native land. She had gone back to France with Vadim after completing her work in the picture. By that time she had begun to believe that her marriage was no longer valid. Vadim was demanding far too much and giving very little in return. To find some peace of mind she went to India and was shocked by the poverty she saw there. But there was one compensation for her; she had some joy in her daughter Vanessa. The child was now one-year-old. Jane left Vadim shortly after she had come to France and returned to Malibu. Fonda was overjoyed to see her. He was outspoken in his praise for a daughter who had proven herself to be so talented as an actress. Jane told an interviewer, "My father and I are very happy with each other now. He's really proud of Vanessa and happy that she is so pretty." She also said that Fonda and Peter had reached a better understanding of each other.

But while Fonda was proud of his children he did not become involved in her politics. Peter, who had other things on his mind, made no attempt to bring his father around to his ideas about life or politics. Jane, on the other hand, had a compulsion to "convert" him to her way of thinking. She once told Fonda that the Russians

164

were charmingly inefficient. They were, she told him, a likeable people. She also proudly reminded him that his grand-daughter Vanessa was one-quarter Russian. He, in turn, was curious to learn why she admired the Russians so much since they were so inefficient. He also asked her why she scoffed at her own countrymen because they were "being efficient for the sake of efficiency."

She claimed that such traits "neutralized the human feelings of a people. Fonda could not follow her line of reasoning. After that discussion it was now more clearly apparent than ever that the gap between them was very difficult to bridge.

Jane soon became involved in the cause of the oppressed native Indians. She met such activists as Donald Duncan the ex-Green Beret sergeant, and Vietnam veteran Fred Gardner, a left-wing organizer. She said that America's moral perfection was not what she had been led to believe. When Duncan described what he had seen in Vietnam to her—especially the atrocities—she was horrified. She asked him to come to her father's house on March 18 and tell him what he knew about the country's military actions in Southeast Asia. Fonda received Duncan politely. He listened to the veteran's account of his own experience in the war and then said, "I am doing all I can speaking up for those candidates who are calling for peace." But Fonda was never a radical nor was he about to become one. He made it quite clear that he still believed in the American system of government, and he told both Jane and Duncan that it was still the best in the complex world we live in today. Jane found herself arguing with a very resolute man. He let her know that, in his opinion, she was being used by a group of self-seeking individuals for their own purposes. While he professed to go along with some of her convictions he deplored the strident way she had projected them to the public. The public image of a well-known person, he said, is as important as the message. In fact, the message would be more readily accepted if she did not jar people with her excessive emotional outbursts.

Fonda's criticism of his daughter's activist role did not deter her from planning to take a trip across the country. She intended to see for herself what was going on at the Indian reservations. Her friends had been telling her how the native Americans were being exploited by an unfeeling government. She also planned to meet with the Black Panthers and find out first hand whether they had a justified grievance against the white majority.

Jane did meet with the Black Panthers and as a result set off a rash of blazing news headlines all over the country. The news accounts grew particularly rancorous when she met with Black Panther leaders at the Green Machine, a coffeehouse near the marine base of Camp Pendelton in San Diego.

That was only the beginning of her travails. She bought a Mercury stationwagon and left with her friend Elizabeth Valland whom she had first met in France, for a tour of the country. Fonda saw her off, snapping pictures of the two while little Vanessa scurried around underfoot. The little girl whispered goodbye to her mother as the car took off.

During her travels her father read the daily newspaper stories about his militant daughter and his anguish increased. Jane returned to Hollywood for a short time to attend the Academy Awards event. It was generally expected that she would win the coveted Oscar for her work in **They Shoot Horses, Don't They?**, but it was given to another actress. Many of her friends thought that it had not been awarded to her because of her political activities and they expressed their opinions publicly. Jane however took it far less seriously. Her thoughts were centered on other matters. She left Hollywood and was soon embroiled in an incident at Fort Carson. She had taken along some books on politics which she planned to give to the prisoners who were being held there. When she tried to drive her car inside the fort the Military Police stopped her. She returned to the local coffeehouse and with the assistance of some of the soldiers, she disguised herself. This time she was allowed to drive into the fort. As soon as she passed through the gate she stopped to deliver a speech to the men and then began to pass out the books. The Military Police seized her and forcibly escorted her and her companions to the guardhouse. She was released shortly after that by order of the base's commandant. He had no appetite for unpleasant publicity.

After passing through a number of communes in Taos, New Mexico, she drove to the University of New Mexico where the student body was planning to stage a demonstration to protest the killings at Kent State; the demonstration was quickly organized and hundreds of students paraded in front of the university president's house. Jane flew to Los Angeles after that protest meeting to attend a press conference that had been called to announce plans for a series of protests against the invasion of Cambodia.

She was now completely committed to the anti-war movement. There were many more trips across the country and numerous speeches delivered to the students and television appearances as well. A very unpleasant experience occurred at Fort Meade. She was manhandled by the Military Police and locked in a small room where she was searched by two female MP's. After she was released she showed bruises she said had been afflicted by the Military Police.

Her tour presented many dangerous moments for her. She was arrested four times while she was working in **Klute** a movie that received great praise from the critics. She joined another organization, the Vietnam Veterans Against the War. That was the time Seymour Hersch wrote about the Mai Lai massacre and shocked an unbelieving America. A number of public gatherings were arranged by the veterans in Detroit. That city was chosen because of its proximity to the Canadian border. It was expected that the Americans who had refused to fight in the war and who were living in Canada, along with some Vietnamese civilians, would be able to cross into the United States and offer testimony via closed-circuit television. Since funds were needed to defray the expenses that would be used to pay for the meetings, Jane offered to tour the country to raise the funds.

On November 3, 1970 Jane was on an Air Canada jet enroute home from a speaking engagement at Fanshaw College. The plane landed at Hopkins International Airport in Cleveland where she planned to rest at a nearby hotel. She walked through customs to be cleared. Generally travelers entering the country from Canada are automatically cleared at their points of departure. But due to the late hour that did not happen. Jane was now at the Cleveland Customs Hall where an inspector whose name was Lawrence Troiano and an Air Canada man stood ready to pass the passengers through. Instead of allowing Jane to pass through Troiano detained her and called his superior in downtown Cleveland. It was now past midnight and Jane was the only passenger not allowed through. When she protested, Troiano told her to keep quiet and started to examine her bag. He also took her address book.

Jane always carried at least 102 vials of organic vitamin pills with her when she was touring. She usually swallowed them instead of taking time for solid food. When the customs official saw the vitamins he assumed, conveniently so, that they were some kind of narcotic. It was obvious that she had been targeted for harassment. Her lawyer could not get inside to talk to her. A police matron made a thorough body search and found some tranquilizers and a bottle of Dexedrine pills which she took as sleeping pills. The pills had been purchased in the United States from a prescription by her personal physician, Dr. J.D. Walters.

Troiano and his colleagues decided to hold her in the Cuyahoga County jail, a rather forbidding-looking building. It was near the Cleveland Central Police Station. Ten hours after she had been incarcerated Jane was released by posting a $5,000 bond pending a probable cause hearing on November 9. Despite the fact that she was innocent of the drug charges leveled against her, the newspapers ran scare headlines announcing "Jane Fonda Arrested; Accused of Smuggling Drugs, Kicking Officers."

Jane was finally declared innocent of all charges. Her lawyer was able to prove that she was on Nixon's enemy list and that orders from Washington had been issued that she be harassed by the government.

Her unfortunate experiences at the Cleveland Airport only served to increase her determination to wage war against the system. The hate mail she received now increased in volume. But it did not deter her from her resolve to stop the war. Her father's remarks did annoy her however.

In an interview with a journalist Fonda complained that he had never received so much hate mail until his daughter had become an anti-war activist. He bemoaned the fact that he was being called a Communist because he had a daughter whose name was Jane Fonda. He bitterly admitted that she was very intelligent but said that someone else was doing her thinking for her. Fonda complained that because she was his daughter, people assumed that he agreed with her political opinions. That was far from the truth.

Fonda was also interviewed by Guy Flatley, a **New York Times** feature writer. Fonda apologized to Flatley for detaining him and explained that he had been on a long-distance call from Washington and had--and then he paused before completing the sentence.

"How shall I put it—I spoke with my erstwhile...alleged daughter. She asked me to put her and her entourage up in my house for a week.'" Fonda said that he would have enjoyed telling her that the house was full but he couldn't refuse to accommodate her and her friends.

Flatley asked him whether there were many people in her entourage—"perhaps too many" for him to house.

"No," said Fonda, "It's not the amount of people. The fact of the matter is that they were very unattractive."

Jane knew well enough by that time that her father still had his prejudices against people who did not share his way of life or believed in ideas which he considered "way out." Fonda, on the other hand, was certain that he knew his daughter better than anybody else, and that Jane had never understood what really motivated her actions. He said that there always had to be someone to start her moving. Her inspiration always had to come from another person whom she respected. It had always been that way, he insisted. First it was Strasberg who encouraged her to become an actress. Then it was Vadim who taught her to be less self-righteous. And now was people like Mark Lane the lawyer and Fred Gardner, the organizer and the other activists in the anti-War movement.

What Fonda could not comprehend was that Jane was her own woman. She did have one weakness if it could be called that. Her brother said that Jane always had a preference for the runt of the litter.

An actress takes on many roles. And Jane had more than her share of them. She had at first been a social butterfly with no aim in life. And then she had been a wife. After that she was a sex kitten, and then an actress and now a political activist. She knew that her father was annoyed and even exasperated by her constant involvements in movements that he did not approve of. He never could understand that it was his own unconscious attempts at manipulating her that aggravated her psyche.

There had always been a love-hate relationship between them. And that held true although to a lesser extent for Peter.

It was rather ironic to see how Fonda could maintain a close and intimate friendship with Jimmy Stewart despite his very conservative opinions and yet found it almost impossible to find some basis for intimacy with his own daughter. His feelings were to change in time. But it did not happen soon enough. There were very long years where the bitterness lasted before the past was forgotten by both of them.

Chapter XXIV
A Matter of Censorship

There were times when the roles offered to Henry Fonda did not arouse his interest or his enthusiasm. But, as he frequently said, an actor must keep working or he is quickly forgotten by those who would hire him. When Fonda was asked to play in a television adaptation of John Steinbeck's novel, **The Red Pony**, he first wanted to read the script before committing himself. After he had perused it carefully he bluntly told the producer that he "had to refuse" the offer; he didn't like it. Had he known that the script had been written by his friend Bob Totten he might have made less scathing remarks about it.

Totten had been asked to direct the play. He had read two drafts of the script prepared by William McCormack and Ron Bishop and had found them wanting. He suggested that he be allowed to write another version of the Steinbeck work. That was the script that Fonda had read. After Fonda learned that Totten had written the script which he had criticized he called him and apologized for his remarks. "I can't accept the script," he said to Totten. The writer, not a bit put out by his friend's statements agreed that he was right. The effort he had made and the work he had produced wasn't good enough apparently. A week after the two men had had their conversation Totten wrote a fifth draft and handed it to Fonda, who then found it satisfactory. When Fonda discussed the script with an interviewer he told him that "It was Bob's script and it was a completely new one and I fell in love with it right away."

The film was to be an NBC special, sponsored by the American Telephone and Telegraph Company. It was to be released by British Lions of London and would be produced both as a television show and a movie to be exhibited in the commercial theaters in Canada and the British Isles.

The movie version was to run for two-and-a half hours in the theaters, but it would be cut twenty minutes on television in order to provide time for commercials.

The really serious problem the producer, the writer and Fonda would be faced with was the fact that the American Telephone and Telegraph Company executives objected to the script; they were shocked by a scene showing the birth of a foal on a stud farm in California.

The director had chosen three mares at a thoroughbred farm. They were all photographed while giving birth to their foals. All in

169

all about four hours of film footage was shot while a veterinarian stood in for Fonda, who was playing the part in the picture, and carried out the actual deliveries.

"Horrors," exclaimed the sponsors when they were told that the birth of a foal would actually be shown on television. Fonda was surprised; he could not understand why they reacted in that way.

"They had read the script over at NBC," he said, "and they were in Sonora (Mexico) with the rest of the cast and saw everything that was being shot and never by word or deed did they indicate that they found that scene objectionable. And then when the picture (was) finished and delivered to them, they suddenly arbitrarily decided they would not accept the explicit birth scenes."

The sponsors obviously assumed that the morals of men, women and children would be affected by the scenes. Totten and producer Fred Brogger left for New York to discuss the matter with the sponsors and NBC. It should be noted that although the network executives had already indicated their approval of the uncensored version, the sponsors prevailed and the offensive scene was cut. In the new version Fonda and the other actors were in the tack room and the labor scene was cut. Fonda's voice was heard narrating what was going on and urging the mare to make a greater effort. He was saying, "Good girl, c'mon, push girl." The camera was never focused on the animal. As Fonda later explained, "Originally both Bob (Totten) and I naively felt that they would say, 'Gee, I think they will want to see what is going on.' But they didn't so we lost the fight."

The moviegoers in Canada saw the uncensored version of **The Red Pony** but the morals of the television audiences in the United States were protected by the overly solicitious corporation executives.

When the producer and Fonda wanted to know why the company had found the scene objectionable Paul Lund, a ninth vice-president of the company and his associates, Walt Cannon and Frank Lane, freely admitted that they were afraid of losing what they said was Corporate Communications. That division of the giant company watched over the making of films, travelogues and maps and its budget amounted to $35 million a year. There had been some criticism from its affiliates that far too much money was being spent frivolously on projects that were of no benefit to the stockholders. The sponsors made it quite clear that the birth scene in **The Red Pony** would irritate many of the company's affiliates and they didn't want to take a chance. "We don't want to take the risk," they admitted. Fonda was not too surprised. "I always thought that there were four areas of censorship—never five--but you can't show the birth as far as AT&T is concerned."

News that the film had been censored brought a flood of letters from many of the people at the preview. They reached the desk of an NBC vice-president who thereupon announced that he could not be held accountable for the cutting of the scene. That was to be expected. The underlings in corporate America, like many politicians are thus brothers under the skin. Both have been forced to take the responsibility for ill-conceived actions of their superiors.

The highly-regarded **Scholastic** Magazine which is circulated nationwide to 16 million students who range in age from ten to eighteen endorsed the uncensored version of the film. The editors had laid out a curriculum in which all kinds of questions were asked about the birth scene. The students were puzzled when they saw the censored film. The questions that were asked about the foal's birth appeared to have no relevance to what they were seeing on the tube.

Surprisingly enough NBC's official censor, Travestis, had approved the original scene when he saw it in the screening room. He had even said that he had "seen this birth sequence five times."

"I not only feel that it should play as it is, but have to question myself and say, 'Travie, possibly you didn't tell your own children the proper thing about the birds and the bees.' "

Althouth he urged that the scene be kept in the picture Lund, the unflappable AT&T President did not change his opinion.

NBC, not at all embarrassed by the fact that it had been caught up in the crossfire now attempted to convince the skeptics that the sponsors never dictated policy. But Fonda insisted "it had been AT&T every foot of the way. They cut it right out and forced NBC to take the burden of it."

Despite the battle that was put up by Fonda and Bob Totten, the sponsor's will prevailed. The scene was cut as ordered and the innocence of all Americans was protected against the corrupting influences of the producers of the film.

To put it bluntly the network could have lost a sponsor who doled out millions of dollars for the time on the air. And a scene that depicted the birth of a foal wasn't worth taking that kind of a risk.

Chapter XXV
Hassles with a Writer
The Caine Mutiny Court Martial

Fonda found his experience acting in Herman Wouk's **The Caine Mutiny Court Martial** a rewarding one. But nothing seemed to run smoothly in any of the productions Fonda was involved in. This time it wasn't the director nor the producer who was creating the problems for him. It was the writer.

Herman Wouk is an orthodox Jew who respects authority. When he wrote the play he insisted on including an epilogue, in which he had his hero, Lieutenant Greenwald, castigate those individuals who tend to besmirch those in authority. Judging by what Wouk stated in the epilogue that would be equivalent to sacrilege.

In the first act of the play Fonda as Greenwald sits quietly, listening to the proceedings of the trial and doodling on a piece of paper. Greenwald doesn't come to life until the second act when he takes over the questioning of Queeg, the officer being tried. The play was first staged in Santa Barbara, California. After a brief run there the company went on a tour for the next fourteen weeks.

Charles Laughton had cancelled his tour to take up the directorial chores. But just before the New York opening Laughton had to leave because of his own commitments to his own project. This left Fonda the director.

The company traveled by bus across the country. Fonda usually sat near a member of the cast for a few minutes and then walked over to another actor to discuss some of the problems that concerned his work.

The critics praised the play but they were all in agreement that the epilogue was sticking out like an extra appendage.

"It was," they agreed, "embarrassing, gratuitous, and unnecessary."

Fonda read the reviews and planned to show them to Laughton when the company arrived in Boston. A day after the company arrived there he met with both Laughton and Wouk and talked about the epilogue. He asked both men to read the reviews. And after they had done it, he said, "Not only the critics but our friends who have come backstage to talk to us said that we do not need the epilogue."

Laughton concurred with what Fonda had said and wanted to eliminate it. But Wouk insisted on keeping it in. He told them that the only reason he had written the play was to give himself the opportunity to express his ideas in the epilogue. He told both men that if they continued to insist on eliminating it he would have it shut down.

Laughton recognized a determined man when he saw one. He knew that Wouk could have the entire project finished off. He reluctantly agreed to include the epilogue, but he insisted that certain changes would have to be made so that the play would not disintegrate before the very eyes of the audience. He told Wouk that it was necessary to write some sort of scenes "through the body of the play which would make the audience totally satisfied, still unresolved, so that at the end there still was the question—what's eating Greenwald. There's something the matter with Greenwald."

The audience, he said, would then be ready for an answer to its question and would be pleased to listen to the epilogue—an epilogue that would clarify to the audience what was on Greenwald's mind.

Wouk said he would write some new lines and scenes. The play opened and this time there was no carping from the critics. The twelve New York newspapers agreed that the epilogue was an essential part of the play. As Fonda exclaimed, "Not one critic said the epilogue was unnecessary. On the contrary, they said, 'Son of a bitch! He hits you with one climax, then hits you with another on top of it!' "

Fonda later talked about the acting problems he had had to work out. They stemmed from the fact that while the audience was momentarily mesmerized by the play and the epilogue, they had different thoughts about it later on. He said that some of his friends came to him after the curtain had been rung down and told him how good it was with such expressions as "You son of a bitch!"

But Fonda believed that "after the impact of the play had worn off, a day or two later, they would say 'goddamn that was a great night, but you know, I don't think I buy that epilogue.' Thus you can see my problem. I had to play on their emotions during the play and into the epilogue and never allow them to start intellectualizing. I had to grab them and the only way I could do that was to grab them emotionally."

Fonda said that if you were able to maintain control of an audience in that way it would not be able to stop and say, "I do not comprehend what the writer is trying to tell me and I simply won't go along with him."

When Jane was starting to take her work seriously he drew on his vast experience in the theater and cited an example of how to take firm control of a particular scene and build up its tempo, "I used the simile of an amphibious plane that has a special design of the hull. There's a step and it's called a step, underneath the keel. The plane doesn't respond so well when it is in the water. But when the pilot attains a certain speed he is able to pick it up onto the step. At that point it's just riding on the step. It is still in the water but ready to take off.

"That's the way I feel if I really got it going when I started that scene. I was up on the step. Then it was all up to me to maintain my control of it. Just stay there because I could now really, go, go, go. But all the time you had to know that the reins were held tightly in your hands and that you were in complete control."

Fonda criticized the way some actors allow their feelings to run riot and begin to slobber. "One can't continue to watch them at work after that. When the actor controls himself the audience will respond as he wants it to. They will not listen to every word that is spoken on stage but will react emotionally to what is being said.

"It is not necessary," he said, "to write such lines as 'his mother being melted down into soap' to whip up an audience's emotions." He was, of course, alluding to Wouk when he said that.

"Why," he asked, "would a writer have to give us such shit! It isn't necessary. The following day or perhaps after that is when one thinks about it. And because Wouk took such means to arouse the audience's emotions in his epilogue," said Fonda, "most people took exception to the play."

Chapter XXVI
A Role to Relish

Fonda had now reached the biblical age of 70. For most men it means a time to retire and live a leisurely life. Perhaps some fishing, a bit of reading, traveling with Shirlee to far off places and a time to enjoy his grandchildren. But that was not in the cards for Fonda. Work had always been his pleasure and acting his compulsion.

The times, he complained to a friend, had become lean, and he was becoming restless. He had had only a few cameo roles, nothing more. And then, to his surprise, he was offered an important role—that of Clarence Darrow, the great dissenter who had fought for the underdog and for his many legal battles. His court battle with William Jennings Bryan, the silver-tongued orator of the Platte, for the right of a young teacher to teach the theory of evolution in the schools had made newspaper headlines all over the western world.

When David Rintels wrote a play about Darrow that had been based on a novel by Irving Stone, he visualized Fonda as being perfect for the role. John Houseman who was to direct the play also believed that he was tailor-made for the part. But when he first broached the idea to Fonda the actor exclaimed, "Imagine, getting Darrow when you're seventy years old!"

Here is how it all started. John Houseman flew out to California and saw Fonda. When he discussed the play with him, Houseman candidly admitted that it was far too long. He also said that he didn't like the way the first act had been written. But he also assured Fonda that the subject matter was so engrossing that it was bound to hold an audience spellbound.

When Fonda discussed the part with a colleague he said that he had fallen "in love with Darrow as a man and as a script. He was a man of tremendous heart. I wish I was a man like that. Now I'm about to be that man every night."

The play dramatized the high points in the great lawyer's career. It addressed itself to the judge, the jury and to the audience as spectators and it all added up to the role of a great liberal lawyer. One wondered why Fonda had been chosen for the part since he bore no resemblance to Darrow. He said, "I wondered why it was sent to me but I was willing to be persuaded."

For that role Fonda had a lock of hair fixed to his forehead. He also wore a pad which served as a paunch which the lawyer had acquired over the years. And his clothes were wrinkled. After he had been made up to look the part he began to memorize the lines.

175

Henry Fonda as Clarence Darrow at Helen Hayes Theater.

He explained how he went about that, "I learned the first line and then the second and then put them together. I turned the page. For weeks I was turning the page in my mind and I saw the cross-outs— 10 pages, 20 pages, 35 pages—finally the entire first act, 53 pages. That was half way through the second act. It was like eating three Thanksgiving dinners and if you swallow you'll throw up. Finally, I got to the last page and I learned the whole thing."

That was only a start. There were countless rehearsals. The revisions were made while he was on stage.

"I can't let up for a split minute," he said, "because I was afraid I would lose my intensity as well as my place in the script."

Fonda was twenty weeks on the road with the play. He performed in Boston, Detroit, Denver, Los Angeles and New York. The people who saw him enacting the lawyer were amazed with his virtuosity. His own personality actually receded into the background as he transformed himself before the eyes of the audience into the famous lawyer.

One critic observed, "Watch the way he voices Darrow's fey and country-style humor. Listen to his voice, never too much inflected, never coarsely characterized yet always lyrical. The face becomes old. The expression one sees is too self-aware to be smug. And with the laughter even of a man who believed that compassion was higher than justice—if Clarence Darrow was not like that he should have been."

He continued, "Darrow spoke 'for the poor and the weary.' I urge every man woman and child interested in justice to see this play."

And another critic said, "It is impossible to remember that it is a theatrical performance—a strange sense of acting as if Darrow himself were in front reminiscing about his life and career with urbanity and compassion."

As the play unfolds one sees Darrow nee Fonda talking about the ten-year-old children who sorted slate from coal. He also speaks about the plight of the coal miners in the company towns of Pennsylvania and is also identifying with them.

The critic, Walter Kerr, who is never easily taken in by slick performers wrote, "He (Fonda) creates the character on stage not by using his charm but by an intellectual metamorphosis."

John Houseman in explaining just how Fonda was able to manage to create so sharply etched an image of the great counselor-at-law said, "You don't direct Fonda. You sort of sit out front and act as ·a mirror for him and then tell him your impressions. He never blocked a piece. I don't think any foreign actor could do it like Hank does.

"After we opened I had the Juilliard (school) kids go and look at him. It's peculiarly an American acting. He'd wander about and I'd say that looks good, or no, you have spent an awful lot of time in that place, I would stay there. The whole thing was very pragmatic."

In an interview Fonda again said how thrilled he was to be playing Darrow and added, "The wonderful thing about playing Darrow is that, although not many people ever heard of him, what he stood for is universal. So I will probably do Darrow some part of every year of my life from now on, as long as I can stay on my feet."

Chapter XXVII
First Monday in October

A new play, **First Monday in October,** starring Henry Fonda and Jane Alexander, was being staged at the Majestic Theater in New York on the night of October 5. The title of the play has a special significance since it is the day when the Supreme Court annually convenes.

Fonda, who had been acting for 53 years when the play opened was now in his 73rd year. He had been playing in the production for nine weeks to great acclaim at the Kennedy Center in Washington D.C., the preceding winter. And now it faced its critical test on Broadway with Fonda enacting the role of Daniel Stone, a Supreme Court Justice, a part that was clearly patterned after the late William O. Douglas, the famous dissenter.

"I play the great dissenter-liberal in a head-on conflict with a reactionary female judge. It's a very funny play," he said, "not a fall-down comedy, but the scenes and situations and the way the man talks I have never heard audiences, even in **Mister Roberts** rock and roll with laughter and break into applause in the middle of scenes the way they do in this play."

When he was asked whether he planned to retire after the play closed down he said that he saw "no reason to retire. Work is a holiday." The minute it ceased to be fun he could quit and devote his time to his hobby, painting.

"Other people are different." He said that "Cary Grant still has all his apples and marbles" and he's a healthy and happy man, and if Jimmy Cagney "got a script he wouldn't even read it; he's too busy painting on Martha's Vineyard."

Very definitely, Fonda had no idea of retiring—ever. And with a hit play on his hands he believed that he was on his way to greater triumphs.

The basic ingredient in the play is the confrontation between two Supreme Court justices—a recently appointed female member of the court, and Stone, an aging classic liberal. The battle between the two on most of the issues is predictable. When the play dwells on serious issues it makes some kind of a point, but when it tries to interject some humor, as when the female justice and her colleagues have to look at a porno film in order to determine whether such pictures should be allowed to be exhibited it becomes quite labored.

The first woman to be nominated to the Supreme Court is a California conservative, and as she is portrayed by Jane Alexander she comes over as a crisp and clear-headed devotee of the rightest

178

principles she stands for. As expected when oil and water mix they find that their ideas do not jell very well. There are some lively goings-on between the two when they fight out their differences about such issues as censorship. She supports state laws that will enable local authorities to prosecute porno film producers, and he abides by the Constitution that guarantees free speech.

In another case the two antagonists clash about a suit against an automobile company that ostensibly does not want an inventor to get a patent on a "momentum-engine" which promises to put an end to the energy crisis and change the face of the free enterprise system.

The playwrights were really reaching very far out when they based so much of their play on so impossible a premise!

In Act Two it becomes painfully apparent that the playwrights have almost lost control of their material and are looking for some kind of device that will keep the plot moving. But in the end everything works out happily. Justice Stone has a heart attack. That causes the lady justice to see the human qualities in the ailing man. And her reaction helps him to see the light about her character.

One realized as the play progressed that Fonda was really playing himself. He was that kind of a man himself, a lifelong liberal.

In **The Grapes of Wrath** he played the disinherited Okie who waged a war against powerful interests who were exploiting the people. In **Twelve Angry Men** he was the dedicated citizen who wanted to see that justice was done to a man standing trial. In **Mister Roberts** he stood up to a power-mad sea captain and waged the good fight for his crew. In **The Young Mr. Lincoln** he portrayed an American leader who was to become the Great Emancipator and in the **Ox-Bow Incident** he tried to stop a lynching of two innocent men. It was no accident that Fonda preferred roles like those.

And it was also no accident that he enjoyed playing the role of a classic liberal in **First Monday in October.**

Walter Kerr, the eminent critic, who had always been impressed with Fonda's work wrote after seeing him in **First Monday in October,** "there he is, rock-solid, instinctively and irremediately erect, a shaft of steel, holding the stage in place—and the audience."

Kerr wasn't all that kind to the two playwrights, Robert E. Lee and Jerome Lawrence. He said that they had let the "play threaten to drift into a blank" while Fonda is "clinging to his position as the eternal dissenter, the classic liberal, the professional curmudgeon of the Supreme Court who is waiting to see how the court's balance will be affected when the new justice is appointed to fill the vacancy.

". . .[F]ootless as it is, Fonda will not yield the play," Kerr wrote. He mentioned Fonda's fortitude and skill as attributes that saved the play and kept it from disintegrating into chaos.

"He is," Kerr continued, "the captain who won't go down with his ship."

Chapter XXVIII
The Adopted Daughter in the Shadows

Both Jane and Peter were always in the limelight through the years. But Fonda's adopted daughter Amy, whose mother was Susan Blanchard, his third wife, was the girl in the shadows for most of her young life. She lived with Susan for several years until she married again. Her new stepfather had a daughter from a previous marriage. The two girls could not get along and Amy was sent to a boarding school. In a sense it was a rejection of a kind, and apparently it had a searing effect on the child. She saw Fonda now and then but the father-daughter relationship was at best a tenuous one. Many people were unaware that Fonda had another daughter until they saw her at the American Film Institute's event when Fonda was awarded a "Life Achievement" recognition.

Peter was there looking his usual handsome self. Jane was also there with her children. Yet Amy who appeared to be somewhat uncomfortable was trying to make herself as obscure as possible. When her father announced that he had a daughter named Amy who was about to receive her doctorate in clinical psychology she was embarrassed at the attention she was receiving.

Amy, like many other children of famous fathers never had a stable homelife. Her mother Susan (she had adopted her) had divorced Fonda and married again. It did not work out well. There was a third marriage. She acquired more step-sisters and step-brothers and two fathers to boot. But she was never able to establish a good relationship with any of her new parents.

Fonda because he was so remote did not encourage her to seek help from him. She said, "Father has a quietness and reserve and modesty that I like. But he is too closed for me. He doesn't show emotion."

Amy's relations with Jane and Peter was friendly enough, but never really close. The differences in their ages—she is about fifteen years younger than Jane and thirteen years younger than Peter—was too much of a gap for her to bridge.

She began to feel the urge to find out who her biological parents were and started to search for them. She found out that she had been born in Miami, Florida, when her mother was 31 years old. Her father, a soldier, had been only 24. She also discovered that her name at birth was Beverly. But despite all her efforts she was never able to locate either of her parents. In the end she had to acknowledge herself that her parents were Susan and Henry. She learned to live with that fact.

Amy admits that she had arrived at a point in her life where she had to forgive any responsibilities her real parents had shirked towards her. She has come to understand that her adopted father's remoteness did not spring from a lack of love for his children. It was not in his nature to act differently; he was a very private person.

After Shirlee came into his life Fonda tried to be more outgoing. He succeeded in some measure. He had "grown to know Tom Hayden, Jane's husband, and admired him very much."

He was in need of love and was fortunate enough to get it from all of his children, including Amy. And in his will he left her $200,000. It was his way of telling her that he did indeed love her and was concerned about her future financial security.

Epilogue

Life never intended to have Henry Fonda retire for good. Work for him was therapeutic. He had been geared for work and found an intense joy in it. At an age when many men and women are resigned to retirement he sought out new projects to engage his energies. And when his daughter Jane, who is not only a superb actress but a producer of motion pictures as well, decided to film **On Golden Pond** she knew that her father would be more than pleased to play the part of the elderly professor who resented the fact that his days on earth were drawing to a close. In presenting him with the opportunity to play the role she had displayed an instinctive understanding what had really motivated him for the past few years. What could be better than to have him in a sense play himself as he did in that particular film? And have Katharine Hepburn enact the role of a devoted wife.

In a way the story of **On Golden Pond** was the true to life story of all three leading members of the cast. Jane who was to play Chelsea, a young woman who had never been able to communicate with her father, knew that that had been her problem for the greater part of her life. Fonda, who was just as grumpy in real life as the character he was portraying, and who as we know had never been able to understand what was troubling Jane through the years, was getting a much needed lesson. And Katharine Hepburn, because of her own experiences with Spencer Tracy, was able to comprehend just what kind of a person the testy professor was.

The idea of acquiring the rights to **On Golden Pond** occurred to Jane back in 1970 when she was working on the movie, **The Electric Horseman** in Utah. She read the playscript one day and became completely enthralled with Ernest Thompson's story about a retired New England professor who resented getting old. Jane had read many plays hoping to find a proper vehicle for her father to work in. **On Golden Pond** was just what she had been looking for.

During an interview with a reporter she talked about the ever-complaining professor Norman Thayer and said that he reminded her of her father when he was in one of his moods. She also said that the good professor's moments of anger and his insensitivity to the feelings of those near and dear to him were also typical of her own father. And she concluded with a statement that the differences between Fonda and herself were gone with the wind now.

According to her, there had only been two periods in her life when Fonda did not see eye-to-eye with her. The first period was when she started to work seriously as an actress. And the second was when she was an activist during the Vietnam War. But that statement was not entirely accurate. They did quarrel on many other occasions. Her father's lifestyle, particularly his many marriages, had been a source of emotional disturbance both for her and Peter. And his overbearing attitude towards her was still troublesome.

It had been many years since she had acted with her father at the Omaha Playhouse. It was her debut at the tender age of eighteen. And now, after all those years had passed, she was to work again with him. During the shooting of one scene, the one that disclosed the hostility that existed between father and daughter, Jane asked Fonda to look into her eyes. She thought that it would lend some credence to the emotions they were feeling. But Fonda bruskly told her that he would have none of that. He said, "I don't need to look at you. I am not one of those actors."

Jane's first reaction to that rebuff was one of extreme anger. She later revealed that tears had welled up in her eyes. And then a thought crossed her mind. He was probably right. And at the same time she was irritated about her own emotional reaction. Here she was, a woman in her middle age and he still had the power to reduce her to "helplessness." It was so reminiscent of what had happened so many times in the past.

Her savior during the filming of the picture was Katharine Hepburn. She saw what had happened and walked over to Jane, embraced her and confessed that she had been subjected to the same putdowns by her friend and lover Spencer Tracy.

Jane later said that it was imperative that she should be emotionally naked so that she could bring some substance to the character she was enacting. Both father and daughter were frequently moved to tears. At dinner one night in Fonda's cabin they were so overcome with their emotions that neither of them said a word to each other. It was now clear enough to both of them that the experience of working together in the film was really autobiographical. The acting stirred them profoundly. But despite all, nothing had actually changed in the actor's relationship with his family. He was, Jane admitted, still remote. But she did manage to comprehend the inner man, his basic honesty and sincerity.

There was another woman who came to respect and in a sense love Fonda. It was Katharine Hepburn. She had never worked with him. It was a first time for both artists. For a woman who was generally given to a certain amount of reticence she surprised all within speaking range of her voice with her enthusiasm for a man she once acknowledged she could have married had she met him years ago.

"He is an unusual man," she said. "He loved to work for its own sake." She also expressed her astonishment for a man who was born in Nebraska who had had five wives. But now, she said, he was most fortunate in having Shirlee for a wife. She was a dedicated one who always took special pains to minister to his needs. And she also took note of the fact that his daughter Jane was very much like him in character.

She works and loves it and also walks the straight line just like her father, figuratively and literally, according to Hepburn.

She also agreed that Jane's relations with her father had bloomed during the filming of the picture.

Jane enjoyed talking about what had happened during what her father said was "the enchanted summer" on a beautiful lake in New England.

"The director said that I wanted to do this sort of resolve-an-unre-solved thing with my father. That's not what I wanted to do. I didn't think about it at the time. But as we began to rehearse—as we got into the filming there things started coming up. . .they just started surfacing. Tremendous wells of love and anger and awe. . .things I wanted to say that hadn't been said. As these things got played out the director would say 'cut' and I would look around the room and the faces of the crew, the people around him. This is lots of people. Not just fathers, sons and daughters, mothers and sons, it's a universal thing."

Fonda, reticent as always, did not reveal his emotional state that readily during that summer. But after he had been awarded the Oscar for his performance in the film he did give vent to his feelings.

He said, "I thought that's the peak. I don't have to reach higher than that." And recollecting how he felt during the shooting of the film he said, "In **On Golden Pond** I got emotional just saying the words. This is a play I did this summer with my daughter Jane who was the producer, and Katharine Hepburn. It was the most magic summer, but I know from the people who have seen it that the magic has got on to the screen too. And I can't wait and see it."

Before the news of the award had become official Jane said, "If my father were to win it would be the stuff that dreams are made of, that I could provide for him the vehicle for which he would win the Academy Award. Add to that the fact that he was getting sick. How often does a kid get a chance to give a gift like that to a parent?"

His being awarded the "Oscar" was, he said, the high point of his life—a life that was to end in the not too distant future. His family knew that with his badly damaged heart the end was near. During the last year of his life he was in and out of the hospital a number of times. Shirlee, his devoted wife, later revealed that she slept on a cot near his bed night after night so that she could help him when he was in pain.

In the end it was his wife Shirlee who knew best how to relate to him. That was far more than Jane had been able to achieve. During the last year she admitted that to some extent he was still a stranger. "I will go over and see him (at the hospital) as soon as this interview is over. I will sit and watch him and wonder who he is. There are parts of him I understand very well because I am very much like him. But I never understood entirely why he is so shy, why he fears that he has nothing to say, nothing to teach, because he does."

And she concluded with the thought that "he becomes liberated when he can hide behind another person. He's too uncertain of who he really is. He is tremendously lacking in self-confidence, a sense of his identity."

His son Peter shares her opinions about his father. He said, "Henry is Henry. He's not a person who wants people to know or knows how to let people know, including me, Jane, all of us. He's a very shy person, you understand. The thing that drove him to be an Eagle Scout, a scoutmaster, the thing that drives him as an actor, that's the way he can communicate and converse."

In his last will and testament he left $200,000 to his adopted daughter Amy and the remainder of his estate to his wife Shirlee and explained why he had disinherited his two children. "They know how to take care of themselves." It surprised many people. Even if they did not need his money, some sensitivity on his part would have enabled him to understand that even a token share in the estate would have told them that he cared.

Until the end of his life he expressed his regret that he had been married five times.

"It's a shameful thing to me," he confesed. "It's not like me. It's not like my family and how it all happened I don't know. I don't dwell on it."

After saying that, he reminded himself that now he was a very happy man because he had chosen Shirlee to be his wife. And he shouted for all to hear, "I'm the luckiest man in the world that I have the wife I have today. That I met her 18 years ago, that she is my wife."

During the past few years Shirlee had to live with the knowledge that he would soon be leaving her for good. And on the day of his death she was standing by his bedside watching him breathe his last. When the reporters who were waiting outside the hospital asked her what had happened she said, "He died comfortably. He was in no pain. He had a very good night the night before. He talked to all of us and was not unconscious at any time. He woke up this morning, sat up in bed and quietly stopped breathing."

Index